This book is presented to

_____

name

_____

date

_____

by

May the Holy Spirit use these meditations to
    keep hope before your eyes,
      provide guidance for your daily living,
      give courage within your inner being,
    and strengthen your faith
as they direct your thoughts and prayers to God's grace
and love in your Lord and Savior, Jesus Christ.

A Year in the Word

Reflections from *Portals of Prayer*®

Edited by Rudolph F. Norden

SAINT LOUIS

1 2 3 4 5 6 7 8 9 10   08 07 06 05 04 03 02 01 00 99

A New Name

He was called Jesus. Luke 2:21 RSV

A new year begins today. But how much newness will the days ahead bring? *New* implies something we have not experienced before. For the Christian, newness is not turning a page on a calendar. Newness is wrapped up in a person: the new man, Jesus Christ. God gave Him to the world so we might experience what we have never experienced before—life.

The name *Jesus* means Savior. Life that is separated from its Creator is not life; it is not even a poor imitation of life. The Scriptures call this life "death." But Jesus is the Savior from death. He becomes part of our death. He empties Himself of His relation to God. That is what the cross means. But the resurrection introduces a truly new thing, not just hope of life after the grave, but the hope of life before the grave and despite the grave.

In Jesus, God's new creation has begun. We who believe what God has done in Jesus also have been raised from death to life. We are saved to experience what we have not known before—life. Baptism gives us a new name. We are Christ's, sons and daughters of God.

This will be a happy new year if each day we are buried with Christ and raised with Him through God's good Word of forgiveness.

Lord, we thank You for our new name and new life. Amen.

Kenneth Schueler/Jan. 1, 1970

GOD'S NEW YEAR'S RESOLUTION
FOR YOU

I will strengthen thee; yea, I will help thee;
yea, I will uphold thee. Isaiah 41:10 KJV

*T*hese are the days of New Year's resolutions. In all of our resolving, we never forget that "man proposes, but God disposes." After all is said and done, the course of our life during this year, either for good or ill, is not dependent on our resolutions, but on the resolutions of our Father in heaven.

How fortunate that we already know His resolution for us in the new year! It is true, we do not know every step of the way that lies ahead. We do not know every piece that He will fit into the pattern. But we do know the pattern. It is the pattern of a gracious God, who has revealed Himself to us in Jesus Christ, His Son.

He has given us His Word that in all the changing scenes of life, He will strengthen us, help us, uphold us. And God can never lie. Paul says: "If we are faithless, He will remain faithful, for He cannot disown Himself" (2 Timothy 2:13). In other words, God keeps His resolutions, and He has resolved to shower with endless mercy all those who embrace His Son as Lord and Savior. Our puny resolves may fade with the drooping tinsel and broken toys of Christmas, but God's resolve is eternal and unchangeable. We place our highest hope in Him.

"Be our joy throughout each year. Amen, Jesus, hear us." Amen.

Herman W. Gockel/Jan. 3, 1975

GOD'S CONCERN FOR HIS PEOPLE

Who shall separate us from the love of Christ?
Shall tribulation, or distress, or persecution,
or famine, or nakedness, or peril, or sword?
Romans 8:35 RSV

*A*nother year has begun. For some it may be an unusual year filled with blessings. These will be so remarkable that they will be remembered. For others it will be an ordinary year. Nothing special will take place. Still others will experience sorrows beyond measure.

Floods, earthquakes, and other natural disasters that strike in an irregular fashion; unexpected sickness and death; as well as other usual and unusual concerns, may touch us this year. All over, discouraged people will ask, "How? How can I find peace for my grief-torn heart? Where? Where can I find assurance as life adds affliction to adversity?"

St. Paul has news for us. He reminded the Romans, and he reminds us as this year opens, that there is nothing that can separate us from God's love in Christ. Throughout this whole year, our Lord offers us the important blessings He has provided for us: forgiveness of sins, salvation, eternal life. He reminds us of His concern for us.

What an important bit of information! Surely this message is much more important to us than having our favorite teams win the bowl games.

Lord, open my eyes that I may see Your love. Amen.

Max G. Beck/Jan. 1, 1978

Safe in the Everlasting Arms

I will never leave thee, nor forsake thee.
Hebrews 13:5 KJV

*I*t is inevitable that in our weaker moments we scan the horizons of the future with apprehension and foreboding. There is no doubt that the year that lies ahead will have its anxious hours: hours of sickness, perhaps even death; sleepless nights; friendless, lonely hours; moments when that lump within our throats begins to swell and those teardrops in our eyes refuse to be concealed.

But as the redeemed of Christ, we can place our hand into the hand of God and march courageously onward! When days of sickness come to us during the year, we hear His voice whispering to us the sweet assurance: "I am the LORD that healeth thee" (Exodus 15:26 KJV). If the wings of the angel of death can be heard around our home, we hear the voice of Him who sent that angel still proclaiming: "I am the resurrection and the life" (John 11:25). And when that friendless lonely hour comes to us, we hear His cheering voice say: "I will not fail thee, nor forsake thee" (Joshua 1:5 KJV). "I am with you alway, even unto the end of the world" (Matthew 28:20 KJV).

Throughout the year that lies ahead, we will experience the glorious truth that the Christian's cross and Christ's comfort leave God's throne at the same time.

Lord, be with me in the coming year. Amen.

Herman W. Gockel/Jan. 1, 1979

SOMETHING TO TAKE HOLD OF

*Into Thy hand I commit my spirit; Thou
hast redeemed me, O LORD, faithful God.*
Psalm 31:5 RSV

One day when Rudyard Kipling, the well-known English writer, was ill and not expected to live, his nurse bent over him and asked, "Is there anything you want?" The sick man whispered in reply: "Only my heavenly Father."

To be in close friendship with God in life and in death—a child of God wants no more and is satisfied with no less.

"Can't you give me something to take hold of?" cried a brilliant but unbelieving woman as she felt the waves of death closing over her. Christians, and only Christians, have just that: something to take hold of; strong arms that will not let them go; the firm anchor of hope; a loving bosom on which to pillow their weary heads and sleep a sleep that is not death. Christians have a Father to whom they can say with Jesus, who was obviously quoting from the psalm: "Father, into Thy hands I commit my spirit!"

Christians can have full confidence in the heavenly Father and in His power and love to receive them because in Christ Jesus they are redeemed and made His dear children.

"Lord Jesus, since you love me, Now spread your wings above me And shield me from alarm. Though Satan would devour me, Let angel guards sing o'er me: 'This child of God shall meet no harm.'" Amen.

Oswald G. Riess/Oct. 24, 1981

11

THE CHRISTMAS OF THE GENTILES

There came wise men … saying,
"Where is He that is born King of the Jews?"
Matthew 2:1–2 KJV

*T*oday is the festival of the Epiphany. Epiphany is a Greek word that means "appearance" or "becoming public." The festival commemorates the appearance of Christ as the promised Savior of the Gentile nations and, therefore, to all the peoples of the world. That is why this day has become known as "the Christmas of the Gentiles."

Everything about Christmas has a distinctly Jewish aspect. The parents of Jesus, the town of Bethlehem, the shepherds, the circumcision, the temple scene—all combine to make a purely Jewish story. But the child of Bethlehem was to be the Savior of *all* people of *all* lands and of *all* ages. So the Christmas story is followed immediately by the story of the Epiphany.

Wise men in a distant land, not members of the Jewish race, see His star and are led by the Holy Spirit to a living faith in the Savior. Bethlehem's child was *their* Redeemer! Today we thank God for that revelation. In a sense, today is *our* Christmas. We are the Gentiles who have been called out of spiritual darkness into His marvelous light. With grateful hearts we can pray:

"As with gladness men of old Did the guiding star behold; … So, most gracious Lord, may we Evermore be led by thee." Amen.

Herman W. Gockel/Jan. 6, 1979

THE GIFT OF FRANKINCENSE

*And when they had opened their treasures,
they presented unto Him gifts ... frankincense.*
Matthew 2:11 KJV

The gift of frankincense to the Christ Child at Bethlehem by the Wise Men was a symbol of their worship and adoration, adding meaning to their gift of gold.

The use of incense in the Old Testament worship of God was fixed by mosaic law. Pure frankincense, mentioned as one of the four ingredients of the incense to be burned, was especially costly.

The priest Zechariah was burning incense in the temple when the angel Gabriel appeared and revealed to him that his wife, Elizabeth, would bear a son, who was to be the forerunner of the Messiah. Such burning of incense in the temple of old, its smoke rising heavenward, was symbolic of worship, of the prayers of the faithful rising up to the throne of grace. The psalmist said, "Let my prayer be set forth before Thee as incense" (Psalm 141:2 KJV).

In the busy schedule of our activities, reserve sufficient time for worship of Christ in the beauty of holiness. In the house of God, let the frankincense, the very best of our faith and devotion, rise heavenward in grateful hymns of prayer and praise to the gracious Lord for sending His Son to be the Savior of us all.

Accept, we pray, O God, our worship of You, Father, Son, and Holy Spirit, to Your glory and our good. In Jesus' name. Amen.

William H. Eifert/Dec. 21, 1967

13

NOTHING BETWEEN US

*All that the Father giveth Me shall come to
Me; and him that cometh to Me I will in no
wise cast out. John 6:37 KJV*

*T*here is a story about a woman who was trying to find
God. In a dream, which she dreamed more than
once, she was standing in front of a thick plate glass window. As she looked at it, she seemed to see God on the
other side.

She hammered on the window, trying to attract God's
attention, but without success. Finally, she found herself
shrieking at the top of her voice. In a quiet, calm voice,
God said to her: "Why are you making so much noise?
There is nothing between us."

Nothing is between us and God, if we only knew it!
Everything that might stand between us and God, Christ
has taken into His own heart. He died for us, and He lives
for us. All He asks is that we come to Him as we are, recognizing our need for His forgiveness, accepting His forgiveness, and living in that forgiveness.

To know Christ is to say to Him: "You died for me. You
paid the price for me. I trust You." That is faith—personal trust in Jesus Christ. Faith lets us be ourselves without
pretense, lets us be sons and daughters of God with nothing between us except love.

*Lord God, forgive us all our sins and give us all the
new life that is in Christ. Amen.*

Oswald C. J. Hoffmann/June 9, 1981

THE BASIS OF COURAGE

They who wait for the LORD shall renew their
strength, they shall mount up with wings like
eagles. *Isaiah 40:31 RSV*

O ften when we think of courage, we think of it in
connection with someone else and not ourselves.
We might think of the soldier who gives his life to save his
platoon. We think of firefighters, police officers, and others who risk their lives for welfare of the public.

Is real courage restricted to such displays of valor? Real
courage runs deeper than specific heroic acts. As a matter
of fact, heroic courage often goes unnoticed and unpubli-
cized. Think of the wife who doesn't give up after her husband dies. Think of the person with a terminal illness who
nevertheless maintains inner peace and concern for others. This list can go on and on.

The above instances have a common denominator:
courage. Courage comes from trusting in God or, as our
text puts it, "waiting for the Lord." Christianity doesn't
ask us to overlook our difficulties nor does it teach simply
the power of positive thinking. It does teach us to face our
problems by relying on God's promises. This is courage.
It is not something developed by us. Real courage is
given—from God Himself. We receive this courage
through God's Word and the sacraments. We join the
apostle in asserting, "If God be for us, who can be against
us?" (Romans 8:31 KJV).

*Lord, You alone can make us strong and courageous.
Amen.*

Daniel P. Aho/June 21, 1975

15

The King with the Golden Touch

Jesus put forth His hand, and touched him.
Matthew 8:3 KJV

*P*ossibly we have all heard the legend of the king who, because of some act of kindness done to one of the gods, was granted whatever favor he desired. The foolish king begged that everything he touched might become gold.

What fun he had for a while! But he was shocked out of his nonsense when, reaching for food and water, he found they also became gold. What really shook him was when his daughter climbed into his lap and at once became a lump of gold. In panic, he implored his god to be delivered from this curse.

We know of another King who, in all the lovelier moral and spiritual sense, is in very truth "the King with the golden touch." When He touches a soul, He blesses and transfigures. He bestows forgiveness, restoration, healing. He transforms paralysis and moral leprosy into spiritual health, vitality, and wholeness. He imparts faith, love, joy, goodwill, and hope. He dissolves prison chains, frees prisoners, and gives power to live victoriously. We know this King. He is Jesus. This wonderful King is the friend of sinners who brings cleansing through His blood; healing and restoration to the sin-sick and the fallen; light and hope, life and victory, to those who receive Him.

Precious Savior, let Your touch ever be upon us to heal, to cleanse, to illumine, and to renew. Amen.

Elmer C. Kieninger/Jan. 10, 1964

PROMISE TO THE PURE IN HEART

Blessed are the pure in heart, for they shall see
God. *Matthew 5:8 RSV*

What is God like? To many folks with a blurred
Christian background, God is a kindly Father
who is full of light and who draws to Himself happy, trusting people. To the ungodly, He is a fearsome, angry being
who threatens to bring punishment and destruction on
the wicked. To some philosophers of religion, God is a
moral being who loves goodness but hates evil. To hea-
then people, God is not well-defined, so He can be anything they imagine and fear. But what is God as He has
revealed Himself, and what is our prospect of seeing Him
as He really is?

The Bible tells us that the believers, the pure in heart,
will see God. But aren't their hearts also defiled with hate,
envy, covetousness, and other sins? Doesn't Jesus include
Christians when He says in Matthew 15:19: "Out of the
heart come evil thoughts, murder, adultery, sexual
immorality, theft, false testimony, slander"?

True, but God has intervened. He renews our hearts. It
is He who cleanses us from all sin through the blood of
Christ. Believing this, we are declared righteous. Now we
grow daily in purity of heart, and we truly see God.

*Heavenly Father, cleanse and purify our hearts
more and more that we may see You with better
vision. Amen.*

Alvaro A. Carino/July 9, 1978

17

Genuine Love

Let love be genuine; hate what is evil, hold
fast to what is good; love one another with
brotherly affection. *Romans 12:9–10 RSV*

*T*he steeple of a partially demolished church in a bombed German city remained standing after World War II. The roof had buckled, and a figure of Christ over the altar was covered with debris. In restoring the building, workmen discovered that the statue was undamaged except for the hands, but the hands could not be found. It was suggested that the figure of Christ remain as it was. It would preach a sermon. Instead of replacing the hands, the words "You are My hands" were lettered in the base of the statue.

We sing: "Take my hands and let them do Works that show my love for you." Ours are the hands by which God's love and mercy are extended to others. If our own love for our God is genuine, it cannot be concealed. It will reveal itself in our actions toward others, as well as in the satisfaction, joy, and peace to be experienced for ourselves. In the introduction to his German translation of the New Testament, Martin Luther provided the reason: "For where works and love do not appear, faith is not genuine, the Gospel has not taken hold, and Christ is not recognized aright."

Take my life, O Lord, renew, Consecrate my heart to you.

Milton S. Ernstmeyer/Oct. 26, 1978

A Little Quiet All Around

*The words of the wise heard in quiet are better
than the shouting of a ruler among fools.*
Ecclesiastes 9:17 RSV

*I*t has been noted that occasionally when someone
speaks English to a person who does not understand
the language, the speaker raises his or her voice. The
implication is that shouting may help the listener comprehend the message.

We tend to be addicted to noise. We are impressed by
the loud mouth and intimidated by the sharp tongue. Our
text, however, reminds us that those who are truly wise
speak softly and listen quietly. Foolish thoughts rattling
around in our heads can create such a racket that we cannot hear the quiet voice of God.

God regularly speaks to us in the still small voice of His
Word and works. There was the quiet of His Son's
unspectacular birth. His resurrection was witnessed by no
human eye. His ascension was accomplished without the
fiery roar of a liftoff. In it all, God quietly says yes to us:
"Yes, I have forgiven your sin. Yes, I know about your
unfortunate lapses, and I invite you to repent and live on
in forgiveness." All God's promises find their yes in
Christ, our Savior.

*Lamb of God, You did not open Your mouth but
went quietly to the cross. Help us cultivate the
quietness of faith. Amen.*

H. Armin Moellering/Oct. 24, 1980

ANOTHER CHANCE

*The vessel he was making of clay was spoiled
in the potter's hand, and he reworked it into
another vessel, as it seemed good to the potter
to do. Jeremiah 18:4 RSV*

God sends His prophet to a potter's shop for a learning experience. As he watches the potter at his
wheel shape a lump of clay into a symmetrical vessel, a
sudden slip ruins the vessel. Does the potter toss it aside
as worthless? No, he takes that same clay, squeezes it, and
fashions another vessel.

That was Jeremiah's message to God's people. Though
they had marred their lives by sin and repeated failure,
God would not discard them. He would make them over
and give them another chance.

Who of us is not painfully aware of having marred the
vessel of life by misuse and abuse? If it were possible,
wouldn't we like to be made over again? That is exactly
what our gracious God tells us He will do through Christ,
His Son and our Savior. It is the whole theme of the
Scriptures: "If any one is in Christ, he is a new creation"
(2 Corinthians 5:17 RSV). Although we have sadly
defaced our lives by wrongdoing and have slipped and
strayed, the all-merciful God still says: "Where sin
abounds, My grace abounds much more."

*Lord, "Thou art the Potter, I am the clay; mold me
and make me after Thy will, while I am waiting,
yielded and still." Amen.*

Albert W. Galen/March 11, 1987

20

LOVE BEGETS LOVE

"But I say unto you, Love your enemies …
do good to them that hate you.
Matthew 5:44 KJV

*A*braham Lincoln once said: "The best way to make a friend of an enemy is to love him." It is likewise true that hatred begets hatred. If we hate a neighbor who hates us, the furrow of hatred will grow deeper and wider.

"Love your enemies," says Jesus. Do we always do this? Is it easily done? Obviously not. We need God's help. He gives us this help by setting the example. As humans, we are by nature at enmity with God, but God loved us even when we hated Him. "Herein is love, not that we loved God, but that He loved us, and sent His Son to be the propitiation [payment] for our sins" (1 John 4:10).

God gives further help. He directs our attention to many noble examples. Jesus prayed: "Father, forgive them; for they know not what they do" (Luke 23:34 KJV). Stephen prayed for his enemies: "Lord, lay not this sin to their charge" (Acts 7:60 KJV).

God does even more. He gives us the power to love our enemies. The Holy Spirit brought us to faith and placed the gift of love in our hearts. Why do we love our enemies? We love them because Christ has led us to love. Love begets love. We pray for God's Spirit that we may love those who hate us.

Precious Savior, give us great love for You and for those who hate us. In Your name we pray. Amen.

Leonard H. Aurich/Jan. 19, 1968

Dorcas

This woman was full of good works and
almsdeeds which she did. *Acts 9:36 KJV*

he seaport of Joppa will be remembered to the end
of time because many centuries ago a faithful church
worker lived there. Her name was Dorcas.

This woman is remembered especially for her almsdeeds, her works of charity. She was rich both in giving
and in personal service, finding her supreme joy in hon-
oring God and helping her neighbor for Jesus' sake. In the
midst of her labors of love, she became ill and died. The
widows she had befriended wept bitter tears as they
showed Peter the coats and garments Dorcas had made. It
was through Peter that God restored her to life so she
could continue her service of love for the needy.

There are many people in this world who need the love
and assistance of others. There is no end to the call for
charity. God's redeemed children consider it a glorious
privilege to assist others who are less fortunate than they.

Services of love performed in the name of the Savior
will not go unrewarded. There is no more genuine satisfaction than that which comes to us from diligent practice
of Christian benevolence. Moreover, service rendered to
others often is rich in returns of affection and gratitude.
Above all, the Lord Himself has promised in grace to
reward the faithful deeds of love performed by His children.

Teach me, Lord, to practice love's sacred act. Amen.

Gustav Lobeck/Jan. 11, 1961

THE GOSPEL NEEDS NO TEETH

*I declare unto you the Gospel ... that Christ
died for our sins according to the Scriptures.*
1 Corinthians 15:1, 3 KJV

A militant defender of the "faith" was overheard to
say with no small amount of indignation: "What
we need is to put more teeth into the Gospel!" We may
attribute his remark either to an imprecise form of speech
or to a complete ignorance of what the Gospel really is.

The Gospel needs no teeth. In fact, it would not know
where to put them. Instead, the Gospel is a pair of extended arms (God's arms) and a pair of inviting hands (God's
hands), inviting the sinner to come home to the Father's
house.

In its strictest sense the Gospel is a simple declarative
sentence that can be summed up in five short words:
"Christ died for our sins." Even in those few instances
where the Scripture uses the imperative—for example,
"Believe on the Lord Jesus Christ"—it is using what the-
ologians call the "evangelical imperative." It is inviting the
unbeliever to believe the good news about Jesus Christ
and His substitutionary death for sinners.

No, the Gospel never needs "more teeth." It needs
more outstretched arms, more loving hands that will
extend the Gospel invitation.

*"Take my lips and keep them true, Filled with mes-
sages from You." Amen.*

Herman W. Gockel/Jan. 15, 1979

We Can Tell Others

*Go therefore and make disciples of all nations
… and lo, I am with you always.*
Matthew 28:19–20 RSV

Once God appeared in a burning bush calling, "Moses, Moses!" Moses replied, "Here am I." When God informed him that he had been chosen to lead God's people, Moses came up with excuses. "I just can't do it. I'm not a good speaker. Please send somebody else." Moses was convinced that he could not do what God asked of him.

Isn't that the way we react? Jesus wants us to tell others about His love for us and for them. Yet we often feel reluctant to talk about our faith in the Lord Jesus. Although our faith is meaningful to us, we fear that the person will not appreciate what we say.

Throughout his career, Moses was aware of his limited ability. Therefore he spent a tremendous amount of time talking to God. He lived so closely to his Lord that he was called a "friend of God." Small wonder this reluctant servant of God became a spiritual giant!

Our Lord commanded us to go into the world and tell others what Jesus taught us. To strengthen us, Jesus promised that He would be with us always. When God tells us to do something, we can go ahead with the task, assured that His Spirit will give us the power to carry it out.

Spirit of the living Lord, when we speak to others about Jesus, please give us the right words to say. Amen.

Alma Kern/Feb. 14, 1975

CHRIST LIVES IN US

I bow my knees unto the Father ...
that Christ may dwell in your hearts by faith.
Ephesians 3:14–17 KJV

*P*aul does not pray for Christ to *visit* or to *sojourn* but to *dwell* in our hearts by faith. Christ is to make His home in us. We sing: "Abide, with us, our Savior, Nor let your mercies cease." We pray: "Come, Lord Jesus, be our guest."

What a blessing it is to have Christ, the Savior from sin and Lord of life, live with us! He comes as the bearer of many gifts of grace. When He makes His abode with us, He endows us with strength to pray to Him, to follow Him as His disciples, to extend love and forgiveness to others. Because of His presence, we have guidance for life and peace for troubled consciences.

We show courtesy when we tell a guest, "Please, make yourself at home." But would we want our friend truly to make himself at home? If he were at home, he would rearrange the furniture, reshape the home, and perhaps discard mementos we treasure. Likewise, when Christ dwells in us, things cannot stay the same. He comes to renew us. He wants to reshape our lives, hearts, and homes. He wants to influence us for good. He wants to live in our hearts not only as guest, but also as host. To pray for Christ to dwell in us involves both a privilege and a responsibility.

Lord, we are not worthy that You should live under our roof, but we ask You to continue to live in our hearts. Amen.

George W. Bornemann/Oct. 6, 1970

Too Much for God?

Thy daughter is dead; trouble not the Master.
Luke 8:49 KJV

*J*ave we ever felt that our troubles were too big, even for God? The friends of Jairus felt that way. That is why they said to him: "Thy daughter is dead; trouble not the Master." Don't bother Jesus anymore, the case is beyond even His power to help.

But the Savior felt differently. He recognized no limitation on His power to help. Jesus said: "Fear not: believe only, and she shall be made whole."

We are reminded of the state of the desperate Israelites. With the Red Sea before them and the chariots of Pharaoh behind them, they were afraid and cried to God for help. Even divine help at that moment seemed out of the question, yet they *prayed!* And God said, "Fear ye not, stand still, and see the salvation of the LORD" (Exodus 14:13 KJV)

There are times in life when we must learn to stand still and to let the Lord take over. It is when we acknowledge our own complete helplessness and surrender ourselves totally to the redeeming and protecting love of Christ that we see His abundant power to help. Have we learned to stand still and let Him take over?

"Be still, my soul; your God will undertake To guide the future as He has the past. Your hope, your confidence let nothing shake; All now mysterious shall be bright at last." Amen.

Herman W. Gockel/July 13, 1976

WHO DID SIN?

His disciples asked Him, "Rabbi, who sinned,
this man or his parents, that he was born
blind?" John 9:2 RSV

*D*ay after day, a blind beggar sat at one of the temple
doors in Jerusalem. Nearly all the city's inhabitants
knew the man from their visits to the temple. The disciples, who also knew the man, were troubled by a question.
One day they asked Jesus: "Rabbi, who sinned, this man
or his parents, that he was born blind?"

Their question is so human! It showed no love or concern for the man's burden. It showed that they believed
the burden was deserved.

Note Jesus' reply: "It was not that this man sinned, or
his parents, but that the works of God might be made
manifest in him" (John 9:3). Jesus did not say that the man
and his parents were not sinners. He asserted that this
man's burden could not be traced to some *specific* sin.

What Jesus did to the blind beggar showed how He
looked at his affliction. Jesus saw an opportunity to be of
service. He healed the man, even as by His death He was
to heal him from sin.

This is the object lesson Jesus teaches us. Instead of
looking for the cause of our neighbor's afflictions, let us
see in them golden opportunities to perform Christian
service.

Lord, enable us to help our neighbor always. Amen.

Lewis E. Eickhoff/Sept. 20, 1979

DON'T WORRY!

*Have no anxiety about anything, but in
everything by prayer and supplication with
thanksgiving let your requests be made known
to God. Philippians 4:6 RSV*

"Don't worry" might seem like the silliest advice anyone could ever give. Yet here it is in black and
white, inspired by the Holy Spirit: "Have no anxiety about
anything."

Worry has got to be one of the most common problems
of the human race. It is almost a daily companion in one
form or another for many of us. Still Paul says, "Don't do
it; don't worry."

Does he suggest an alternative? Yes, and one that works
according to the testimony of many Christians: "But in
everything by prayer and supplication with thanksgiving
let your requests be made known to God." Telling God
about your problem is the alternative to worry. He cared
enough to send Jesus, His Son, to be our Savior. If He
cared that much, can't we trust Him to take care of us, to
deal with the problems that worry us?

As human beings, maybe we'll still toss and turn occasionally. But we've all seen the calm that comes to those
who commit their concerns to the Lord and wait patiently for His gift of peace. What a difference it makes! What
a basis for thanksgiving!

*Heavenly Father, give me the confidence in You
that I need so I may cast every care of mine on You.
In Jesus' name. Amen.*

Daniel A. Reeb/July 25, 1986

THE NEED FOR FAMILY

God setteth the solitary in families.
Psalm 68:6 KJV

*F*amilies are God's idea. He has ordained life that every civilization has a family system of some kind. "God setteth the solitary in families." In that sense, marriages are made in heaven, but family life is often lived in hell! That is, instead of family members pulling together, they often pull apart and against one another. As Thomas Merton wrote: "Hell is where no one has anything in common except the fact that they all hate one another and cannot get away from one another and from themselves."

Among the papers found after the death of author F. Scott Fitzgerald was a suggestion for a possible story: "A widely separated family inherits a house in which they have to live together." That would make quite a story!

Every family has tension and disagreements. But faith gives us a way to face these differences so they don't need to become divisive. First, our faith invites us to be humble, not know-it-alls. We can respect the opinions of others in the family. Second, our faith calls on us to forgive as Christ has forgiven us. How can we refuse to forgive family members when we recall the cost of our own forgiveness? Third, reconciliation—the experience that results when we have learned to communicate our differences humbly and forgivingly.

God, as You are reconciled to us, let us be reconciled to one another. Amen.

Edward W. Wessling/June 21, 1959

HONEST CONFESSION

I acknowledge my transgressions: and my sin
is ever before me. *Psalm 51:3 KJV*

*I*magine, if you will, a man kneeling in profound grief
and sincere repentance. His name is David. He is
remembering with deep shame and sorrow great sins he
has committed.

Suppose that you and I were kneeling at that altar.
Would we also have reason to think with shame and
remorse about what we have done? Have we ever used
God's holy name for profanity or harbored feelings of
hatred, bitterness, vengeance, pride, selfishness, greed, or
miserliness in our heart? If so, then we will know something of what David felt.

David wants to tell God what is on his heart, and this is
what he says: "I acknowledge my transgressions: and my
sin is ever before me." David realized that he was not only
born in sin, but also a sinner by practice. He had been
working at it. He was so acutely conscious of this that he
had to tell God about it.

You and I also humbly, sorrowfully tell God about our
sins. The man who once stood in the temple and said to
God, "I thank Thee that I am not like other men," (Luke
18:11 RSV) may have talked to the moon but not to God.
To reach God's ear, sinners say, "I acknowledge my transgressions." Then they plead, "God, be merciful to me, a
sinner, for Jesus' sake."

*Dear heavenly Father, by Your Holy Spirit, grant
us in grace the ability honestly, penitently to lay our
sins at Your throne of mercy, for Jesus' sake. Amen.*

Otto A. Geiseman/March 16, 1961

30

GRATEFUL WITNESS

Restore unto me the joy of Thy salvation …
Then will I teach transgressors Thy ways.
Psalm 51:12–13 KJV

Great joy and a deep sense of peace came into the heart of David when he threw himself on God's mercy. This was an experience so thrilling and reassuring that David found it necessary to tell other sinners about it.

This explains why he so often spoke of God's mercy and forgiving love in the many beautiful psalms or hymns. No one but God could begin to count the vast numbers of people who have learned about His love from David. Even now, multitudes of people love to sit with the hymnbook of the Old Testament, the Psalter, and allow David to tell them about God, sin, and the mercy of a forgiving heavenly Father.

David's mouth spoke out of the fullness of his heart. Our mouth will do likewise if we feel any comparable sense of thanks to God for His love to us. This does not mean that we will mount a soapbox and behave ourselves like fanatics. It does mean we will eagerly and happily witness with our lips and lives to God's forgiving love in Christ.

"Oh, that I had a thousand voices To praise my God with thousand tongues! My heart, which in the Lord rejoices, Would then proclaim in grateful songs To all, wherever I might be, What great things God has done for me." Amen.

Otto A. Geiseman/March 18, 1961

31

THE REAL PROMISE OF CHRIST

And this is the promise that He hath promised
us, even eternal life. 1 John 2:25 KJV

*T*he temporal blessings and benefits of Christianity are frequently overemphasized. Certain spokespeople hold out the promise that once a person believes in Christ, there will be no worries, no troubles.

Certainly, belief in Christ as Savior and Lord brings peace of mind and serenity. The Savior's promise "My peace I give to you" holds true also for His people in modern times. However, our Lord also warns us *not* to look for temporal or material rewards when we follow Him. He cautions all who believe in Him that the cost of discipleship in this world will be high.

The real promise that He holds out, however, is far more wonderful than any immediate earthly gain. That promise is nothing less than eternal life. It centers in the forgiveness of sins. It is fulfilled in the new relationship with God that forgiveness brings, where we are accepted as God's dear children—whom He still chastens in love but upon whom He looks with favor and everlasting mercy. This new relationship with God will last forever. It is the precious gift that Christ bestows on all who believe in Him.

This means a new life, beginning right now. Despite our problems, we are filled with courage, hope, and joy. God is for us—now and forever.

Lord, let me hide myself in You. Amen.

T. A. Weinhold/May 11, 1959

UNCEASING PRAYER

Pray without ceasing.
1 Thessalonians 5:17 KJV

*P*rayer is a good spiritual exercise. St. Paul tells us, "Pray without ceasing." Pray every day, every hour, in the name of the Lord Jesus. Pray in good times and in bad.

Too often we treat God like an attendant in a hospital emergency room. We run to Him only when we are in trouble, when the marriage isn't working out, when we get sick, when we lose our job, when we have trouble at school, or when we go to the funeral home to make arrangements for the burial of a loved one.

We can, of course, come to our gracious God in the time of trouble and the hour of sorrow. Jesus gives this invitation, "Come unto Me, all ye that labor and are heavy laden, and I will give you rest" (Matthew 11:28 KJV).

We also can come to Him in good times. We can share with Him our joys; invite Jesus to weddings, birthdays, and anniversaries; thank Him for all of His beautiful, bountiful blessings; and thank Him for the greatest gift of all—our eternal salvation.

Pray without ceasing, and "What things soever ye desire, when ye pray, believe that ye receive them, and ye shall have them," said Jesus (Mark 11:24 KJV).

Dear Lord Jesus, we thank You for the privilege of prayer that You have given us as the children of God. Amen.

Victor F. Halboth Jr./Aug. 13, 1981

Our Hardest Subject

Even though the desire to do good is in me,
I am not able to do it. I don't do the good
I want to do; instead, I do the evil that
I do not want to do. Romans 7:18–19 TEV

While looking over his daughter's report card, Father suddenly frowned. "Looks good, Ruthie," he said, "but what about this D in conduct?" "But, Daddy," came the reply, "conduct is my hardest subject!"

So it is for all of us, even for St. Paul. "What a wretched man I am!" he berates himself (Romans 7:24). "What I want to do I do not do, but what I hate I do" (Romans 7:15). The wide inconsistency between faith and performance is no doubt the most frustrating problem in life for all of us.

In struggling through the problem, Paul comes up with the answer: "Thanks be to God—through Jesus Christ our Lord!" (Romans 7:25). Like Paul, we must be ready to admit frankly and openly that of ourselves we simply can't make the grade. Humbled by our inability, we draw strength from knowing that through Christ our failures are covered by His spotless perfection.

Not I, but Christ! He is the source of our power to do the good and not the evil. Only as we rely on His power can we progress in our hardest subject.

Grant me grace each day, dear Lord, that Your strength may be made perfect in my weakness. For Your love's sake. Amen.

Albert W. Galen/March 28, 1987

34

A Time to Forgive

Love does not insist on its own way.
1 Corinthians 13:5 RSV

*T*here are times when we allow the other person—a child, a spouse, a congregation member—to make a mistake. Continuously correcting a person robs him or her of dignity. It says, "You are free to act only as long as you are right." Sometimes "right" is no more than opinion.

God does not deal with us that way. He does not reject those who have done wrong and seek His forgiveness. He is always there to forgive, to heal, and to show mercy. Jesus describes the Father in this way in the story of the prodigal son.

There are times when we are called to speak right judgments. Loveless judgment, on the other hand, is all our old nature understands. Such judgment may seek to kill what is wrong in our relationships, but it also threatens what is good.

Words of judgment, having brought about a changed heart, need to be followed by forgiveness. Forgiveness binds together the relationship. God daily forgives us through Christ's sacrifice on the cross. Daily we forgive others as God forgives us. We say, "I, too, am a sinner. I forgive you."

Lord, forgive me for all that I have done wrong today. Move me to forgive others and so extend Your forgiveness into their lives. Amen.

C. Leo Symmank/July 20, 1987

GOD'S PERSONAL CARE

The LORD shut him in. *Genesis 7:16 RSV*

*P*ersonal care is the hallmark of love. Witness it in the instance of a mother attending to an injured or rejected child, or see it as a nurse ministers to the ill.

In the narrative of Noah, witness God Himself bending down from heaven toward a violent and corrupt world. With extraordinary tenderness, He reaches out to Noah and his family to rescue them from certain destruction.

Noah is warned, seemingly before others, of the impending catastrophe. He is chosen not only to be saved, but also to be an instrument to save his family and two of "every living thing of all flesh." God personally provided the plan, the dimensions, and the design of the lifesaving ark.

God aided Noah by giving the animals a voluntary impulse to come to Noah. He also provided everyone in the ark, human being and beast, with food for the 150-day, or 5-month, stay. When the rains came and everyone was in the ark, God personally shut the door—a most tender touch!

God also chose us and saved us by the flood of our Baptism. He provides us with all we need to sustain—yes, even enjoy—life. And He often shuts the door to adversity to protect us. In Christ we are safe.

We thank You, Father, for a lifetime of personal care. Amen.

Bernard H. Arkebauer/Aug. 11, 1982

THE GLORY OF CONVERSION

They glorified God in me. *Galatians 1:24 KJV*

*I*t was a great day for the early Christians when it became known that Paul, the bitter enemy of Christianity, had become the greatest defender of the Gospel. Neither he nor they, however, had any false notions about the reason for this radical change. Paul says of himself: "God called me by His grace." He says about the Christians: "They glorified God in me." The conversion of Paul was not the choice of a free human mind but a miracle performed by God Himself.

It is no different in our case. Our ancestors may have been pious Christians. We ourselves may have lived all of our lives in a Christian environment. We may devote all the talents of our gifted minds to the study of spiritual things. We may even spend our years in the ministry. All of this does not assure our conversion or make us Christians. Rather, these are the fruits of our conversion. Our conversion was and is the work of God alone. It is another revelation of the glory of our Lord that He takes those who are His enemies and makes them His friends and followers by the converting grace of His Holy Spirit. To God we owe thanksgiving, prayers for His continued grace, and the finest gifts of our devotion to His service.

Spirit of God, by whom alone we are converted, grant us grace to know this, faithfulness to persevere, and a heart to worship and serve You with the Father and the Son, Jesus our Savior. Amen.

Daniel E. Poellot/Dec. 15, 1981

She Got What She Asked For

Thy will be done. Matthew 6:10 RSV

An elderly woman lay sick in a hospital. Her talkative neighbor went to great lengths to express her sympathy. "It's a shame this had to happen to you"—and so on and on.

Finally the woman in bed interrupted. "Ellen, I don't see it that way at all," she said. "I'm getting exactly what I asked for. For many years I've been ending my evening prayers with: 'Nevertheless, not my will, but Thine be done.' The way I see it, even my present illness is part of God's answer to that prayer. It's His will that's being done, and I know that His will is always for my best."

Have you and I learned to look at our crosses as part of God's "good and gracious will"? We who have seen the God of heaven in the face of Jesus Christ need not be afraid of committing our lives entirely to His will. We know that His will for us is one of love and tender mercy. Through Christ we know that God is on our side. If God is for us, who or what can be against us? Because we know that we have a gracious God in heaven, we can pray with confidence: "Thy will be done." When we pray this, we get what we ask for.

Lord, because of Christ, I know that You are my loving Father. Therefore I pray with confidence: "Your will be done." Amen.

Herman W. Gockel/Oct. 28, 1987

WE BELONG TO GOD

[Mary and Joseph] brought [Jesus] to
Jerusalem to present Him to the Lord.
Luke 2:22 RSV

*T*he last plague to come on the Egyptians was the
killing of the firstborn. Among the Israelites, the
firstborn sons were mercifully spared. Therefore, God
claimed them for special service to Himself.

Later only the sons of the tribe of Levi were accepted
for this service; all others had to be redeemed. Therefore,
Mary and Joseph brought Jesus to present Him to the
Lord and to offer the required payment of redemption. In
the church calendar, February 2 is the day on which we
celebrate this event.

On this occasion, God would remind us that we belong
to Him by virtue of Christ's redemption. See the dignity
conferred on us! Our bodies have been redeemed with the
blood of Christ. We are not our own. Too often people
say, "My body is my own. I may do with it as I please."
Wrong! We have our body and life as a trust from God.
They remain His possession. We are only stewards who
must give God an account of how we have used His possession. What a challenge for daily Christian living! The
apostle says, "Ye are bought with a price: therefore glorify God in your body and in your spirit, which are God's"
(1 Corinthians 6:10 KJV).

*Lord God, help me so to use my body and life that
I need not hesitate to give You an account of my
stewardship. Amen.*

Herbert W. Berner/Feb. 2, 1978

39

Praising God in Music

*Praise the Lord with the lyre, make melody
to Him with the harp of ten strings!*
Psalm 33:2 RSV

*T*oday marks the birthday of the well-known Lutheran composer of the 19th century, Felix Mendelssohn. Already at the age of 10, he appeared as a concert pianist. By the age of 12, he had written several compositions.

Mendelssohn placed his talents into the service of the church, doing much to revive interest in and appreciation for the music of Bach. He also wrote several oratorios as well as the music for the well-known hymn "Hark! The Herald Angels Sing."

The Lord delights in the music His children make to Him. We have every reason to sing when we remember what great things God has done for our salvation. In Christ He has made us His children. It puts a song in our hearts and on our lips when we remember the enemy of our souls has been defeated and the victory is ours.

The singing of hymns constitutes an important part of our worship. What a thrill fills our hearts when we recall that we have this opportunity to join the communion of saints in worshiping our God in this manner! We respond joyfully to the invitation: "Praise the Lord with the lyre, make melody to Him with the harp of ten strings!"

Dear Lord, accept the song of our hearts and the praise of our lips, for You have redeemed us. Amen.

Herbert W. Berner/Feb. 3, 1978

Out of the Depths

Out of the belly of hell cried I. *Jonah 2:2 KJV*

*N*o words uttered by our dying Savior on the cross are more mysterious and yet more comforting than these: "My God, My God, why have You forsaken Me?" Who can fully understand this—Christ completely forsaken by His heavenly Father? Yet that is what our sins did to Him. He had to drink the cup of suffering to its last bitter drops. The pains and terrors of hell took hold of Him. He was completely forsaken by God so you and I need never be abandoned in hell.

No matter the depths to which we may fall, if we turn in faith to our Lord, we have help and forgiveness in Jesus' name. David found this to be true. "Out of the depths" he cried in his extremity and God heard Him. That, too, was Jonah's experience. In his helplessness and hopelessness in the fish's belly, he cried *to* and not *against* the Lord. He acknowledged his disobedience and threw himself on God's mercy, and the Lord heard him.

Certainly a fish's belly is a strange altar for prayer! Sin can bring horrible and strange circumstances. Yet if Jonah could cry to the Lord from the depths of the sea and be heard, there is no place, either high or low, that will keep us from calling on our Lord.

In the shadow of the cross, we draw near to You, dear Savior. Increase our faith that no suffering may darken our trust in You. We know You will never forsake us; have mercy on us, and grant that we may never be separated from You. Amen.

Stratford Eynon/March 16, 1960

ONCE MORE, WITH THANKSGIVING

Let the word of Christ dwell in you richly,
teach and admonish one another in all wisdom,
and sing psalms and hymns and spiritual songs
with thankfulness. *Colossians 3:16 RSV*

We've probably done it many times: Read the Bible, discussed the message of God's grace, and said our prayers in the company of fellow believers. We have felt the encouragement of our corporate response to God's gift of salvation. Shall we keep doing it? Yes, because there is so much more of God's Word for us yet to receive.

If we are content with crumbs, we will starve. If we fail to exercise, we will shrivel and die. If we neglect the rich fullness of God's Word, we impoverish our faith. If we fail to bless God for His goodness toward us, our resolve to serve Him shrinks. So once more, with thankfulness to God, let's not forget to get together to worship Him. He has provided the refreshing waters of life in Christ to revive our parched hopes. By the promise of His grace, He relieves our guilty consciences. Through Christ, He pardons all our sins. We are made new.

We come together because we have so much to learn. There's more joy in Christ yet to uncover. More power from Him is yet to be received.

Implant Your rich Word in us, O God, that receiving it more fully we may teach and sing of Jesus more joyfully. Amen.

Victor A. Constien/April 7, 1979

Soil Conditions

But those that were sown upon the good soil
are the ones who hear the word and accept it
and bear fruit, thirtyfold and sixtyfold and a
hundredfold. *Mark 4:20 RSV*

*A*lmost all of us have planted a package of seeds. Even in this small agricultural effort, we may have discovered the importance of soil conditions. The seed in too-shallow soil grows quickly but soon dies. The seed sprinkled in a rocky area germinates very sparsely. The seed in a weedy spot is choked out. But ah, the sweet success that comes when good seed is planted in fertile ground!

What kind of ground are we? Countless times each week God's Word is "planted" in our hearts through sermons, Bible studies, devotional readings, and the like. Has it taken root? Have our hearts been fertile soil, prepared and ready to foster growth in Jesus, our Lord and Savior?

The Holy Spirit prepares the soil of our hearts as we continue to study God's Word. We pray that God will let His Word speak to us. We provide ourselves with tools such as commentaries, different translations, and study guides to assist us in understanding and growing in the Word. Then we "dig in." Christ's love will become a power in us. God's Word will grow in our lives. We will see the fruit of that Word mature in us and bring us closer to our Lord and Savior, Jesus Christ.

Lord, prepare my heart to receive Your Word. Let it ever grow within me and bring forth good fruit. Amen.

Jeanette L. Groth/Aug. 10, 1986

Down from the Mountain

*When they lifted up their eyes, they saw no
one but Jesus only.... They were coming
down the mountain. Matthew 17:8-9 RSV*

Can you recall a mountaintop experience in your life?
A celebration or reunion, a time of special sharing
with a loved one, a beautiful vacation sight? Those precious
moments are over too soon. Unfortunately, like the bear
who went over the mountain in the old nursery rhyme, we
reach the other side and have to come back down again.

The disciples were overcome with Jesus' glory, but as
suddenly as it happened, it was gone. Likewise Jacob
awoke from his vision of a ladder to heaven and proceed-
ed on his journey to a strange land and a frightening,
unsure future.

Praising God with His saints on earth and receiving
His love and forgiveness in Word and Sacrament are
mountaintops God offers us every Sunday. But it is not
only on the mountaintops that God is with us. Jesus came
back *down* the mountain, back to dusty roads and demanding crowds and long days of teaching and healing, back to
His suffering and death for them—and for us!

Jesus comes back with us to our valleys, back to the
burdens we left behind and have to pick up again. Isn't it
great that through them all we too can look up and see
"Jesus only"?

*We praise You, O Lord! You come down from the
heavens to our earth. You lift us to the mountaintops of Your presence. Amen.*

Louise Mueller/July 15, 1984

44

The Ears of Jesus

O Thou that hearest prayer, unto Thee shall
all flesh come. *Psalm 65:2 KJV*

*I*t is a noisy world we live in: TV, radio, traffic noises,
bells, whistles, the roar of jets overhead, the shrieking
of children at play. When Jesus moved among people, He
heard the hum of human life around Him. These took on
a special meaning for Him, for He had come to share fully
the life of fallen sinners.

Jesus' ears heard words of human kindness, love, cheer,
comfort. But they also heard many words spoken in anger,
in lust, in envy, in selfishness, in blasphemy. These were
only some of the sins for which He made atonement.

Often His ears heard a call for help, for forgiveness, for
divine guidance and comfort. His ears were sensitive to
such sounds. The cry of one lone beggar in the crowded
streets of Jericho was enough to stop Him in His tracks.
The unspoken cry of a little man in a sycamore tree
prompted Jesus to look up and say, "Zacchaeus, make
haste, and come down; for to day I must abide at thy
house" (Luke 19:5 KJV). Even on the cross His ears were
quick to hear the cry of the lonely heart, "Lord, remember me when Thou comest into Thy kingdom" (Luke
23:42 KJV).

On His throne of glory, Jesus continues to listen for the
call for help coming from the hearts of those who believe
in Him. His ears are always open to our prayers.

Lord Jesus, teach us to pray. Amen.

Herbert A. Mueller/May 9, 1961

LISTEN!

A voice came from the cloud, saying,
"This is My Son, whom I have chosen;
listen to Him." *Luke 9:35*

*T*he transfiguration brings Jesus into focus. Our Lord takes Peter, James, and John up onto a mountain to pray. Jesus' prayer time was, it seems, nap time for the disciples. But as they rest, Jesus is transfigured. The appearance of His face changes; His clothing glitters like lightning; and Moses and Elijah appear in glorious splendor and talk with our Lord. A cloud settles over the scene.

A voice from the cloud echoes the words spoken by the Father at Jesus' baptism: "This is My Son, whom I have chosen; listen to Him."

The transfiguration is a sign that points to Jesus, the promised Messiah, who would deliver His people from the bondage of sin. The transfiguration points to Jerusalem and the exodus, or departure from life, that the Lord Jesus would make there as the true Passover Lamb.

As we prepare for the Lenten season, we learn anew to listen to the Son. His words tell us how He suffered under the weight of our sin so our life, as poor and covered with shame as it is, might be transfigured by His cross and empty grave.

King of Glory, keep our ears tuned to Your voice, that our hearts may know Your peace and joy. Amen.

John T. Pless/Feb. 5, 1989

On Getting Lost

I tell you, there is joy before the angels of God
over one sinner who repents. Luke 15:10 RSV

I had never read a sadder letter. It told of the sudden
death of a father—a man who years before had drifted
from church and God but because of unfulfilled intentions
and repeated postponements had never made it back. The
last words still linger in my memory: "It's so easy to get lost
from God. Some forget how easy it is to return."

Yes, many know how easy it is to get lost. As they
become more enmeshed in the daily grind, obstacles pile
up. It grows harder and harder to find the way back to
God.

Yet God is always near—nearer than they think—
yearning for them, seeking, searching, calling them back.
That is the picture of God that Jesus places before us in
the three stories of Luke 15: the seeking shepherd, the
searching housewife, and the yearning father. In each
case, the seekers celebrate with spontaneous joy when the
search and the wait are rewarded.

Dare we ever forget how much we mean to God? How
very much we mean has been proved by the price He paid
to get us back: Not with "silver or gold, but with the precious brood of Christ" (1 Peter 1:18–19 RSV).Who can
refuse a God like that?

Thank You, gracious God, that Your Welcome
Home *sign is always out for every penitent sinner.*
Amen.

Albert W. Galen/Jan. 22, 1982

A Coin to Be Spent

When ye pray, say, ... forgive us our sins;
for we also forgive every one that is indebted
to us. Luke 11:2, 4 KJV

*F*requently the newspapers bring us the story of some eccentric who died of malnutrition while surrounded by riches. The victim is usually found in a shabby apartment crowded with the odds and ends with which the person could not part. In the mattress or a cupboard is the fortune that could have bought a comfortable life, but all the person did with the money was count it.

We shake our heads and remark, "What I would not do if that money were mine!" Money is to be spent purposefully. We cannot quite understand the miser who deprives himself of the essentials of life. Yet many of us are like this when it comes to God's forgiveness. We seek it over and over again. We talk about it, treasure it; we would not be without it. But forgiveness is not a keepsake. It is a coin to be spent in the course of daily living. God forgives us for Christ's sake so we might forgive those who trespass against us.

Grudge bearing and the demand of an eye for an eye spoil friendly relationships. Forgiveness dissolves the discord and lets us and our neighbor begin again with a clean slate and pursue healthy relationships.

One can become impoverished by spending money, but one never goes bankrupt by lavishing forgiveness on others. "Give, and it shall be given unto you" (Luke 6:38 KJV).

Gracious Lord, help us enjoy Your forgiveness purchased by Christ by passing it on to others. Amen.

Jack H. Ruff/June 21, 1964

48

OUR BROTHER

*Since therefore the children share in flesh and
blood, He Himself likewise partook of the
same nature. Hebrews 2:14 RSV*

*B*rotherhood awards are associated with February 12,
the birthday of Abraham Lincoln, because the great
emancipator was far ahead of his day in recognizing the
unity of humankind. The color of one's skin doesn't stand
in the way of true unity. God has made of one blood all
nations on our small planet.

But after creation, sin came into our hearts and ways,
and unity became a myth. Cain killed Abel. Isaac got into
trouble with Ishmael. Joseph's brothers sold him into slavery So it goes: Arabs vs. Jews. Catholics vs. Protestants.
Orthodox Christians vs. Muslims.

True unity can be restored only when we recognize
Christ as our big brother who "died for sins once for all,
the righteous for the unrighteous, to bring you to God"
(1 Peter 3:18). Another reference says, "Ye are all the children of God by faith in Christ Jesus" (Galatians 3:26
KJV).

Here's how we prove Jesus is our brother: "Whoever
does God's will is My brother and sister" (Mark 3:35).
Again, "Jesus Christ laid down His life for us. And we
ought to lay down our lives for our brothers" (1 John
3:16).

*Brother, help us love all our brothers and sisters.
Amen.*

Bertwin L. Frey/Feb. 12, 1972

A Good Work

Why trouble ye the woman?
for she hath wrought a good work upon Me.
Matthew 26:10 KJV

What a waste! It might have been sold for much and given to the poor. This was the reaction of the disciples when Mary of Bethany anointed Jesus' feet with precious ointment. When something is proposed that shows great love for Jesus, His house, or His kingdom, do we, too, think of the poor? Yet how often do we think of the poor when we are about to make an expenditure for ourselves?

But Jesus said Mary had done a good work. And it was so beautifully timed. His enemies were plotting His destruction, and He knew it. Before Him lay Gethsemane, the horror of courtrooms, the way of sorrows, crucifixion, death. He appreciated the love of Mary, which forgot about cost. He would remember this act of love amid the dark hours of His passion, when no one would seem to care. And to the end of time the church would remember it and be encouraged to follow Mary's example.

Today, when there are things that can be done for Jesus, let us, like Mary, eagerly seize the opportunities. Today may be the day to speak the Gospel to someone groping in the dark, to help a person in need, to visit a home of loneliness. Let us use this day for good works for Him, remembering not the cost or effort.

O Jesus, help us to love You, not counting the cost but only rejoicing in this, that we can serve You. Amen.

Louis W. Grother/March 1, 1962

50

God's Valentine

God so loved the world, that He gave His only begotten Son. John 3:16 KJV

*F*or many of us, our earliest recollection of Valentine's Day was the heart-pounding anticipation of getting a valentine from the one we secretly "loved." How we read all kinds of hidden meanings into the printed card or candy heart! How crushed we were if we didn't get the valentine we hoped for!

"Dearly beloved," God addresses every one of us, "I have loved you with an everlasting love." We would have been elated if He had merely acknowledged our existence. But to have Him care enough about us to put His love in writing—and to go beyond that to prove that He means it when He says, "I love you," by giving us His most precious possession, His only Son—that makes God's the best valentine of all.

God did not leave us guessing as to how He feels about us, each and every one of us. In our Baptism He told us personally, "You are My beloved child." Publicly on Good Friday, He said, "This is how much I love you."

When we feel unloved, all we have to do is open God's valentine, His holy Word—and take each promise personally.

You really meant it when You said You loved me, Lord Jesus. Help me mean it when I say I love You too. Amen.

Jaroslav J. Vajda/Feb. 14, 1987

Seeking First God's Kingdom

Seek ye first the kingdom of God, and His
righteousness; and all these things shall be
added unto you. *Matthew 6:33 KJV*

*T*he story is told of a couple on a Caribbean cruise. To
cut down on the cost of their meals, they took along
a supply of "junk" food and prepared their own simple
meals in their cabin. On the very last day of the cruise,
another couple asked them why they were not eating their
meals in the dining room. The frugal pair confessed that
they were eating "junk" food in their cabin. You can imagine how disconcerting it was when the couple learned that
the price of their ticket included all meals aboard ship.

There is something even more disconcerting than that.
Too many people live out their entire lives existing on
"junk" food when they could be enjoying the Bread of
Life.

Life is more than things. We enjoy all the material
blessings of life—TV, stereo, golf. But such things cannot
bring real happiness. We need the good news of God's
love for us in Christ Jesus. The blood of Christ cleanses
us from all sin. The cross brings purpose to our life as we
serve Jesus and our fellow human beings in God's kingdom. When we put this first, we have the promise of
God's blessings given us by grace.

*Dear Lord Jesus, help us to live one day at a time
and to bask in the sunshine of Your love. Amen.*

Victor F. Halboth Jr./Aug. 5, 1981

"Be Not Afraid!"

*Immediately He talked with them,
and saith unto them, "Be of good cheer: it is I;
be not afraid." Mark 6:50 KJV*

*H*ave you ever been afraid, really afraid? Many things can strike terror into our hearts. The doctor says in a quiet voice, "It's malignant." Or the supervisor says, "I'm sorry, we must make some cutbacks. We hope the layoff is only temporary." The telephone rings in the middle of the night, and a strange voice says, "There has been an accident. Can you come to the hospital?"

The disciples in today's reading were afraid. They were in the midst of a terrifying, turbulent storm. Then Jesus came to them, walking on the water. Jesus, true God and true man, can perform mighty miracles. "He went up unto them into the ship; and the wind ceased" (Mark 6:51).

"Be of good cheer: it is I; be not afraid." We have this reassurance of our radiant Redeemer. When we are bothered and bewildered by fear and anxiety, Jesus comes to us with His love. He brings calmness and courage to our hearts. We focus our eyes of faith on the Lord Jesus. He will bring relief and release. He has removed fear and guilt. He died on the cross for all our sins. We can cope with life when we realize that we are God-made, God-saved, and God-loved. The Gospel has the power to chase away our fears.

Dear Lord Jesus, we thank You for Your redeeming love. Amen.

Victor F. Halboth Jr./Feb. 9, 1984

The Word of Forgiveness

And when He saw their faith He said, "Man,
your sins are forgiven you." Luke 5:20 RSV

Just imagine how the doctors and nurses in your local hospital would react if you walked up to the bed of a paralyzed patient, placed your hands on the still body, looked into the person's eyes, and said, "My son, your sins are forgiven." Whoever heard of such a thing?

Such surprises entered the hearts of those in the city of Capernaum who saw Jesus do that very thing to a man who was paralyzed. They expected the miracle-working Christ to deal first with the paralyzed limbs that condemned this man to a bedridden existence.

"Son, or daughter, your sins are forgiven." Is that what we expect from Jesus Christ today? Does that word take us by surprise, too, when we consider all of the social and emotional problems that plague the world?

Christ's first word is forgiveness because only that word penetrates to the root of our problems. We are confused and perplexed because we are adrift from God. That is why the greatest word of all remains this declaration of Christ: "Son, your sins are forgiven"—forgiven because He died for them.

Blessed Lord, we receive from You pardon for all of our sins. Thank You for that word of grace. Amen.

John F. Johnson/April 3, 1987

TRIUMPH IN DEATH

Thanks be to God, who gives us the victory
through our Lord Jesus Christ.
1 Corinthians 15:57 RSV

*T*oday marks the anniversary of Martin Luther's death. In a sense he really began to live when he discovered the meaning of Christ's righteousness imputed to us through faith. A whole new world was opened to him. It was one of the early steps that set him on the way to becoming the great Reformer of the church. Now he realized what a blessed truth lay in the words, "The just shall live by his faith" (Habakkuk 2:4 KJV). This removed the fear of death for him. He saw in Christ not only his Judge, but above all his Savior.

In this faith, Luther could write: "Christ became our Substitute and let the Law, sin, and death fall upon Him in our behalf. He not only removed them from us but utterly conquered them so that they should possess neither right nor power over us and that we might have complete victory in Christ." As he lay dying, Luther confidently confessed: "I pass away; Father, I yield up my spirit into Thy hands; Thou hast redeemed me, Lord, Thou faithful God."

What Scripture says of Abel is certainly true also of Luther: "He died, but through his faith he is still speaking" (Hebrews 11:4 RSV). What he says is this: "Thanks be to God, who gives us the victory through our Lord Jesus Christ."

Dear Lord, give us the faith not only to live but also to die confidently and victoriously. Amen.

Herbert W. Berner/Feb. 18, 1978

PORTRAIT OF A CLIMBER

He ran on ahead and climbed up into a
sycamore tree. *Luke 19:4 RSV*

Some selfish climbers do not hesitate to step on others
to rise above them. But Zacchaeus was not a member
of this club.

Conversely, Zacchaeus ignored damaged dignity and
invited criticism to meet Jesus, his Savior. Zacchaeus, an
Israelite, belonged to the despised class of publicans and
sinners. He had a desire to meet Him who had elevated
Matthew, a fellow tax collector, to discipleship. As
Zacchaeus' climb illustrates, a person's entry into the kingdom of God is sometimes preceded by unusual action.

Christ knew Zacchaeus because He called him by
name. Zacchaeus' climbing changed the Savior's plans
because He now announced, "I must stay at your house
today." Those who through the power of the Holy Spirit
seek Christ find that He first sought them.

Zacchaeus paid a high price for climbing: loss of dignity and wealth, community eyebrow raising, ridicule. But
his "high price" was nothing compared to the precious
pearl he found: Jesus Christ. Salvation came to his house
that day. That blessed day Christ, the Morning Star, rose
to shine in his life, never to set again. What a glorious
climb!

*Grant us the power, O Lord Jesus Christ, constant-
ly to climb nearer to You, so day by day we may grow
in the certainty of salvation in our house. Amen.*

Bernhard H. Arkebauer/Nov. 23, 1979

Putting Christ First

Let the dead bury their dead. Luke 9:60 KJV

O nce we have heard Christ's command, "Follow Me," it echoes within our hearts. We remember the man who answered Jesus' command to follow Him by saying, "Lord, suffer me first to go and bury my father." Jesus' answer was clear and decisive: "Let the dead bury their dead: but go thou and preach the kingdom of God." For ancient Jews, no obligation was more sacred than burying the dead.

To follow Jesus indeed calls for self-denial and even more because Jesus demands first place in our lives. Our natural feelings must be set aside. He calls us into a relationship with Him that is higher than family, state, and world.

This is a rude shock to the mental pictures we have of the Christian faith. Life is not essentially more pleasant and easy. In absolute, almost shocking terms, Christ insists on total devotion. He will not be a means to another end. He is the end and object of faith and trust. We do not hold to Him because of some future benefit. There is no bargaining involved. We love Him for who He is. We worship the God who fashioned us. We adore Him who died for us. We dedicate ourselves to Him who daily guides us. His call to discipleship—to follow Him—takes precedence over every other duty in life.

We put Him first!

Fasten our eyes more firmly on You that our love for You may deepen. Amen.

David S. Schuller/Aug. 13, 1959

LIVING FOR JESUS

*He died for all, that they which live should not
henceforth live unto themselves, but unto Him
which died for them, and rose again.*
2 Corinthians 5:15 KJV

Over the door of a church in Germany, a lamb is cut
in stone. This is the story. While a man was at work
on the church steeple, he lost his footing and fell. He
struck a lamb grazing in the churchyard. His fall was broken and he escaped death, but the lamb died. In gratitude
the man had the figure of a lamb cut into the stone above
the church door. It was his monument of gratitude to the
lamb that had lost its life in saving his.

There was another Lamb that gave His life for us. It
was Jesus, the Lamb of God. He died for all. We were the
sinners who deserved to die, but Jesus bore our sins and
died in our place. By His death, He won eternal life for us.

For that, we owe Him a debt of gratitude we can never
repay. What monument shall we raise to Him who gave
His life for us? Let it be the monument of a life lived in
love and gratitude to Him. When we have learned the
meaning of the statement "Christ died for me," our
response will be, "Henceforth I will live for Him. As I
travel the highway to heaven, my life will be spent in loving service to Him who loved me and died for me and set
my feet on the way to heaven." We can do no less than
that for Him who has done so much for us.

*"Take my life, O Lord, renew Consecrate my heart
to you." Amen.*

Felix Kretzschmar/Sept. 11, 1963

THE POWER OF FAITH

All things, whatsoever ye shall ask in prayer,
believing, ye shall receive. *Matthew 21:22 KJV*

To understand, we must note the word *believing*. To believe means to trust, to have confidence in someone. When we pray, we pray in faith. We trust our Lord.

We have confidence in His wisdom as well as in His power and love. We do not know for what to pray because we do not know what is good for us. But He knows, and in His wisdom, He will grant us exactly that. This is why the best prayer is always the prayer of our Lord in Gethsemane, "Your will be done."

We can pray that prayer with full confidence that we will receive all things that are best for us. The Bible promises, "All things work together for good to them that love God" (Romans 8:28 KJV).

This Lenten season reminds us that there is one thing that we truly need: God's forgiveness for our sins. We have this forgiveness through Christ. Scripture says, "He that spared not His own Son, but delivered Him up for us all, how shall He not with Him also freely give us all things?" (Romans 8:32 KJV). God has given us His dearest and best in Jesus. He will not fail to give us gifts of less value as we need them.

"Lord, give us such a faith as this; And then, whate'er may come, We'll taste e'en now the hallowed bliss Of an eternal home." Amen.

Henry F. Wind/March 2, 1959

59

The Gift of Forbearance

Forbearing one another and forgiving one another. Colossians 3:13 KJV

*I*n these days of Lent, God's love is much on our minds. So is His infinite patience. He has for ages been patient with this world. He has been patient with you and me, who have sinned against Him, sometimes ignorantly, but too often in full awareness.

God has been merciful because He has permitted us time for reflection, for repentance, and for our pleas to Him for forgiveness. He has not cut us off and cast us away, though He has had thousandfold reason to do so.

Our text says that Christ has forgiven us. He asked His Father to do so, then paid for our transgressions so the justice of God could and might yield to His love.

Now God asks us to show forbearance and forgiveness to one another too. He asks us to show meekness and patience rather than the flintlike hardness of pride, which strikes off sparks to set our unity in Christ in flames.

Two factors loom large in this plea. One is humility; the other is obedience. Both of these are Christlike things. "He humbled Himself, and became obedient unto death, even the death of the cross" (Philippians 2:8 KJV). Are we to be humble as He was? We need to be because after His humiliation, He has been highly exalted. Before the throne not pride, but humility and obedience are honored.

Dear Father, let this mind-set be in us that was also in Christ Jesus. Amen.

Richard A. Jesse/April 8, 1965

A Friend of Sinners

The Pharisees and the scribes murmured,
saying, "This man receives sinners and eats
with them." *Luke 15:2 RSV*

A favorite accusation that Jesus' enemies made against Him was that He befriended sinners and associated with them. They meant it as a reflection on Him. By this charge they sought to undermine His influence and authority. The charge was true. He was a friend to all who would welcome His friendship. He had friends and loyal followers among all classes of people. But He did not mingle with sinners to be like them or to approve of their sins. His purpose for associating with sinners was to help them and to save them.

Thank God that Jesus is still the friend of sinners. For countless people this truth is precious. Instead of despairing in their sins, these people have found hope and consolation in the friend who gave Himself into death for their salvation and who gives them strength to lead nobler and better lives.

These words are precious to us, too, because they show that He is also our friend. We all have sinned, and our only hope is in Jesus Christ, the friend of sinners. He will receive all who sincerely repent of their sins and look to Him in faith.

How wonderful, dear Jesus, that You are the friend of sinners! Make me more worthy of Your friendship. Amen.

William A. Lauterbach/Aug. 2, 1978

61

It's an Accomplished Fact

*By one offering He hath perfected for ever
them that are sanctified. Hebrews 10:14 KJV*

How often don't we find ourselves starting something that never seems to get finished! So many projects begin with good intentions, but the finished product sometimes never sees the light of day. There are times when we start something and find that we cannot complete it by ourselves. We need help from someone else.

Not so with our God! Already before the foundations of the world were laid, He had determined to redeem and save His people. His plan was perfect and complete. He promised to send a Savior, one who would be the substitute and sacrifice for all people. That's what Jesus means to us. He bore our sins in His own body on the cross, and by His stripes we are healed.

Nothing can be added to His perfect sacrifice. We cannot cooperate with or assist God in His great work of saving us. There was one offering. In that gift of His Son, God has perfected those who are His through faith. We need not try to make ourselves "more right" with God. In fact, that is impossible. While we daily grow in our response to God's love, His sacrifice is complete. Through our Substitute we are perfect—forever!

Lord Jesus, thank You for the perfect righteousness You have gained for us, which is ours by faith in You. Amen.

August T. Mennicke/May 1, 1984

WHEN A DEAR ONE DIES

Jesus told the synagogue ruler, "Don't be
afraid; just believe." *Mark 5:36*

*T*he fear that passed through the heart of the synagogue ruler on receiving word that his daughter had
died is no stranger to us. Those of us who have experienced the death of loved ones know that fear: "What will
I do without them?"

The difficulty may be in loading too much meaning
into future plans. "When I retire, my wife and I are going
to travel," we say. Or "When my son is a man, he'll run
the family business." Then death strikes! How will we
cope with the future? All is changed. The anticipated
meaning is squelched. Then fear sets in. "It won't be the
same," we cry. Truthfully, it probably will not.

Death does change the planned future, but it does not
change the one who holds the future. He is Jesus Christ,
our Savior and Lord. He says in the face of death, "Don't
be afraid; just believe." As God, one with the Father, Jesus
holds the future and knows what that future really is. Our
real future is eternity; in heaven, plans will never be shattered again. Thus the days, months, and years beyond the
loved one's death need hold no fear for us. God will never
forsake us. Only believe!

*My future is secure with You, Lord Jesus, because
You hold it in Your loving hand. Help me to believe
it and fear no more. Amen.*

Norbert C. Oesch/Sept. 17, 1988

The Problem of Evil

You are dust, and to dust you shall return.
Genesis 3:19 RSV

*T*here are times in life when these words of the poet Robert Browning almost seem appropriate:
The lark's on the wing,
The snail's on the thorn
God's in his heaven,
All's right with the world.
But these moments don't have much staying power. A person does not have to live very long before discovering that everything is not quite right with this world. Broken relationships, accidents, pain, and death enter into each of our lives. Sooner or later we are all tempted to ask the question posed by Rabbi Kushner at the death of his son from progeria, the disease that causes children to die of old age: "Why do bad things happen to good people?"

The question is falsely put. Because of the disobedience of our first parents, there are no "good people" in this world. "All have sinned," says St. Paul (Romans 3:23). The curse spoken to Adam and Eve, "To dust you shall return," applies to all.

The surprise is not that evil exists but that God has overcome evil. This is the message and the miracle of the cross. In Christ the all-powerful and all-loving God has defeated sin and its consequences and brought healing for hurting sinners. There is, therefore, hope for us.

Thank You, Lord, for solving the problem of evil for us through Christ's death and resurrection. Amen.

Samuel H. Nafzger/Oct. 2, 1988

Amazing Silence

But Jesus gave him no answer. John 19:9 KJV

*T*here is a proverb "Silence is golden." Silence is golden at times. But frequently it is also significant. It was a singular feature of our Lord's passion that He rarely spoke during the 12 hours preceding His death. Occasionally He refused even to answer. In so doing He fulfilled Isaiah's vision of the Messiah: "He was oppressed, and He was afflicted, yet He opened not His mouth" (Isaiah 53:7 KJV).

But His silence was not that of defeat. It was the willing silence of the suffering Savior. As the Son of God and the substitute for sinful man, He had come to achieve the world's redemption. Had He answered the false accusations of His enemies, pleaded innocence, and demanded justice, He would have defeated the purpose of His mission.

His was an atoning silence. "The LORD hath laid on Him the iniquity of us all" (Isaiah 53:6 KJV). By His silence He bore also our sins of the tongue. In a day of lies and gossip, curses and filthy jests, we need greater faith in our Lord's atoning silence and firmer determination to use our tongue for His glory.

Today Jesus is no longer silent. Day and night He pleads our cause as our Mediator before the throne of heaven. Through Him the burden of our sins and the sorrow of our heart come before the Father and are heard and answered. Today He also invites us: "Come unto Me ... and I will give you rest."

Even so, Lord Jesus, I come, I come. Amen.

Julius W. Acker/April 8, 1963

Leap Year

I trust in Thee, O Lord, I say,
"Thou art my God." My times are in Thy
hand. Psalm 31:14–15 RSV

O nce every four years, a 29th day is added to February, thus lengthening the year from 365 to 366 days. "Leap year" we call it. Some people are very conscious of it, especially those who observe birthdays or other anniversaries on the 29th. They must either observe them on the exact day every four years or celebrate them every year either a day early or a day late.

While we may add a day to a year, we cannot add a day to our lives. There may be those difficult moments when we truly wish that we could die and shorten the hopelessness and pain of living. There are other times when we might wish we could postpone the inevitable death that faces us—a day perhaps, or a month or a year. There are days that can't end soon enough for us, and there are other days that we wish would never end.

In all instances, though, our times are in God's hand. Whether a day more or a day less, it is important that we see the grace of God in Christ Jesus through all of the circumstances we face. Underneath us at all times are His everlasting arms, supporting, sustaining, and strengthening us.

Hold me always, Lord, in the right hand of Your power. Amen.

Wilbert J. Fields/March 20, 1977

LET US DRAW NEAR

Let us draw near with a true heart in full
assurance of faith. *Hebrews 10:22 RSV*

*I*n the Old Testament the high priest on the Day of
Atonement entered the Holy of Holies, which con-
tained the ark of the covenant. Only he could enter the
Holy of Holies and that once a year. He came into the
very presence of God to pray and to offer sacrifices, for
himself and his people.

How grateful we should be to our High Priest, Jesus
Christ, who through His death and resurrection makes it
possible for each one of us to come into the very presence
of our God!

Through the perfect sacrifice of Christ our sins are no
longer charged to our account. "God was in Christ, reconciling the world unto Himself, not imputing their trespasses unto them."

The greatest transaction in the world took place on
Good Friday: the sins of the world were charged to Jesus
Christ. By His death He paid all our debts, and now God
no longer holds our sins against us. As a result, we can and
should confidently enter into the presence of God, knowing that Jesus has removed our sins from our account and
has revealed to us a Father who loves us and hears our
prayers. We all need to remind ourselves that we should
daily enter into God's presence through prayer.

*Lord, forgive me for being so remiss in entering into Your
presence. Let me call upon You every day of my life. Amen.*

Andrew Simcak Jr./Oct. 19, 1976

JAMES BEN-ZEBEDEE

*And He took with him Peter and James
and John, and began to be greatly distressed
and troubled. Mark 14:33 RSV*

*E*very great venture has an executive committee of
some sort. The Twelve were no exception. Peter,
James, and John stand out in the gospels as the "big three"
who attended our Lord on special occasions: up on the
Mount of Transfiguration, for example, or down in the
Garden of Gethsemane. The three were to provide Him
the very human sort of support we all need in crises.

Even though the three failed Him in the garden by
promptly falling asleep they remained as leaders among
the apostles. Did the other nine disciples envy them?
Quite possibly. We know how disgruntled they were at
Mother Zebedee's campaigning for her James and John.

Envy, however, is one of the most useless emotions to
afflict humankind. It hurts us, not the object of our envy.
Take James as a powerful example. No one envied James
eight years later, in A.D. 41. Why not? Because King
Herod Agrippa I cut off his head (Acts 12:2). How ridicu-
lous are our transitory jealousies, our envies-of-the-
moment! James followed Christ into eternal life, and so
can we. Christians who have life in Him need never be
jealous.

*Thanks be to You, O God, for Your unspeakable
gift! Amen.*

Paul L. Maier/March 10, 1979

The Hem Of His Garment

*If I may but touch [the hem of] His garment,
I shall be made whole. Matthew 9:20–21 KJV*

*T*here come times, even in the life of the believer, when every door seems to be closed; when there seems to be no escape from the troubles that beset us: a loved one lying on a sickbed for years, a broken marriage which has resulted in untold grief and pain, a wayward child for whom we had such rosy hopes.

Where to turn—when every door seems closed, when there seems to be no God in heaven who is conscious of our need, or who, if He is really there, seems to turn a deaf ear to our every plea? The unnamed woman in our text provides us with an excellent example.

Jostled by a milling crowd, she approached Jesus from the rear, saying to herself: "If I may but touch the hem of His garment!" There was no spoken prayer, in fact there was no prayer at all. It was merely a sigh of faith, a confession of trust in the love and omnipotence of the Son of God to whom she had drawn so close.

"If I may but touch the hem of His garment!" You and I can do just that. His omnipotence, His wisdom, and His love are just that close to us!

"When all things seem against us, To drive us to despair, We know one gate is open, One ear will hear our prayer." Amen.

Herman W. Gockel/July 11, 1980

THE INEVITABLE CROSS

From that time Jesus began to show
His disciples that He must go to Jerusalem
and suffer many things. *Matthew 16:21 RSV*

Where did the road to Calvary begin? Did it begin in Caesarea Philippi when Jesus told His disciples that He was going to Jerusalem? or in the Garden of Gethsemane ... when He was arrested? or when He was born in a Bethlehem manger?

Actually it began in God's eternal grace before the foundations of the world were laid. God's great plan of love and mercy revolves around the cross of Christ. Jesus must go to Jerusalem! He must suffer! He must die! It was all inevitable according to God's plan.

What compelled Christ to take the way of the cross? Not the hatred of His enemies or the schemes of politicians. It was Christ's mission to bear our sin and guilt because God loves us. "All we like sheep have gone astray ... and the Lord has laid on Him the iniquity of us all." God's eternal purpose is revealed in the cross of Calvary. His death is not to be seen as tragic. Rather, the cross means victory. This was God's plan for the salvation of our souls. We cannot explain it. We can only praise it.

Everlasting God, who delivered the children of Israel from captivity, may we be delivered from sin and death by Your power and grace in Jesus Christ, Your Son. Amen.

John F. Johnson/April 13, 1987

RESTLESS FEET

*As long as it is day, we must do the work
of him who sent me. Night is coming, when
no one can work. John 9:4*

Isaiah had spoken of the feet that bring glad tidings. Back in the old days people often traveled on foot— certainly not by airplane or railroad or automobile. One wonders at the miles covered by that great missionary St. Paul. And we could say the same about Jesus. He had restless feet. He had a message to bring to a world under Satan's control. He knew that His time was short. And so He moved steadily from place to place with the Good News of the kingdom of God's grace and forgiveness.

So it is with us. We have been given a certain time span to serve as ministers of Jesus in this world. No one knows how soon the night will come for any of us. But while it is day, let us be about our business.

We, too, have been sent to bring healing to the sin-sick, to comfort those who sorrow over their sins, to help those who struggle against the devil, the world, and the flesh.

We ourselves, and also those whom we send, can be the men and women of restless feet in our day, bringing the Gospel of life and light to those who are in darkness.

Lord Jesus, keep us restlessly on the move with Your saving Gospel. Amen.

Herbert A. Mueller/April 26, 1988

THE GOOD NEWS

God so loved the world that He gave His only begotten Son that whosoever believeth in Him should not perish but have everlasting life. *John 3:16 KJV*

*T*his statement of Jesus gives us the Gospel in a nutshell. It tells us all we need to know about God. It takes us to God's heart by bringing God's heart close to us. It is not enough to know that God is love. We must also know that God in love comes to us. This is the good news precisely.

The love of God is not an emotion which stays locked up within His mysterious person. This love takes on flesh-and-blood form; love becomes a person—Jesus Christ, God's Son and Mary's Son.

Love also acts: His love does not simply stand about waiting to be noticed. With power Jesus begins to roll back the forces which torment and enslave all of us. He forgives sin, casts out devils, heals the sick, comforts the despairing.

God's love is costly: Jesus suffers and dies. Because He loves His Son, God accepts the sacrifice of Jesus and shows it by raising Him from the dead.

Because God's love is a giving love, it is saving love. We are embraced and held safe in the arms of God, not because we ran to Him in our troubles but because He did not hesitate to pursue us and to pay the full price of such pursuit until He found us. The measure of God's love is that "He gave His only Son."

Lord God, let nothing separate us from Your love in Christ Jesus. Amen.

Kenneth R. Schueler/Feb. 11, 1962

"Lord, Have Mercy"

Blind Bartimaeus shouted: "Jesus, Son of
David, have mercy on me!" *Mark 10:47*

Early in the church's history, Bartimaeus' prayer became the daily prayer of all believers. When we ask for mercy, we do not ask only for forgiveness or deliverance. We also ask for sight and healing. We ask for the peace of God that passes all understanding and embraces our entire existence. We ask for our salvation. We ask for peace in every part of the globe. We pray that Christ's church may be well. We plead for unity among the children of God on earth. We pray for our congregation. We ask that God will help, save, comfort, and defend us when we pray, "Lord, have mercy"—have mercy on us for the sake of Jesus Christ, who gave His life to redeem us.

God always hears us when we echo blind Bartimaeus' words. When we come as beggars who cannot live without the mercy of the Lord, He always sends us on our way with the blessing of His Word. We approach Him in faith, trusting that He will again dispense His mercy, flowing like a river over our lives. Drenched in His love, confident that it will continue forever, we go our ways living out a life certain of His mercy and therefore willing and able to show mercy to others in Jesus' holy name.

Have mercy, Jesus, and empower us through Your Holy Spirit to show Your mercy to those around us. Amen.

Robert A. Kolb/Nov. 3, 1988

The Zero Hour

The hour is come, that the Son of Man should
be glorified. *John 12:23 KJV*

We are in the midst of the Lenten season. We go to Calvary to behold a love most amazing, yes, divine. Without the suffering and death of Jesus on Golgotha's cross, we would have no hope; heaven would be closed. Our faith would be meaningless, our life despairing. Through Jesus' death we find peace with God because Jesus is the Lamb of God who takes away the sin of the world—*my sin*. Nothing is left undone.

At the cross we find healing for our soul and are restored to grace. We dwell in the presence of Jesus and live in that faith that saves. The burdens of the day become lighter, the uncertainties are removed, and our ordeals are more readily met because Jesus is our friend, who sticks closer than a brother.

That hour when Jesus gave Himself for our redemption is the zero hour in history. Although Jesus went down into death and hell, He came forth triumphantly to be proclaimed victor for time and eternity.

Today angels and saints and all Christendom give Him glory and honor as the risen Lord. He has given us peace with God and hope in the darkest hour of the night, and He guarantees us salvation through His resurrection.

Lord Jesus, continue in me that I may be with You forever. Amen.

Alfred Doerffler/Feb. 25, 1959

COME, MEET OUR GOD

*You shall be to Me a kingdom of priests
and a holy nation. Exodus 19:6 RSV*

*I*n ancient myths people went to the mountain to find their gods or built towers by which they might storm the ramparts of heaven. And from the security of their lofty perch, the gods toyed with the lives of mortals.

It was not so when the children of Israel, outward-bound from Egypt, came into the wilderness of Sinai. They came not to seek the Lord because it was He who had called them. Confronted by the awesome power of God—lightning flashing on the mountainside and a deep mist veiling its face they were afraid. "Let not God speak to us," they cried. "Let Moses be our eyes and ears." Moses, who had once been God's spokesman before Pharaoh now became the people's voice before God.

God spoke with Moses—words of covenant and expectation: "I am the LORD your God, who brought you out of the land of Egypt" (Exodus 20:2). These words, passed from Moses to the people and from generation to generation, continue to remind us of the presence of God, who has called us to be a treasured people, a kingdom of priests, a holy nation.

To another mountain—to Calvary—God called His people to create for Himself the true church, which Christ loved and for which He gave His life.

Teach us to live in the Gospel, O Lord Jesus, as a kingdom of priests and a holy nation. Amen.

Alston S. Kirk/May 16, 1989

The Handwriting against Us

[God] blott[ed] out the handwriting of ordinances that was against us ... nailing it to His cross. Colossians 2:14 KJV

*T*he words quoted above remind us of a beautiful Palestinian custom. When a debt was paid in full, the creditor who had received his money would nail the canceled note over the door of the man who had owed it. Thus the public knew that payment had been made and all was settled.

The debt of our sins is staggering. We could not pay for our own sins or for the sins of others. "None of them can by any means redeem his brother nor give to God a ransom for him: (For the redemption of their soul is precious ..." (Psalm 49:7–8).

Jesus, our precious Savior, shed His blood for us, and our heavenly Father has written across the handwriting against us, "Paid in full." The Gospel presents this truth to us in all its beauty. From the very heights of heaven is proclaimed the truth: "The blood of Jesus His Son cleanses us from all sin" (1 John 1:7 RSV). Our forgiveness is sealed with His blood.

The devil and our conscience can no longer accuse us. Our Mediator offered one sacrifice for sin that is good forever. All who accept this message are blessed with peace, joy, new life, new hope. All this is ours by faith in Jesus.

Lamb of God, pure and holy, grant us blessed peace in the knowledge that our sins have been blotted out. Amen.

Victor L. Brandt/June 3, 1976

A Religion That Rolls Up Its Sleeves

Wherefore gird up the loins of your mind.
1 Peter 1:13 KJV

*I*n the opening statement of his first letter (vv. 3–12) the apostle Peter described the Christian's hope, the heavenly inheritance purchased for us by Christ. But what happened in the past involves the present. Because we have a living hope through Christ's resurrection, *therefore* "gird up the loins of your mind."

In the ancient world men wore long robes. When getting ready for energetic work, a man would gather his loosely flowing robe close to him and tighten it with his belt. A modern equivalent of this custom might read, "Roll up the sleeves of your mind."

When does the Christian mind have its sleeves rolled up? When the believer, being alert, cultivates a mind that will dig down into the rich truths of the Bible. This means that the Christian is not satisfied with vague and hazy notions or slipshod thinking about our Christian faith. Modern church life often clamors for shorter and easier sermons, for bright and light services. But pastors and people with mental sleeves rolled up will not yield to the popular demand for a watered-down Christianity. Christ's life, teachings, death, and resurrection are hard facts. They are news-flash material. Getting the facts straight and getting at their meaning calls for clear thinking on our part. God wants both my heart and my head.

Lord, help me to think deeply and clearly as I follow the footsteps of Your thinking in the Bible. Amen.

Ewald J. Otto/Oct. 13, 1959

Blessed by Body and Blood

The cup of blessing which we bless, is it not a participation in the blood of Christ? The bread which we break, is it not a participation in the body of Christ? 1 Corinthians 10:16 RSV

*I*n one-to-one ministry, no one equals our Lord Jesus. He knows us from the inside out. He is fully aware of what we need. He guides us through the experiences that will best equip us to serve Him and our neighbors.

Especially at the Lord's Table does He show His personal concern for us. There together with the wine He gives us His true blood. Together with the bread He gives us His true body. It's the same body and blood He yielded into death on the cross for the forgiveness of our sins.

Because Jesus wants to make certain that we know He died and rose again for us as persons, He invites us to Holy Communion. No doubt about it! One by one, person by person, He assures us that what He did, He did for us. He guarantees that His gift of life and salvation through the forgiveness of sins is meant for all and that He personally offers and conveys it to us.

We are ready to receive the blessing of Christ's body and blood in the Sacrament when we trust that they were given and shed for us.

O Holy Spirit, lead us to repent of our sins and to trust altogether in the forgiveness Christ gives us at His Table. Amen.

Victor A. Constien/April 12, 1979

The King Whom Men Would Teach

I will therefore chastise Him and release Him.
Luke 23:16 RSV

After Jesus was sent back by Herod, Pilate called the ruling priests and the other leaders and the people together. "You brought this man as one who turns the people against their government," he told them. "Now look, I have examined Him before you but haven't found Him guilty of any of the things of which you accuse Him. Nor did Herod because he sent Him back to us. You see, He has done nothing to deserve death. So I am going to teach Him a lesson and let Him go."

This is the best that human justice can come up with when it must judge Jesus. He does not deserve to die because He is a good Man who does so much good; at least, He does no real harm. But He does need a lesson because He obviously goes too far when fine, respectable people must bring charges against Him.

This sounds so modern that it might have been written in our newspapers this morning. Our world would teach Jesus something, even about Himself, instead of learning only of Him. "Listen to Him," says the voice from heaven. Sin is refusal to hear Him. Sin would rather teach Him a lesson. But if we believe the first part of the voice from heaven, "This is My beloved Son," we have no problem with the second part: "Listen to Him!"

Lord Jesus, by the Holy Spirit help us always to hear You to the exclusion of all else. Amen.

William A. Buege/April 9, 1962

KNOWING WHAT CHRIST HAS DONE

He said to them, "Do you know what I have done to you?" John 13:12 RSV

A few hours before our Savior knelt in the agony of Gethsemane He performed a most menial service by washing the feet of His disciples. When He arose after the completion of His servile task, He sought to impress on His disciples the meaning was of the practical example of humility they had just witnessed. He asked them: "Do you know what I have done to you?"

This Lententide, a season of solemn heart searching, we are urgently moved to apply this question to ourselves and ask: What is it that Christ is doing as He serves us and suffers for us? What are we to learn in a personal, intimate way from what He has done for us?

Surely the Holy Spirit impresses this truth on us: "Where sin abounded, grace did much more abound" (Romans 5:20 KJV). With eyes thus enlightened, we see through tears of repentance the gleaming hope of Christ's cross, which assures us that each appeal for grace, for mercy, for pardon, for redemption has been answered fully, freely, and forever by Jesus' self-sacrificing love.

The upward gaze to the cross reveals love so amazing, so divine that we cannot but give love in return.

Precious Savior, we thank You for all You have done for us. Make our lives eloquent testimonies of Your love. Amen.

Eugene R. Bertermann/March 5, 1976

THE HANDS OF JESUS

And I give unto them eternal life; and they
shall never perish, neither shall any man pluck
them out of My hand. John 10:28 KJV

*D*uring the earthly ministry of Jesus, many felt the touch of His hands. What were they like?

They had known toil. They had worked with rough timber in the carpenter shop in Nazareth. They were not soft hands. They were the hands of a working man.

But they were gentle too. They rested on the heads of little children; they were laid on many a fevered brow; they touched the eyes of the blind, the ears of the deaf, the limbs of the lame, the tongues of the dumb, the remains of the dead. They were hands of compassion.

They were strong hands because they were the hands of God. Under their touch the blind, the lame, the deaf, the dumb, were made whole; and the dead were restored to life!

They were uplifted hands. They were nailed to the cross, pierced and wounded and bleeding for our transgressions. However, on the day He ascended to heaven, these hands were lifted to bless us as we travel through this world of sin. His abiding presence in our lives and our homes blesses us with endless benedictions to keep us on the narrow way of life. Then on the other side these hands will be lifted to welcome us home to live in the eternal glory, where sin and death and sorrow cannot touch us.

Lord Jesus, bless us always with Your grace. Amen.

Herbert A. Mueller/May 11, 1961

81

GOD'S SEAL

God is faithful, by whom ye were called unto the fellowship of His Son Jesus Christ our Lord. *1 Corinthians 1:9 KJV*

*L*ook to the cross! See Jesus hanging there? What is that, really? It is God's seal that whatever Jesus said and did is true.

Do you know how in years past people who couldn't write signed their names to legal documents? They made a cross, then somebody filled in, "John Smith, his mark." That's it.

The cross is "God's mark." The cross is God signing His name to all of Christ's claims. "Blessed are the meek." How do you know that's true, that God means it? Because He signed it once with a cross, His mark. "Lo, I am with you always," and there to back it up is a cross, God's mark. "Thy sins be forgiven thee," "In My Father's house are many mansions"—God signed it all with a cross, His mark.

When will we realize that God is in earnest? Jesus didn't go to Gethsemane lightly. He didn't put up a cross as collateral when what He said was guesswork. If Jesus says a word to you about forgiveness, He backs it up with His agony and blood. He means it. If He tells you He will give you victory by His cross, you know that He is serious about it. The cross is God's mark that tells you He means what He says.

Lord Jesus, fasten our eyes on Your cross, that there we may find the certainty that all Your promises are sure. Amen.

Arnold G. Kuntz/March 22, 1974

The Divine Magnet

*I, if I be lifted up from the earth, will draw all
men unto Me. John 12:32 KJV*

*T*here are industrial magnets so powerful they can lift
tons of steel. The earth's gravity, still more powerful, mightily pulls all things toward the earth's center. But
God has created a unique drawing power: the cross of His
Son. This is the divine magnet.

When was Christ's drawing power greatest? When He
stilled the raging tempest? banished evil spirits? fed the
multitudes? raised the dead? was transfigured? held the
crowds spellbound with the power of His message?

He Himself supplies the answer. When He was lifted
up on Calvary's cross, suffering and dying, He would draw
all people to Himself.

The uplifted Christ draws us by His love. The love that
caused Him to bare His back to the lash, to offer His head
to a crown of cruel thorns, to allow spikes of death to be
driven into His quivering flesh, has magnetic power.

The uplifted Christ draws us by His matchless life. His
greatness and goodness, His humility and truth, attract
people from all walks of life. Young and old, rich and poor,
educated and illiterate—all are found at Calvary. The
uplifted Christ draws us by the power of His death and
resurrection. He saves us from ourselves and gives us
power to live victoriously in and for Him.

*Blessed Redeemer, ever draw me graciously to You.
Amen.*

Julius W. Acker/April 3, 1963

COMPLAINING?

*I loathe my very life; therefore I will give
free rein to my complaint and speak out
in the bitterness of my soul. Job 10:1*

How common our complaining! The weather always seems too hot or too cold, too wet or too dry. We always need more money and more time. We complain about sickness, job stress, family conflict, and church coldness. Then when even more serious problems arise, we complain on a deeper level.

You know the plight of Job, who suddenly lost his possessions, his children, and his health. Sitting in rags on a dung heap, he faced stark reality and cried out in his bitter complaint. He did not understand and asked God why he was suffering. He wondered when God would vindicate him.

Ultimately Job learned to accept God's authority. He also learned to trust in God's love. We sin and deserve nothing but punishment. Like Job, we complain against God and others. We despair of ourselves and wish to place the blame on someone else. God silences our complaints. We realize that we are sinful and that God is holy. But we listen to His voice and hear a word of love. His Son endured all the pain, injustice, and punishment of a sinful world. Silent before His tormentors, He went willingly to death on the cross for us. He lives, and so shall we. Complaints transformed to thanksgiving and praise!

Lord, thanks for Your uncomplaining death. Amen.

Stephen J. Carter/July 14, 1988

BROTHER LAZARUS

*So the chief priests planned to put Lazarus also
to death, because on account of him many of
the Jews were going away and believing in
Jesus. John 12:10 RSV*

*F*our crosses could have been standing on Calvary on Good Friday—the extra one for Lazarus, the brother of Mary and Martha.

When Jesus worked the ultimate sign on His friend Lazarus—raising him from the dead—He set in motion a chain of events that would culminate in His own death. Bethany was so near Jerusalem that news of Lazarus' resurrection sparked a reaction in the holy city powerful enough to frighten the priestly establishment. Now they also marked Lazarus for death.

Why Lazarus escaped the priestly plot is not clear in Scripture. Perhaps the religious authorities had enough trouble getting Jesus condemned. Another victim would only have complicated their case. A more important question is whether Lazarus' resurrection was a blessing or bane to him. Death is so terrible, some would argue, that the man should not have had to die twice.

The example of Lazarus assures us that Jesus is indeed the resurrection and the life. Because of what Jesus did for us, death becomes the door to God's blessed eternity.

We thank You, O Lord, for taking the sting out of death. Amen.

Paul L. Maier/March 4, 1979

85

24-Hour Service

I will therefore that men pray every where.
1 Timothy 2:8 KJV

*T*he passion of Jesus reveals to us a *praying* Savior. As Jesus gathers the disciples in the Upper Room, He makes His High Priestly Prayer, pleading for those who have come to faith that they, being *in* the world, be not *of* the world. Then Jesus goes to the garden to drink the cup of agony and asks that it be removed. However, if there be no other way but by the shedding of His blood, He goes willingly to Calvary to die for the sin of the world. There on the cross we behold Him in prayer, even holding fast to His Father in the three hours of darkness. To His dying hour Jesus prays.

Throughout His public ministry Jesus prayed. He made a profound impression on His disciples with His prayer life. Therefore they came to Jesus with the plea: "Lord, teach us to pray!" He taught them *and us* His marvelous prayer, the "Our Father."

Prayer is a vital part of our Christian living. Everywhere we should pray, Paul urges. If we cannot pray where we are, we had better get out at once because we are in the wrong place.

Nothing is too trivial, nothing too unusual to take to God in prayer. And "Oh, what peace we often forfeit; Oh, what needless pain we bear—All because we do not carry Ev'rything to God in prayer!"

Lord, today teach me, too, to pray more fervently. Amen.

Alfred Doerffler/Feb. 23, 1959

CELEBRATE A MIRACLE

Now the parable is this: The seed is the Word
of God. *Luke 8:11 RSV*

Spring begins during this time in March. We take the day of the vernal equinox in stride, perhaps with brighter eyes but with little ado. For the alert individual Christian, however, might it not be a celebration day anyway?

In this hemisphere, spring marks the recurrence of several billion mini-miracles as tiny seeds spring into life. Despite the buffeting of an unfriendly environment, many survive and grow into plants of remarkable beauty and productivity.

In sermon and parable Jesus often likens spring's miracles to a more awesome miracle: the seed of the Word of God springing into living faith in human hearts, bearing fruits of love, and growing to eternal life. Wonderful beyond comprehension!

Now wouldn't the first day of spring be just the time to celebrate personally that miracle of grace in our lives? Surely, faith in our Lord Jesus, planted through Holy Baptism and God's Word and nourished by the Holy Spirit, which has survived and grown through the years to make us walking miracles of God's grace, calls for celebration.

Let's do it now as we welcome spring again.

I praise You, Lord, Creator, Redeemer, and Sanctifier, for making me a miracle of Your grace to share Your glory. Amen.

Albert W. Galen/March 21, 1987

FIRSTFRUITS FOR THE LORD

Honor the LORD with your substance
and with the first fruits of all your produce.
Proverbs 3:9 RSV

We may not speak about firstfruits very often, but every Jewish family in Old Testament times certainly knew what they were. Firstfruit is simply the first fruit that appears on a tree.

Imagine that you have a peach tree in your backyard. In spring you notice the many blossoms, and you predict there will be many peaches. You are right. The little peaches grow bigger and bigger. Finally, one which is a bit larger than the others begins to show a beautiful color that tells you it is time to help yourself.

If you lived in Old Testament times, you would not casually eat that first peach from the tree. You would carefully pick it and give it to the Lord. The Lord received the first of any harvest. That is what Proverbs 3:9 means by suggesting, "Honor the LORD with your substance and with the first fruits of all your produce."

Old Testament worship rules may not apply in detail to New Testament Christians, but the principle of giving the Lord the first and best of our time, talent, and treasure is certainly applicable. The love Christ poured out on us moves us to give Him something better than mere leftovers. We give Him the best.

Lord Jesus, You started the giving when You offered Yourself on the cross. Help us to honor You with our best. Amen.

Howard W. Kramer/June 16, 1969

SONG IN THE NIGHT

*Ye shall have a song, as in the night when a
holy solemnity is kept. Isaiah 30:29 KJV*

O ne of the most beloved songs we can sing in the
"night" of doubt and fear is "Just as I Am, Without
One Plea." One day the hymn writer, Charlotte Elliott,
confessed to a famous Swiss preacher: "I would like to
come to Jesus, as you suggest, but how can I be sure that
He will receive me, a sinner?"

The preacher smiled and answered: "Charlotte, come
to Him just as you are. He will receive you, for He has
promised, 'I will never refuse anyone who comes to
Me,'—not even sinners like the thief on the cross or the
denying disciples." Then Miss Elliott beheld the Lamb of
God that takes away the sin of the world.

Deeply impressed by these reassurances, the poet
reflected on them for many days. Then she immortalized
her newly found acceptance by God in this favorite hymn
of many sinners: "Just as I am, without one plea But that
Thy blood was shed for me And that Thou bidd'st me
come to Thee, O Lamb of God, I come, I come." For millions of believers, "tossed about With many a conflict,
many a doubt," this has been their "song in the night."

*Lord Jesus, Lamb of God, because I believe Your
promise that You bore my sin, I come to You in
confident faith. Amen.*

Elmer E. Maschoff/Nov. 19, 1981

THE FORGIVING FATHER

*Father, forgive them; for they know not what
they do. Luke 23:34 RSV*

Jesus, dying on the cross, asked that His persecutors be forgiven. What an act of divine grace! He was speaking to His Father. He was asking the Father to forgive the people who were killing His Son. What a superhuman request!

Yet this is the nature of the Gospel. This is the basis of the Good News. This is the wonder of the Christian message of divine forgiveness. The divine Father and Son forgive the Son's own slayers. And since every human being is involved in the death of Jesus Christ, the Bible announces that every human being is forgiven. In fact, the strange yet comforting truth is that it was the very act of Christ's dying that won forgiveness and life for those who contributed to His death. The Gospel proclaims: "The blood of Jesus His Son cleanses us from all sin" (1 John 1:7 RSV).

By the miracle of conversion our heavenly Father's forgiving nature is implanted in human fathers so they can practice the grace of forgiveness toward their children. How important that Christian parents acquire and practice this grace, in response to how their heavenly Father treats them! The grace of forgiveness brings blessings to Christian families.

Dear Savior, we thank You for asking Your Father to forgive us and for Your sacrifice that made forgiveness sure. Amen.

W. Th. Janzow/May 19, 1972

90

LENT AND LOVE

Herein is love, not that we loved God, but that
He loved us, and sent His Son to be the propi-
tiation for our sins. 1 John 4:10 KJV

*L*ent's message has been *love.* Christmas proclaims the love of God the Father, who sent His only Son into the world. Lent tells of the love of God the Son, who died on the cross for the sins of all humanity. Pentecost celebrates the love of God the Holy Spirit, who alone makes possible our acceptance of God's love. There is joy in the Lenten message, the joy in knowing and in accepting God's infinite love for us.

There is also sorrow in the Lenten season, sorrow over our lovelessness to God. Every failure in our love to one another is failure in our love to God. Every sin against God's Law is failure in our love because "love is the fulfilling of the Law." Nothing we give or give up, nothing we do or abstain from doing, can change our lovelessness. But "where sin abounded, grace did much more abound" (Romans 5:20 KJV). "Herein is love, not that we loved God but that He loved us and sent His Son to be the propitiation [appeasement] for our sins."

During Lent we have made in various ways our sincere confessions: "I acknowledge my transgressions, and my sin is ever before me." Always, however, we sorrow over sin as those who live on the Easter side of the cross, as those who accept God's love in Christ Jesus for the forgiveness of every sin.

Thanks and praise be to You, O God of love! Amen.

Robert Schroeter/March 25, 1959

CHRIST'S PEACE FREELY GIVEN

Peace I leave with you, My peace I give unto
you. ... Let not your heart be troubled, neither
let it be afraid. *John 14:27 KJV*

*T*he peace the Savior bestowed on His disciples on
the night of His betrayal was the peace of which the
apostle writes, "Being justified by faith, we have peace
with God through our Lord Jesus Christ" (Romans 5:1
KJV). It is the peace of forgiven sin, the peace that passes
all understanding.

Although this peace cost Christ dearly, we may have it
without money and without price. "Peace I leave with
you, My peace I give unto you." No charge here. It is ours
by faith.

Christ leaves this peace with us and gives it to us in His
Gospel. "These things I have spoken unto you that in Me
ye might have peace." The Gospel tells us that the Father
"made peace through the blood of His cross" (Colossians
1:20 KJV) that there is "now no condemnation to them
which are in Christ Jesus" (Romans 8:1 KJV).

When this peace enters, the troubled and fearful heart
finds rest. It fears neither the present nor the future. In
every situation of life it is tuned to the voice of the risen
and living Savior, "Peace be unto you." "Let not your
heart be troubled; ye believe in God, believe also in Me."
This peace is ours daily throughout the year.

Savior, "Grant us Thy peace throughout our earth-
ly life, Our balm in sorrow and our stay in strife."
Amen.

Otto H. Pfotenhauer/Jan. 8, 1968

A GOOD THING

For me it is good to be near God.
Psalm 73:28 RSV

A pastor whose office was on the second floor of the parsonage was shocked one day. As he lifted his eyes from the book before him, he saw his young son standing on the window ledge. He was terribly frightened because the child was in great peril of losing his balance and tumbling to the ground.

The youngster had wondered just what his father did each day in that room behind closed doors. So he had placed a ladder to the window and climbed up and gazed in at his parent.

As the father pulled the child into the room, mildly rebuking him for his folly, his thoughts were turned in another direction. Often he had sought to enter the secret council chamber of God to see how and why He does things only to discover an easier way. He need only ask the Father for guidance to understand His ways. In His Word God tells us why He acts as He does. Some things we cannot know but important things He reveals to us if we draw near in confidence. It is good to be near God. Things are so much brighter in His presence. In His Word we learn He is constantly at work on our behalf, offering us Jesus as our health and salvation. James tells us: "Draw near to God and He will draw near to you" (James 4:8 RSV).

Help me, my loving God, to approach You with boldness, knowing that it is good for me to be near You. Amen.

Melvin J. Tassler/Jan. 17, 1984

WERE YOU THERE?

I have been crucified with Christ; it is no
longer I who live, but Christ who lives in me.
Galatians 2:20 RSV

O ne of the more familiar Negro spirituals asks, "Were you there when they crucified my Lord?" The believer answers this question in the affirmative: "Yes, I was there when Christ was crucified." We know that Jesus was crucified almost two thousand years ago and that the crucifixion took place thousands of miles from where we live. Yet we say we were there. We don't mean to say that we were physically standing under the cross on that first Good Friday. We are saying that we were there because Jesus took our sins on Himself and was crucified because of them.

We were the ones who deserved to be crucified because of our sins against a holy and righteous God. Jesus took our place and carried our sins with Him to Golgotha. He did that because He loved us and gave Himself for us. Believers throughout the ages join with St. Paul in saying, "I am crucified with Christ, nevertheless I live."

Indeed we live! That is why the believer can answer the question of the spiritual, "Were you there when He rose up from the grave?" also in the affirmative. We were not only crucified with Christ, but we also rise with Christ.

We thank You, heavenly Father, that You did not spare Your Son but delivered Him to death on the cross for us. Amen.

William H. Griffen/Feb. 13, 1986

Meat Instead of Milk

Solid food is for the mature.
Hebrews 5:14 RSV

*B*abies are cute, but we soon long to have them begin to crawl. Then to stand. Then to talk. Then to leave the bottle. The infant Christian progresses from stage to stage, from spoon-feeding to self-feeding of the "sincere milk of the Word" (1 Peter 2:2 KJV). But with growth comes the need for adult food, for meat. "Solid food is for the mature," states the above text.

As we grow spiritually by our feeding on the Word, moving from milk to meat, we become capable of dealing with adult problems and situations. Building a marriage, rearing children, holding a job, governing a community or a country, doing the Lord's work—none of these is child's play. Our Lord Jesus Christ studied hard and trained long before He undertook the salvation of the human race. No weakling could have done it.

Our tasks in life likewise are demanding of spiritual muscle, spiritual stamina, spiritual intelligence, spiritual maturity. The nourishment for such strength is available—it is as near as the Spirit in Word and Sacrament. Eat regularly and well of that food and grow strong. Then see how you are able to fulfill the challenges of life.

Lord Jesus Christ, You are the bread come down from heaven and the manna for which my spirit hungers. Hold me with Your powerful hand and feed me till I want no more. Amen.

Jaroslav J. Vajda/May 4, 1977

95

GOD'S SALVATION LASTS FOREVER

My salvation will last forever, My righteousness
will never fail. Isaiah 51:6

Some people today believe that the end of their life on earth is the end of their life altogether. The best thing they can hope for is that their good name will live on a generation or two after them. This "sophisticated" view of the lack of an afterlife is not much different from what we arrogantly call the "primitive" religion of tribal animists.

God gives us a strikingly different view—that of His design for human life. Even though the heavens will vanish like smoke, the earth wear out like a garment, and its creatures die like flies, His full salvation is on its way. His plan to set our lives aright is reaching total fulfillment.

Anchored in Christ's self-sacrifice for us and in His triumphant reclaiming of life from the grave, His salvation is bearing down on us. It already has us in His grasp, and He will never let us fall from His hands, even though they have nail holes in them. His arm, stretched out on the cross, bestows righteousness on us. His promise guarantees that the salvation righteousness brings will last forever and will never fail. Secure in this promise, we look to Him and hope in His powerful, delivering arm.

We are confident, O Christ, in the might of Your arms, which were spread out on the cross that we might have salvation. Amen.

Robert A. Kolb/Nov. 22, 1988

THE KING, NO MERE MAN

*Have nothing to do with that righteous man,
for I have suffered much over Him today in a
dream. Matthew 27:19 RSV*

*P*ontius Pilate, the Roman governor, is in the midst of
a strange trial. He has tried many cases before, but
none so perplexing and irritating as this. He knows he
ought to release this Jesus, yet his political entanglements
make him hesitate to do what justice demands.

In the midst of these strange proceedings, he receives a
strange message from his wife: "Have nothing to do with
that righteous man, for I have suffered much over Him
today in a dream."

One tradition says she was a convert to Judaism; another says she was a secret disciple of Jesus. Be that as it may,
she passes a verdict all her own: Jesus is a righteous man,
a man with nobility of character. This, however was not
sufficient. Jesus is more than a just, upright, honest man.
He is the sinless Son of God.

"Have nothing to do with that righteous man!" But we
must have something to do with Jesus. We cannot live
without Him; we cannot die in peace without Him; we
cannot enter heaven without Him. Only if we hide in His
sacred wounds and are cleansed from our sin can we have
peace of mind and salvation in all eternity.

*Lord Jesus, we want to have everything to do with
You. Come therefore into our hearts and abide there
in grace. Amen.*

William A. Buege/April 9, 1976

The "Fool-Hearty" and the Wise

He who trusts in his own mind is a fool;
but he who walks in wisdom will be delivered.
Proverbs 28:26 RSV

*F*or some this first day of April has been a fools' day. For others it is a day to be remembered for other reasons.

The writer of Proverbs didn't regard his mention of the fool as very funny. For him, foolishness was a matter of life and death. According to King Solomon, whom the Lord chose to write these inspired and instructive proverbs, those who trust in themselves rather than in God are fools. Such foolish trust proceeds from the vain imaginations in the human heart.

Unlike the faithless fool who places his trust in himself, the faithful Christian, according to the above proverb, "walks in wisdom." This wisdom is found in the Word of God, Holy Scripture, which makes us "wise unto salvation through faith which is in Christ Jesus" (2 Timothy 3:15 KJV).

Our salvation is not in foolish imaginations of our heart but in the very heart of God, who so loved the world that He sent His Son to give us salvation. It is a wise person, not a foolish one, who in faith accepts this gift of God and so finds deliverance from sin. It is a wise person who lives in the wisdom of faith.

"To God, the only wise, the one immortal King, let hallelujahs rise from every living thing." Amen.

Ihno A. Janssen/April 1, 1982

98

THE HUMBLE JESUS

[Jesus] rose from supper, laid aside His garments, and girded Himself with a towel. Then He poured water into a basin, and began to wash the disciples' feet. *John 13:4–5 RSV*

Jesus came, the heav'ns adoring,
Came with peace from realms on high;
Jesus came for man's redemption,
Lowly came on earth to die;
Alleluia! Alleluia!
Came in deep humility.

As an example of humility and service, Jesus, as His last days on earth were approaching, laid aside His outer garments and began to wash His disciples' feet. Not only was this a social custom of the times (it was usually done by servants), it was above all a striking example of Jesus' love for His disciples and of His humility for the salvation of all people.

Jesus tells us: "You also should do as I have done to you." In other words, the most menial tasks, done in love and for meeting human needs, have the Lord's approval and blessing. Not the headline-provoking accomplishments dear to public relations departments, but the kindly oft-unnoticed deeds of thoughtfulness and love are recommended and commended by our Lord.

Teach us, O God, that "the fear of the LORD is instruction in wisdom, and humility goes before honor" (Proverbs 15:33 RSV). Amen.

Andrew J. Buehner/May 11, 1979

WHY TREAT US LIKE THAT?

*His mother said unto Him, Son, why hast
Thou thus dealt with us? Luke 2:48 KJV*

Would any parent, with a spark of love for her child, miss the anguish in Mary's question? For three days she and Joseph had searched for their 12-year-old son lost in the city—or perhaps kidnapped. What an emotional mixture of love, happiness, anger, and relief when the boy was found! But through her anxiety, Mary could not resist the censuring comment. Jesus answered, "There was a reason."

Many Christians have framed Mary's remark in the question, "How could you do this to me?" God's answer is always the same. He tells us that no evil comes from His hand. He assures us that love directs the course of His response to our need. He reminds us that He gives us not what we want but what we need.

There is a great difference between what we want and what we need. An irresponsible parent blurs this difference, but our heavenly Father keeps it straight. For instance: No one wanted a Redeemer, but "while we were yet sinners, Christ died for us" (Romans 5:8 KJV). We *needed* redemption. And no one wants to "walk through the valley of the shadow of death," but God assures us that we need this experience on our way to life eternal. He always treats us right. Trust Him who gave His only Son to save us.

O Lord, our needs and our wants get us so confused. Straighten out our thinking. We ask this in Jesus' name. Amen.

Charles S. Mueller Sr./March 16, 1968

A MEANINGFUL DARKNESS

There was a darkness over all the earth.
Luke 23:44 KJV

*T*he Bible records a number of instances of darkness. At the giving of the Law, darkness in the form of a thick cloud settled on Mount Sinai. That darkness proclaimed the presence of God on the mountain, and all Israel stood in awe around the holy hill. Years later, at the dedication of Solomon's temple, a thick dark cloud filled the holy place. This darkness, too, announced God's presence in His sanctuary. Solomon told the assembled worshipers, "The LORD said that He would dwell in the thick darkness" (1 Kings 8:12). Mindful of instances of darkness such as these, the psalmist was moved to write: "He made darkness His secret place; His pavilion round about Him were … thick clouds of the skies" (Psalm 18:11 KJV).

Similarly God let a deep darkness cover Golgotha. That darkness should have set the people gathered around the cross to thinking. It should have moved them to say: "Truly this is the Son of God." But most of the spectators, though having eyes, did not see that, shrouded in darkness, God was in Christ, reconciling the world to Himself.

That unnatural darkness has a message for us too. In silent but awe-filled accents it says, "Behold your God." Once we have heard the message of that darkness no other darkness can make us afraid, not even the darkness of the valley of death's shadow.

Lord Jesus, help us see You in the darkness of sorrow, trouble, and sin. Amen.

J. Henry Gienapp/April 13, 1960

PHILIP OF BETHSAIDA

Philip said to Him, "Lord, show us the Father,
and we shall be satisfied." *John 14:8 RSV*

*T*he disciple Philip made this request in one of the
most poignant scenes of the passion story. It was in
the Upper Room, where Jesus had just instituted His
Supper.

We might easily blame Philip for posing so naive a suggestion this late in Jesus' ministry. Jesus Himself seemed
taken aback by it, as His response in the reading shows.
Apparently Philip had made precious little theological
progress since the day when he wondered how Jesus
would ever feed the five thousand.

Christians, though, can be grateful for Philip's request
in the Upper Room. It called forth one of the most powerful assertions Jesus ever made to His own divinity. It is
so easy for us to miss the significance of *who* is about to
suffer and die in our behalf on Good Friday: a man named
Jesus, true, but also—ineffable thought—He who is very
God of very God.

No question about God is ever too naive for us to ask,
if it sincerely troubles us. Philip's query received a profound reply. It helps us see the dimensions of the passion
story.

*Let us ever keep in mind the larger perspectives of
Lent, O Lord, so we do not miss its message for us.
Amen.*

Paul L. Maier/March 9, 1979

An Amazing Contradiction

When I am weak, then am I strong.
2 Corinthians 12:10 KJV

*H*ere is an amazing contradiction. It doesn't seem to make sense. How can it be?

The apostle Paul was bothered by a physical ailment that he called "a thorn in the flesh." Its purpose was to keep him humble as he himself tells us. Three times he prayed the Lord to remove it, but the Lord had a different answer for him, "My grace is sufficient for thee, for My strength is made perfect in weakness."

Paul found this to be true. Despite his handicap and weakness, Paul was able to endure many troubles and to accomplish great things through the grace and power the Lord supplied.

You can't fill a glass with milk if it is already filled with something else; you must first empty it. When we confess our sinfulness, God shows us how mightily He saves us through Christ. When we realize our weaknesses, He shows us what His grace can accomplish.

When we are facing some difficult task or bearing some heavy burden, we do not have to pray for an easier task or a lighter burden, but for the strength God is ready to give. Then we learn: When we are weak, then we are strong.

Lord, help us to realize our weakness that we may look to You for the strength we need. Amen.

Felix H. Kretzschmar/Nov. 8, 1977

ONE WHO NEVER CHANGES

I am the LORD, I change not. *Malachi 3:6*

Jesus Christ the same yesterday, and today,
and forever. *Hebrews 13:8 KJV*

Many of us resent change. The networks change our favorite evening TV schedule, and we are frustrated. A wrecking ball goes into action and takes away our favorite corner drugstore; a parking lot takes its place. Our barber or hair stylist retires, and we must find a new one.

An ancient Greek philosopher once made this statement, "You cannot step into the same stream twice." Life is an ever-changing stream.

But there is one who never changes. Jesus never changes. Listen again to this great Word of God, this powerful promise: "Jesus Christ the same yesterday, and today, and forever." Our topsy-turvy world may collapse, but Jesus never changes. His love for us remains the same. His care and concern for us is constant. The saving power of His Gospel never loses its potency. Through His death on the cross all our sins are forgiven. His resurrection from the dead seals for us eternal salvation. These great truths will never change.

"Swift to its close ebbs out life's little day; Earth's joys grow dim, its glories pass away; Change and decay in all around I see; O Thou, who changest not, abide with me."

Our heavenly Father, help us to handle change and to avail ourselves of the stability You give to us in Your Word. Amen.

Victor F. Halboth Jr./Feb. 24, 1984

WHAT A LEGACY TO LEAVE!

I am reminded of your sincere faith …
that dwelt first in your grandmother Lois
and your mother Eunice. *2 Timothy 1:5 RSV*

*P*arents leave various kinds of legacies to their children. Some leave sizable fortunes, or tested values to live by, or the knowledge of Christ and the example of a strong faith in Him, or a combination of these. Or—tragically—nothing.

There are a number of legacies that cannot be measured in dollars and cents: an example of Christian faith and forgiveness, a model of compassion and love, a dedication to ideals, a patient and tolerant attitude, active concern for the weak, or a lively interest in God's plan for the world.

But such a legacy takes years to develop. No one falls into it, drifts into it, or pulls it out of the air. It grows day by day, like compound interest on the investment of daily communication with God; regular eating and drinking at the Lord's Table; conscientious hearing of His Word; attention to one's spiritual health, diet, and habits; and the diligent and purposeful exercise of the mind. It's not too early to begin.

We will leave something of benefit for everyone if we keep growing in Christ during the time we are gathering His harvest.

Holy Spirit, equip us with Your promised gifts that we may leave the world richer than we found it. Amen.

Jaroslav J. Vajda/May 26, 1977

105

IN THE KINGDOM

I will not drink henceforth of this fruit of the vine,
until that day when I drink it new with you
in My Father's kingdom. *Matthew 26:29 KJV*

*J*esus had just instituted the Lord's Supper. Before Him
was Gethsemane with its agony and bloody sweat; halls
of judgment with their injustice and abuse; Calvary with
its crucifixion, being forsaken of God, and death.

The road would not be easy for His followers either.
The events of His passion would deeply shake their faith.
They would rejoice at their reunion with Him beyond the
resurrection, but then they would be parted from His visible presence by His ascension. They would make a hard,
heroic, wearisome journey as His witnesses to the world.
Most of them would suffer much, then there would be
martyrdom.

The church in time to come would be a militant
church, fighting against enemies without and within. The
strife would be hard. And there would be no visible Christ
to encourage and strengthen His own.

Jesus gave us, His church, His disciples of all time, a
vision that gave Him joy and was to be our comfort.
Beyond Calvary, yes, because of it and its victory, He would
be united with His own in glory. He would drink the cup
"new" with us in His Father's kingdom. There we will see
Him face to face and rejoice in the full fruits of His victory.
His Word and sacraments will sustain us until then.

*Jesus, sustain us by the vision of coming glory.
Amen.*

Louis W. Grother/March 5, 1962

In the Time of Sifting

*Simon ... I have prayed for thee, that thy faith
fail not. Luke 22:31–32 KJV*

*I*t was a slow and solemn walk—that eventful trip from
the Upper Room, where Jesus had just completed the
institution of the Lord's Supper, to the Mount of Olives
across the brook Kidron. Jesus had reminded Simon Peter
of the terrible ordeal he would have to face. "Simon,
behold, Satan hath desired to have you, that he may sift
you as wheat." He added, "But I have prayed for thee, that
thy faith fail not."

This was one prayer of Jesus, it would seem, that
almost failed. How close Peter came to falling from faith
we know from the story of his threefold denial of the
Lord. With fear in his heart and profanity on his lips,
Peter denied the Lord Jesus and denied being one of His
disciples. Only the loving look of Jesus rekindled the flick-
er of faith in his heart and brought Peter to deep repentance. From that day on he became a stalwart confessor of
Christ.

In Romans 8:34 we are told that the Christ who died
and rose again is even now at the right hand of God and
"maketh intercession for us." Of this, we can be sure: He
is praying that our faith will not fail. How we need to pray
this prayer also—for ourselves and for others! It can be
the difference between spiritual death and spiritual life.

*Lord Jesus, preserve us ever steadfast in the true
faith. Amen.*

Victor L. Behnken/Feb. 16, 1970

107

No Swords!

Put up again thy sword into its place for all
they that take the sword shall perish with the
sword. *Matthew 26:52 KJV*

When Peter saw the band of soldiers about to seize Jesus, he reached for his sword, probably a short, dagger-type knife such as travelers carried. Peter is ready now to do what he had promised Jesus—die for Him. In the church we need men and women who will dare for Jesus, who will risk all for Him.

But Peter did not understand. Jesus was ready, even eager, to face His captors. This was a necessary part of His work of salvation. What He had to fight could not be accomplished with the sword. Resistance with arms would have defeated the whole purpose of His life.

Still people use the sword. They prefer to do something, fight something, be physically active in gaining salvation. It is hard for people to let Jesus be crucified and by being crucified earn eternal life for them. But so it must be if we are to be saved at all.

Even in the spread of the kingdom, the sword has been used. "Be baptized or die by the sword" was the choice offered the Goths when "Christian" soldiers entered the north country. Nor can gimmicks replace the Gospel in evangelizing the world, as if they were more potent than the simple telling of the story of Jesus. "Put up the sword," says Jesus. "I will win My way."

Jesus, save me by Your Gospel of grace. Amen.

Louis W. Grother/March 17, 1962

The Priest's Maid Was Right

*The maid saw him, and began again to say to
the bystanders, "This man is one of them."*
Mark 14:69 RSV

*N*one of the disciples who fled from Gethsemane
continued in hiding; two disciples, John and Peter,
cautiously followed Jesus at a safe distance. John evidently had some friends among the high priest's staff, because
he was able to gain admission into the palace of Caiaphas,
to which Jesus was brought.

As Peter stood warming himself before a fire in the
courtyard—in early April, nights are still cool in
Jerusalem—he was recognized by a door maid. "You also
were with the Nazarene, Jesus," she challenged.

Although Peter denied it under oath, the servant girl
was absolutely right. She had pierced Peter's pretenses
with uncanny accuracy. Jesus' prediction in the Upper
Room was fulfilled. The nameless maid had played her
tiny part in the greatest drama Palestine had witnessed.
One can only hope that later she saw Peter again in another light and that the Holy Spirit enlarged her role within
the story of salvation.

May God grant us the power of piercing our pretenses
and of seeing Jesus more clearly as our Savior.

*Lord, help me always to declare myself as Your
disciple. Amen.*

Paul L. Maier/March 14, 1979

THE PRICE OF FREEDOM

[God] made Him to be sin for us, who knew
no sin. *2 Corinthians 5:21 RSV*

*A*fter suffering yet another persecution for the mere
fact of being Jewish, Tevye, the main character in
the musical *Fiddler on the Roof*, looks up to heaven and
says, more whimsically than seriously: "I know we are
Your chosen people, Lord, but do You have to choose us
so *often?*"

There is more than a little truth to this if we apply it to
Jesus. He was the "Christ of God," that is, the Chosen
One, the Anointed One, who had been set aside for a spe-
cial task.

We tend to think of the glory and privilege involved in
being the Chosen One. We forget that Jesus was chosen
for a terrifying task. In the Garden of Gethsemane He
would feel sorrowful unto death and sweat profusely at
the thought of what was coming. As our text indicates,
God was going to make Jesus to be sin for our sakes so we
would become God's holy people. God would say, "I no
longer see sin anywhere else but in My own Son. In Him
I see Sodom and Gomorrah and all the evil that exists, and
I will destroy it all by destroying Him."

The Chosen One set us free at His own expense, and
what a price He paid! It was sufficient to make us eternally pleasing to God.

*Lord Jesus, help us appreciate Your love and the price
it prompted You to pay for our salvation. Amen.*

Mark Wessling/Sept. 8, 1982

110

Look Who's Waiting for Us!

*Verily I say unto thee, To day shalt thou be
with Me in paradise. Luke 23:43 KJV*

Of the few people of whom the Scriptures specifical-
ly tell us that they are now in heaven, one was a
criminal. It was to a man who had misspent his life in sin
and shame, but who in his dying moments had come to
faith in his Redeemer, that Christ opened wide the doors
of heaven and said: "To day shalt thou be with Me in paradise." There was room even for the dying thief in the
Father's house above.

Heaven *is* like that! More than we sometimes imagine,
its mansions are peopled with a great unnumbered throng
of converted "dying thieves," "penitent publicans," and
those, both great and small, who have come "out of great
tribulation, and have washed their robes, and made them
white in the blood of the Lamb" (Revelation 7:14).

What an inviting, reassuring picture of our Father's
house above—to remember that "the dying thief" awaits
us there! His Savior is our Savior. The door by which he
entered the heavenly mansion is still open to us; it is the
door of repentance for sin and faith in our divine
Redeemer. Remember who's waiting for us—a sinner,
redeemed, restored by grace through faith in Jesus Christ
our Savior. If he, then also you and I!

*Lord, grant me the same grace You granted to the
thief on the cross. Amen.*

Herman W. Gockel/Jan. 31, 1975

DARKNESS AND LIGHT

*From the sixth hour there was darkness
over all the land until the ninth hour.*
Matthew 27:45 RSV

Calvary was a place of contrasts. While the enemies of Christ stood firm in their conviction that Christ was to die, they stood on unfirm ground because of an earthquake. Although His accusers wanted nothing to do with Him, they swarmed around His cross and wouldn't leave Him alone. While some at Calvary were cheering for Him, others were jeering at Him.

Perhaps the sharpest contrast at Calvary was seen in the three-hour darkness that surrounded the Savior, who said, "I am the light of the world" (John 8:12 KJV). Never before were darkness and the light seen in their contradictory natures.

The darkness on Calvary symbolizes our darkened lives of sin. The light that penetrated this spiritual darkness is the Christ, who conquered sin, death, and the devil in His sacrificial suffering, death, and resurrection.

The German poet Goethe in his dying moments cried, "Light, more light." We too pray for the light of God's love in Jesus Christ, which penetrated Calvary's darkness. We need "Light, more light" until we through faith in Christ will dwell in the eternal light of heaven.

"O Christ, our true and only light, Enlighten those who sit in night." Amen.

Ihno A. Janssen/April 10, 1982

The Hill of Skulls

I will lift up mine eyes unto the hills, from whence cometh my help. Psalm 121:1 KJV

Golgotha; skull. An ugly name, an ugly thought depicting death. As Jesus looked ahead to the hill, He stumbled, and the cross He bore on His whip-torn back fell, and He with it.

After what seemed like hours, He was at the top of the hill. "And they crucified Him." No one was there to help. His own hands, once strong to heal, to hold, to lift, are nailed to the cross.

Even the Father in heaven withdraws His presence and help because Jesus chose to cover Himself with the guilt of our sins. And it is the essence of God's justice to punish sin. Thus the hill of the skull becomes the place of no help.

No help? We lift up our eyes to the hill again, and we see Him who gets no help *giving* help. He prays forgiveness for His enemies. He provides a home for His mother. He cheers a fellow victim of the cross by promising him heaven.

The temptation to weep comes as we see His agony. But we must see more. He became helpless in our place that we might be helped. He helps us with the great exchange in which He died as a sinner that we might live forever as children of God.

"When other helpers fail and comforts flee, Help of the helpless, oh, abide with me!" Amen.

Karl E. Lutze/July 20, 1968

THE TRIUMPHANT SAVIOR

When Jesus had received the vinegar, He said,
"It is finished"; and He bowed His head and
gave up His spirit. *John 19:30 RSV*

After all the gloom and pain, there is heard the shout that reverberates around our world for all time, "It is finished!" Luke tells us that Jesus cried out with a loud voice. When men expected Him to die of exhaustion, He was instead able to shout His triumphant cry of victory. Suffering and torment were behind Him now. He had accomplished the greatest task of all time. He had redeemed the world from sin and eternal death.

It is finished! All the angels in heaven must have echoed and reechoed that cry. We too share in that triumph because our redemption was accomplished. History can know no greater moment of triumph until the trumpet sounds the signal for our Lord's return in glory.

In the words *It is finished!* we find death, hell, sin, and damnation breathing their last, their power broken. Could ever the report be more complete and thorough: Mission accomplished!

It was indeed accomplished, and we are free, released from the bondage and captivity, the penalty and the never-ending despair of sin. Hell itself may mount the full weight of its power against us—to no avail. Our battle is won!

Jesus, our Savior, our conquering hero, keep us safe in Your power that we may ever share Your eternal victory. Amen.

Arnim H. Polster/April 17, 1981

114

BEING FAITHFUL
TO A FAITHFUL GOD

Does their faithlessness nullify the faithfulness
of God? *Romans 3:3 RSV*

What about our faithfulness to God? How does our record read? We know the history of the first man and woman, Adam and Eve, who committed the first unfaithful act in the Garden of Eden when they disobeyed God. David, one of the most gifted leaders of God's people in the Old Testament, became unfaithful but later expressed bitter remorse for the times he deserted God.

The disciples, eager to follow Christ, were to grieve at their lack of faithfulness when they forsook their Lord and fled. Peter, the boldest of them all, wept tears of shame for His denial. Our Lord still asks us, His present-day disciples, to be faithful.

A dramatic scene was enacted in Worms, Germany, on this date in 1521. The world wondered whether Martin Luther would remain faithful to God's Word, which he had previously professed so boldly. He stayed true to God. Before the diet or assembly of the emperor and church dignitaries, he boldly stated, "My conscience is captive to the Word of God. I cannot and I will not recant anything … Here I stand; I cannot do otherwise." This is what it means to be faithful.

Eternal God, keep us faithful in our fellowship with Your Son, Jesus Christ our Lord. Amen.

Milton S. Ernstmeyer/Oct. 6, 1978

The Last Easter

Christ has been raised from the dead,
the first fruits of those who have fallen asleep.
1 Corinthians 15:20 RSV

*C*hrist gained the victory for us all on the first Easter, and every day since then has been touched by its power. The battle against sin and doubt may still go on, but a daily return in faith to our personal "resurrection day," when we were "raised" with Christ in Baptism, renews our strength. Finally, we are cheered on in the fight as we look ahead to the last Easter.

Christ Himself is the firstfruits of that final resurrection day in which all believers shall share. Even as He came forth from the grave, so there will be a joyous Easter Day when He will come forth from heaven, summon us to come forth, and will "change our lowly body to be like His glorious body" (Philippians 3:21 RSV).

Martin Luther movingly invites us to consider the full and eternal implications of that last Easter: "Let us rejoice in this coming day, and let us say: Winter has lasted long enough, beautiful summer once more will come, aye, a summer which will never end, a summer in which not only all the saints rejoice, but all angels as well, a summer for which all creatures wait and sigh, an eternal summer in which all things are made new."

O Christ, our heavenly bridegroom, we eagerly await that great day when we shall greet You. Amen.

Vernon R. Schreiber/April 29, 1974

116

"Who Can Move the Stone?"

Who will roll away the stone for us from the
door of the tomb? *Mark 16:3 RSV*

A great deal of valuable spiritual energy is wasted if
we worry about stones that have been rolled away
by the time we get to them.

Early Easter morning the women were on their way to
perform their last work of love for Jesus, whom they
expected to find lifeless in the tomb. But they worried
about the huge stone they were sure they would find in
front of the entrance.

Formidable boulders block the doorways into our
future. Sin, sickness, and sorrow are real, so are loneliness
and our feelings of inadequacy. As God pushed aside the
stone from the tomb, so He removed the barrier of sin
that blocked our path to Him. The way from our burdened hearts to the heart of God was cleared long before
we were born to worry over sin and guilt. So,

If there's a stone against your heart today,
Look up to Him and it will roll away.

And how about the other stones in our future? "It shall
come to pass, that before they call, I will answer," God
promises (Isaiah 65:24 KJV). His faithful Word and centuries of Christian experience combine to assure us that
"God can remove the stone!" He can push aside the obstacles or provide us with the resources to surmount the bar-
riers in our way.

Exchange our folly of worrying over removed stones
for a greater confidence in Your love and power. Amen.

Robert K. Menzel/April 20, 1961

EASTER PEACE

Jesus ... stood in the midst,
and saith unto them, Peace be unto you.
John 20:19 KJV

Easter Sunday evening as the disciples gathered behind locked doors, there was no peace in their hearts. Their Lord was dead. Fear of their enemies gripped their souls.

Suddenly Jesus appeared and said: "Peace be unto you." This was more than a salutation. It was the benediction of the risen Prince of Peace who had restored the peace of God to the hearts of men.

The risen Christ brings to us peace of conscience. The penalty of our sins had been paid in full. The guilt of our sins is removed. The power of sin in our lives is broken. Now we have full and complete pardon. We are at peace with God.

The peace of the risen Christ arms us with new courage to live for Him. We may face ridicule, rejection by friends, nonpromotion, even discharge from work for the principles of Christ. But with this Easter peace in our hearts, we can face all because we know the peace of God that passes all understanding. As Luther wrote, we can live as though Christ had died yesterday, had risen today, and were coming tomorrow to bring us abiding peace.

Christ, give us Your peace now and always. Amen.

Julius W. Acker/April 16, 1963

118

A Friend to Walk with Us

*Jesus Himself drew near, and went with them
... Did not our hearts burn within us, while He
talked with us by the way? Luke 24:15, 32 KJV*

Two disciples were walking to Emmaus on the evening of Easter. They had heard the news that Jesus had risen from the dead, but they had not seen Him. The news was hard to believe. Their hearts were filled with questions, doubts, and sorrows.

Then Jesus joined them on their journey and opened the Scriptures to them. For some strange reason they did not recognize Him for the time being. But a wonderful thing happened as He walked and talked with them. Their hearts began to burn with new light and life, comfort and hope. When Jesus joined them and walked with them, it made their journey a memorable experience.

The journey heavenward is at times a lonely one, but we Christians never walk alone. There are others traveling with us. And there is one friend on whose companionship we can always count. This friend is Jesus. He is always ready to share His presence and love with us along the way, to share our joys and sorrows, to strengthen us in weakness, to comfort us in sadness, to cheer us and give us hope in moments of distress and discouragement. It makes a world of difference if we begin each day with the thought, "No matter what I have to face today, I am not alone. Jesus is walking with me."

*Be my constant friend and companion, Lord Jesus,
and walk with me every day of my journey. Amen.*

Felix Kretzschmar/Sept. 7, 1963

THE HANDS OF JESUS

When He had said this, He showed them
His hands. *John 20:20 RSV*

*I*t was the first Easter Sunday evening. The disciples,
afraid for their lives, sat behind locked doors. Suddenly
Jesus appeared to them. To assure them that He is their
living Lord, He showed them His hands. The hands of
Jesus! *Mighty* hands they are. They touched the sick and
healed them. They lifted the youth of Nain out of death.
They passed over the eyes of the blind, made them see.

These are *kindly* hands. They rested in benediction on
the heads of little children; they were stretched out to the
weary and heavy-laden. Often they were raised in prayer
and blessing. Always they were dedicated in service to the
Father and to His children.

These were *pierced* hands. He had been nailed to the
cross and had shed His precious blood that we might be
loosed from the power of sin and Satan, that we might be
washed in His blood. His pierced hands make us realize at
what tremendous cost we have been redeemed.

Today the hands of God's people serve as the hands of
Jesus. He will use our hands, cleansed in His blood, for
His service. We dedicate our hands to His service, saying:
"Take my hands, and let them move At the impulse of
Your love."

You have written our names in the palms of Your
hands. Give us the grace to serve You daily. Amen.

Amos A. Schmidt/Nov. 22, 1960

120

Remembering Christ's
Resurrection

*Remember that Jesus Christ of the seed
of David was raised from the dead according
to my Gospel. 2 Timothy 2:8 KJV*

We sometimes speak of Easter Christians. These are people who attend church in all their finery on Easter Sunday, then usually stay away until another Easter rolls around. But these are not the only Easter Christians. Some of us who attend church regularly are really Easter Christians. We give thought to Christ's resurrection only at Easter time, then let this truth lie forgotten for the rest of the year.

The apostle Paul knew the need of keeping the resurrection of Jesus always in mind. From experience he knew how this doctrine had repeatedly filled him with courage to face life's trials and with strength to bear life's burdens. He wrote for our encouragement: "I can do all things through Christ which strengtheneth me" (Philippians 4:13 KJV). And to his young assistant who was taking upon himself the office of a minister, Paul wrote: "Remember that Jesus Christ of the seed of David was raised from the dead."

We do well to remember at all times that Jesus Christ was raised from the dead. Holding fast that truth will take the tensions from our lives and remove all frustrations. It will make living an unending triumph. It gives meaning to the line: *He lives to quiet all my fears.*

In days of sunshine and of shadow help us to remember always Your resurrection, O Lord. Amen.

J. Henry Gienapp/April 21, 1960

THE INTERRUPTIONS

*They glorified God, saying, "A great prophet
has arisen among us!" and "God has visited
His people!" Luke 7:16 RSV*

*L*ife is filled with painful interruptions. The reality of
life is tragedies and reverses. We think of the funeral procession coming out of the town of Nain that Jesus
meets. "As He drew near to the gate of the city, behold, a
man who had died was being carried out, the only son of
his mother, and she was a widow" (Luke 7:12 RSV).

That's the tragic picture—a woman without a son,
without a husband, without a supporter. It doesn't seem
fair that her life should be so upset. But that is the fate of
the sinner—to live with judgment and to reckon with the
reality of death. Every interruption of life confirms that.

Except one! Christ interrupted the interruptions. He
reversed the judgment. He is the conqueror of death.
Halting the funeral procession, He raised the dead man
and returned him to his mother. This was an intervening
act of grace, a sign that our Lord would turn the table of
judgment by His own death and resurrection.

The great interruption has occurred. God has visited
His people. In Jesus Christ God, the Lord and Creator, is
never up against a dead end or a blind alley. He always has
room to act and to save poor, miserable sinners. This is
what He did in Christ.

*God of salvation, in all Your visitations deliver us
at last for Jesus' sake. Amen.*

Ronald Starenko/Feb. 7, 1973

ME, LORD?

Moses said unto God, Who am I, that I should go unto Pharaoh, and ... bring forth the children of Israel out of Egypt? *Exodus 3:11 KJV*

God must get awfully tired of human beings—and their excuses. Paging through the Bible, we seem to find nothing but reluctant warriors for the Almighty. Instead of Isaiah's "Here am I; send me," the more common reply to God's call is "Me, Lord? Not me! Send him!"

Moses was like that. Confronted with God's call to service, he offered the human excuse. He pleaded inadequacy, unpreparedness, and indisposition. But God wanted Moses. Without his knowledge, God had prepared Moses for a task and mellowed him through the years. God was ready to act—through Moses. It was Moses who wanted to hold back.

God still equips those whom He would use. Through the Holy Spirit, operating in Word and Sacrament, God supplies divine power. Using other men and women, God equips us through good example, adequate training, and steady encouragement. In this way He prepares fathers and mothers, citizens and workers, pastors and teachers. All are to do His will, telling the story of Christ.

God urges us to let our light shine. When the divine order comes to blaze forth, we may be sure that He has already supplied the wick, the oil, and the match.

Call us to service, Lord, and by Your Spirit show us how we have been equipped by You. Amen.

Charles S. Mueller Sr./March 27, 1968

123

Portrait of Heavenly Celebrants

There will be more joy in heaven over one
sinner who repents than over ninety-nine
righteous persons. *Luke 15:7 RSV*

God doesn't accept what in the business world we would call a "satisfactory percentage." To lose only 1 percent is an "anticipated risk" that, when added to the price of the other 99 percent, still assures a profitable gain.

Heaven's concern is with the individual, not just with an acceptable majority. "One" is the name of everyone. "One that was lost" is your name and mine. Christ came to seek and to save that one—us! O blessed day when the Good Shepherd found us and laid us on His shoulder!

The lost one is carried directly back to the fold and reunited with the ninety-nine. The ninety-nine are in His protective fold and therefore not less loved. The very fact that He loved the "one" assures the ninety-nine of equal tenderness and shepherdly concern.

Heaven's joy and celebration is intimately connected with Christ's redemptive work. We see heaven's participation at Christ's birth, His temptation, His suffering, His Easter victory, and His ascension. The rejoicing of the saints awaits us, who are wanderers found and returned to the care of the Good Shepherd.

O Good Shepherd, accept us who were lost and now are found. Add us to the circle of heaven's rejoicing saints. Amen.

Bernhard H. Arkebauer/Nov. 9, 1979

Easter Peace—Despite Fear

He said to them, "It is I; do not be afraid."
John 6:20 RSV

A small child may often hear strange noises and imagine horrible monsters in the dark bedroom at night. He or she will cry out in fear for mommy or daddy. And when mommy or daddy sits by the bed, the fears are gone and the child is at peace, able to fall asleep.

Our fears as adults are not so easily routed. We can feel real panic when we sit by the bedside of that same child who is gasping for breath in a critical illness. To see a car out of control crashing toward you is a real cause for terror. A soldier about to go on the attack will have serious fears for survival. We all have our quota of fears, large and small.

There is one who can truly calm our fears and dispel our terrors—the Christ who could still the wind and the waves, who could heal the sick and raise the dead. What have we to fear as long as we hear His reassuring words: "It is I; do not be afraid"? What have we to fear when we know He is at our side, protecting us from all that is truly evil?

Christian soldiers do die in battle. Christian children also die of disease. Christian families become involved in automobile accidents. We share in the miseries of our world. But with Christ at our side, the end will always be a happy and glorious one—eternally.

Lord Jesus, keep us safe in all our terrors and fears. Amen.

Arnim H. Polster/April 26, 1968

A Sign of Life

*Unless I see in His hands the print of the nails,
and place my finger in the mark of the nails,
and place my hand in His side, I will not
believe. John 20:25 RSV*

*D*oubting Thomas is all of us! The good news of the resurrection is drowned out by the noise of our fears. The scars of death are too real to be wiped out by the hope of new life. We belabor the signs of death even when the news of the resurrection breaks in on us.

Death is a scandal for us. We live in a world so drenched with death we are certain that there is no escape from the chilling waves it belches from the deep. We know the familiar marks of death. We accept its reality. Its carnage litters our highways and our battlefields. It is so common that we can expect it any place.

No wonder Thomas does not ask to see the risen Christ. He asks to see the dead Christ. He calls for the signs of death that grip the world, that pinched out the life of the Master. But when He is confronted by the risen Christ, he does not mention his demands for the signs of death.

The risen Christ breaks into our lives in the same way. He comes to bring us the signs of life. He comes to overpower our concern with death. He comes to destroy death's hold on us. Death is no longer our lord, and we are no longer its slaves.

Lord God, help us to live in the freedom from death Your Son has won for us. Amen.

Harry N. Huxhold/April 2, 1967

126

SEE YOURSELF IN CHRIST'S RESURRECTION

We shall certainly be united with Him in a resurrection like His. Romans 6:5 RSV

*P*eople found it extremely difficult to believe that Jesus was alive again on Easter morning and that the tomb was empty. However, many saw Him and touched Him. When they were assured that He was truly raised from the dead, joy and peace filled their hearts, and life took on a new meaning.

Paul reminds us that the miracle of Christ's resurrection belongs also to us who through Baptism went down into death in His crucifixion.

It is hard for us to believe that *we* have had the Calvary and open-tomb experience in our Baptism. We, too, have come from death into a new life. And it is ours as a gift. Peace and joy are ours because for us, who have been united with Christ, the Savior, there is no more crucifixion and judgment to come. We are to proclaim this peace and joy to others.

Easter is more than the historical remembering of Jesus' great triumph over Satan and sin and evil men who plotted to kill Him. Easter means a new life in Christ, not only on Easter day but daily until we reach the fullness of joy in glory.

This new life in Christ appears as we are active in sharing Him and His Gospel with others.

Gracious Savior, help us see in each Baptism an observance of Easter, yielding peace and joy to our hearts. Amen.

Karl E. Lutze/July 29, 1965

LOVE'S EXPLANATION

It is because the LORD loves you.
Deuteronomy 7:8 RSV

*M*oses was trying to explain to the people, whom God had entrusted to his care and leadership why God had selected them for His precious possession, why God had set His love on them.

The people may have had their own explanations of this phenomenon of divine providence and mercy, but obviously they were not the correct ones in God's sight. Guided by the Holy Spirit, Moses presented an unusual explanation! "It was not because you were more in number than any other people that the LORD set His love upon you ... It is because the LORD loves you" (Deuteronomy 7:7–8 RSV).

Human reason questions such an explanation and declares that it is none at all. But it is from God, and it satisfies. God sets His love on His people, on each one of us, because He loves His people, each of us.

Love has its own initiative and reasons for acting. Love is self-giving and self-fulfilling because it springs from God, who is Himself love. In this simply stated but profoundly grounded fact, we find the basis for God's gift of His Son. Christ died for us "while we were yet sinners" (Romans 5:8 RSV). The only explanation is still that of Moses: "He loves us because He loves us."

Our loving Savior, we thank You for loving us so much, despite our sins and weaknesses. Amen.

Melvin J. Tassler/Nov. 5, 1980

What Is Faith?

He that cometh to God must believe that He is, and that He is a rewarder of them that diligently seek Him. *Hebrews 11:6 KJV*

What is this thing called faith? It is not something that we can put in a test tube and analyze scientifically. It is not some vague and hazy virtue that in times of stress people say, "we must have." It is not something magical that we can wear around our neck like a charm to ward off the stings of evil fortune. It is not a process of the mind, not the memorizing of proof texts.

No, faith is "the substance of things hoped for, the evidence of things not seen" (Hebrews 11:1 KJV). Faith is the hand that reaches out into the dark and is grasped by the unseen hand of God.

Faith is not something remote, abstract, learned out of a book, but it is the Spirit's work within us. Faith is personal and real because it brings our Lord so close to us.

Faith offers a challenge to something higher than our reason, than our mental and physical powers alone. The apostle says, "He that cometh to God must *believe* that He is, and that He is a rewarder of them that diligently seek Him." He gives us the power to seek Him, He shows us where to find Him, then He rewards us for it!

The Christian's faith is focused on one object alone—the compelling, magnetic figure of Christ. By faith we enshrine Him in our hearts as the Prince of Life, the Lord of Glory.

O Lord, transform our faith at last into sight. Amen.

Thomas Coates/Oct. 6, 1959

LIVING JOYFULLY

*Restore to me the joy of Thy salvation,
and uphold me with a willing spirit.*
Psalm 51:12 RSV

*J*oy is a gift from God. But if we do not take a gift and use it, it will not benefit us. That is definitely true of joy.

Often we confuse joy with happiness, but there is a big difference between the two. Happiness has its roots in happenings. Happiness is determined by what happens in our lives, which is not permanent. Circumstances change. People fail us. Events don't always happen according to our desires. Because happiness is determined by events, it is temporary.

Joy is rooted in God. God has made us for joy, creating us to live in harmony with Him and all things. Through sin we lost this harmony and this joy. But Jesus Christ, the mediator between God and humanity, restored peace and harmony—and with it, joy. Through faith in Jesus, our Lord and Savior, we are right with God. Joy comes from our restored relationship.

Every day we sin. But every day, as we repent and turn to God, He assures us of His forgiveness. Every day we pray, "Restore to me the joy of Thy salvation, and uphold me with a willing spirit." The result is that we live joyfully.

May our joy, Lord, be full. Teach us to understand the greatness of our salvation through Christ. Amen.

Eldon L. Brandt/Aug. 9, 1985

STAND FIRM!

Moses answered the people, "Do not be afraid.
Stand firm and you will see the deliverance the
LORD will bring you today." Exodus 14:13

The children of Israel were trapped between the Red
Sea and Pharaoh's army. What should they do?

Moses told them to stand firm and they would see the
Lord's deliverance. God opened the Red Sea, destroyed
Pharaoh's army, and led them to safety. Sometimes we feel
trapped with no way of escape. All our struggling only
gets us deeper into trouble. At such times we can stand
firm and await the deliverance of the Lord.

This does not mean that we should sit idly by and do
nothing to help ourselves. But when we are hemmed in by
circumstances that threaten to overwhelm us, we remember how God delivered His people in Egypt.

God knows a hundred ways of escape when we see only
a blank wall. All we can do is pray, "Cover my defenseless
head With the shadow of Your wing."

Spiritually we are also completely helpless. We cannot
come to God or do away with our sins. God draws us to
Himself and leads us to our Savior. This is entirely His
work. "Nothing in my hands I bring, Simply to Thy cross
I cling."

Dear Lord, when we are trapped, help us to stand
firm and await Your deliverance. Amen.

Oscar J. Klinkermann/Jan. 4, 1987

THE ANGELS AND THEIR KING

But to what angel has He ever said, "Sit at My right hand till
I make thy enemies a stool for thy feet?" Are they not all
ministering spirits sent forth to serve, for the sake of those
who are to obtain salvation? *Hebrews 1:13–14 RSV*

*T*here is high drama in the story of the angels. The little glimpses the Scriptures give indicate their unusual calling, the importance of their work, and the joyful
spirit in which they serve.

Recall some memorable occasions. They brought
startling messages to Abraham, Jacob, Zechariah, and
Mary. They showed a mighty arm when they shut the
mouths of lions surrounding Daniel. They gave strength
to Jesus in the garden and to Paul on a stormy sea. They
relayed God's great news near Bethlehem and near the
open tomb.

Yet the continuing activity of the angels is neither
apparent nor dramatic. They serve all children of God,
both young and old. They minister to the redeemed.
Their unnoticed activity on our behalf will be revealed to
us only on the Last Day.

Although angels are agents of God's goodness to us, we
receive an even higher gift. God also gave His Son—more
than an angel: King of the angels, stronger than angels. All
our enemies are under His feet. He is more precious to us
because He Himself is the gift. God gave us not only a message but a Savior-Son, a Redeemer-King, in Christ Jesus.

*We thank You, Lord Jesus, for angel hosts, but we
glorify You for sitting triumphantly at the right
hand of the Father and hearing us pray. Amen.*

Victor L. Brandt/Feb. 19, 1964

The Forgiving Father

*When he was yet a great way off, his father
saw him, and had compassion, and ran, and fell
on his neck, and kissed him. Luke 15:20 KJV*

Many feel the well-known parable in Luke 15 should
be referred to as that of the forgiving father rather
than the prodigal son. The central figure in the story really
is the father. How he longed and grieved and waited
while his wayward son was off wasting his life in sinful
rebellion!

But how the father rejoiced when the son returned! He
didn't walk. He ran, hugged his offspring, kissed him, and
prepared a bounteous and joyful welcome-home party. All
was forgiven. The son, who had been lost, was found.
What the father longed for and wanted more than anything else had come to pass.

It still happens that way today. There is still joy in heav-
en over one sinner who repents. And God does more than
just kill a fatted calf for an evening's party. He has prepared the eternal banquet in heaven that will never end.
All who return to Him through repentance and faith will
share in it. There is no cost. No credential is required
other than that we wear the garment that God Himself
has provided: the righteousness of Christ. And He still
calls out, "Come, for all things are now ready."

*Heavenly Father, thank You for welcoming us home
and for receiving us with joy. In Jesus' name.
Amen.*

August T. Mennicke/May 8, 1984

QUESTIONS AND ANSWERS

*After three days they found Him ...
sitting among the teachers, listening to them
and asking them questions. Luke 2:46 RSV*

Good teachers use various teaching methods. Sometimes they lecture. Or tell stories with a pointed meaning. Sometimes they chat about the day's news. Various methods are used to make teaching effective.

Jesus was a good teacher. He used all those methods—and one more. He taught by questions and answers, challenging listeners to consider God's plan of redemption for them. He made them think about the life that brings wholeness.

The question-answer method of teaching is still effective. Through the strengthening pressure of good questions, we are forced to think and are kept from turning exciting understanding into dull repetition.

Who asks the questions? The world. We ourselves. But the clearest questions come from Scripture. Today, as was the case two thousand years ago, we either ignore these pointed questions or seek meaningful answers. God's people seek answers.

Our only satisfying answers are from the Word of God, telling us that the blood of Jesus, shed on Calvary, cleanses us from all sin. We listen to this Word and become wise to salvation by faith in Christ. Therefore, search the Scriptures.

O God, by Your Holy Spirit lead us to confront all valid questions, and grant that we may find Your answers. Amen.

Charles S. Mueller Sr./March 1, 1968

134

"He Means It"

The wrath of God is revealed from heaven against all ungodliness and unrighteousness of men. *Romans 1:18 KJV*

*T*he children were playing rather noisily while their mother, too sick to be out of bed, was trying to rest upstairs. They had been warned several times by their father to quiet down but continued, as youngsters sometimes do. All at once the voice of their father was heard a final time. One of them looked quickly towards the others, "Hey, we better be quiet. Dad really means it this time."

When God speaks to us in His Word, "He really means it" too. There He has set forth His holy Law. We sometimes gain the impression that God is inclined to be softhearted and indulgent toward disobedience. He is pictured as the "Man upstairs" who looks the other way when His children sin.

Nothing could be farther from the truth. When we realize how deep and fierce is His wrath against sin, we do not pass the cross of Christ in pride and self-righteousness. Not one of us can come into God's presence with clean hands and a pure heart. When God judges, "He really means it."

How much He means it was vividly revealed on Calvary. There His wrath against our sin was visited on His Son. Here we begin to see how—wondrous fact!— His love is stronger still. Of this love, then, it is all the more true—"He really means it." He gives us a Savior.

Let me understand Your wrath, O God, that I may better comprehend Your love. Amen.

T. A. Weinhold/May 13, 1959

WASTE AT ITS WORST

In our work together with God, then, we beg
you who have received God's grace not to let it
be wasted. *2 Corinthians 6:1 TEV*

*T*here probably isn't a pastor in the world who can
page through the parish records and membership
rolls without feeling much of the deep sadness that moved
St. Paul to write the above words.

Paul thinks of God's grace—so shining, so beautiful, so
truly amazing! Then considers our neglect and refusal—
so perverse, so foolish, so terribly wasteful! He pleads and
begs: Let's stop that waste!

To reject offered love is never a light matter. To reject
love divine leads to the darkest of consequences—to reject
the love of God who so loved the world that He gave His
only Son; the love of the Son who gave Himself in the
greatest of sacrifices to give us eternal life; the love of the
Holy Spirit who searches out our heart with God's Good
News to bring us God's gift of unending life. That is why
the apostle makes his earnest plea all the more compelling: "Listen, *now* is the time to accept God's grace.
Look, *now* is the day of salvation."

By God's grace His *now* is still ours. Not to use it would
be waste at its worst.

*Heavenly Father, to the large measure of grace You
have given us add the special grace to treasure it
and never let it go to waste. Give us power to go on
from grace to glory! Amen.*

Albert W. Galen/Jan. 30, 1982

WATER AND THE WORD

Rise and be baptized, and wash away your sins,
calling on His name. *Acts 22:16 RSV*

We were baptized with ordinary water, the same water with which we quench our thirst and wash our hands. We do not know why God chose ordinary water for this baptismal sacrament of initiation into His kingdom. He could have chosen the nectar of some rare flower or the melted snows of Mount Hermon.

But the power of forgiveness does not rest in the water—when the water was applied, these words were spoken: "I baptize you in the name of the Father, and of the Son, and of the Holy Ghost."

Later, as I grew older, I learned from the Bible that "he that believeth and is baptized shall be saved" (Mark 16:16 KJV). This tells us of the promise of Holy Baptism: It is "a gracious water of life and a washing of regeneration in the Holy Ghost."

I believe this promise. In faith I take hold of my Lord Christ and all He has done for me in His life and suffering and death. In faith I receive in the water of Baptism all that He has promised. The life I now live in the flesh, I live by faith in the Son of God, who loved me and gave Himself for me.

"With faithful heart, O God, I pray: Grant me Thy Holy Spirit; Look Thou on my infirmity Through Jesus' blood and merit. Grant me to grow in grace each day That by this Sacrament I may Eternal life inherit." Amen.

David A. Preisinger/Aug. 20, 1961

137

Regular Rest Stops

And He went to the synagogue, as His custom
was, on the sabbath day. *Luke 4:16 RSV*

*M*ountain hikers appreciate regular rest stops. A few
minutes every hour helps one to relax, to appreciate the new view, and to regain energy for the trail ahead.
To walk to the point of near exhaustion before resting will
destroy the joy of the whole hike.

Along life's trail we also need regular rest stops. We
need to take time with God's Word, to relax in His forgiveness through Jesus, to realize His love and power, and
to be strengthened for following in His footsteps.

Most important is the weekly "rest stop" of public worship. God commands our coming together to hear the
preaching of the Gospel, both because we thereby confess
our faith in Jesus as Savior and because we need it. Those
who refuse public worship despise God as well as His
Word.

Our weekly public worship, which also was Jesus' custom, is like the overnight rest between hikes. In addition,
we need at least a few minutes daily with God's Word, as
in these devotions. This is not a drudgery but a service of
joy and a delightful exercise of faith.

Help us, Lord, so we both hear and follow Your
Word joyfully each day as long as You give us life.
Amen.

Theo. E. Allwardt Sr./Aug. 9, 1987

What I Have I Ought to Give

Peter said, "I have no silver and gold,
but I give you what I have; in the name of
Jesus Christ of Nazareth, walk." *Acts 3:6 RSV*

*T*he crippled man had been sitting at the gate of the temple long years. Many worshipers, as they passed by, gave him alms—some small, some bigger. But all of the alms were ineffective to meet his greatest need.

St. Peter had a gift. Its value was greater than millions of dollars. His gift met the man's need. It did not consist in sharing a brilliant culture or a theological tradition. That would not fill the man's need. The apostle shared the riches of the Lord Jesus Christ and the power of His name. He gave his gift simply and effectively. He said, "Walk." He meant: Get free in the Lord's name from your condition.

All this happened at the ninth hour, late in the day. For us it may be later than we think, but it is not too late. Now is the day of our salvation. Now, from all the crippling chains of our selfishness, the Lord offers immediate freedom.

The healed and freed man blessed the Lord for His gift. Holding their hands, he entered with the apostles Peter and John into the temple to worship. Those who are redeemed and freed always join together to worship the Lord for His grace.

Speak Your healing Word to us, O Jesus, and let us join our hands with other redeemed people to do Your will. Amen.

Carl F. Weidmann/April 8, 1970

139

THE EMPOWERING WORD

When [the shepherd] has brought out all his own,
he goes before them, and the sheep follow him, for
they know his voice. *John 10:4 RSV*

One of the great differences between the Law and the Gospel, both God's Word, is that the Law demands but does not help us perform what it demands. The Gospel, on the other hand, is the power of God for salvation to those who believe. It enables us to be God's children and to do what God desires.

The Law insists that we be holy as God is holy. But it ends up condemning us for not being holy and does nothing to make us holy. The Gospel brings us to faith in Jesus Christ and in Him declares us to be holy with the very holiness of the Son of God, who loved us and gave Himself for us.

The Gospel is the voice of the Good Shepherd. He who laid down His life for the sheep calls us in and through His Word. We know that voice. It designates us as God's beloved in Christ. The Gospel is the rod and the staff with which our Good Shepherd comforts us throughout life and even in the valley of the shadow of death.

Faith clings to Jesus Christ. His Gospel calls and empowers us to follow Him. His voice both invites and enables us to come to Him and to follow in His steps.

Lord, guide us by Your Word and bring us at last into the eternal sheepfold of God. Amen.

William A. Buege/April 29, 1971

A Promise Given, a Promise Kept

[Abraham] was strengthened in his faith and
gave glory to God, being fully persuaded that
God had power to do what He had promised.
Romans 4:20–21

*P*eople do not seem to take promises as seriously today as they once did. In years gone by, when a person made a promise, he or she took it as a serious vow to carry out. No promise was made if its fulfillment was deemed doubtful. Today, an unkept promise does not seem to be of much concern, and in many instances, people even expect promises to be ignored.

God promised Abraham that he and Sarah would have a son, and Abraham believed God. He was "fully persuaded" that God had the power to keep His promise. God did, and Abraham became the "father of many nations," as God had promised.

Today God still makes countless promises to you and to me in His Word, and He keeps them. In His Son, our Savior Jesus Christ, He has promised to grant forgiveness and eternal life to those who believe in His name and who in faith are "fully persuaded" that He can and will keep His promise. "No matter how many promises God has made, they are 'Yes' in Christ," St. Paul assures us in 2 Corinthians 1:20.

We thank You, O Lord, our heavenly Father, for keeping Your promises to us despite our constant failure to remain faithful to You. In Jesus' name. Amen.

Carlos H. Puig/Jan. 2, 1988

141

TROUBLED BUT HOPEFUL

Man is born to trouble. Job 5:7 RSV

*B*irth is a joyous event. Parental faces beam. Families celebrate. Yet birth ushers the infant into an existence that is bound to include trouble, pain, and sorrow. Job knew this from personal experience. He saw his oxen, sheep, and camels devastated. He saw his home blown down by a great wind. He saw his children killed in a storm. His own body was so tortured with boils and pain that he wanted to die.

Job sensed, however, that his was not an isolated instance. He recognized trouble as a universal condition. All humanity is born to trouble.

Why, then, is birth met with such universal rejoicing? First, because we are incurable optimists. We hope and, in a sense, believe that the suffering of the coming generation will be less than our own. Second, because God's earth, sky, and universe provide, on balance, a good dwelling place.

The greatest reason, however, to rejoice in a human birth is rooted in God and His Gospel. The infant is God's creation. The infant has been redeemed by Christ. God wants the infant to come to faith and enjoy what Christ has earned: forgiveness, life, and salvation. We are born to trouble, but in faith we are reborn to hope, joy, and eternal life.

Lord, we thank You for having created, redeemed, and given us eternal life. Amen.

W. Th. Janzow/May 1, 1972

THOSE GOOD, STRONG HANDS

In the shadow of His hand He hid me.
Isaiah 49:2 RSV

*A*lbrecht Durer painted the famous "Praying Hands." They were his brother's hands. The artist decided to make them memorable because the hard, life-long labor of those hands made it possible for him to study art and achieve fame.

The hands of Jesus are worthy of immortal fame. They put the planets into orbit and touched the straw of Bethlehem's manger. Thirty years later His hands, tough-ened by hard labor, gave help and healing to young and old. They touched the "untouchable" leper and cured him. They were placed on the brow of children.

The same hands were held by spikes to the cross, heavy with the world's sin. Truly the whole world lay in those hands. And they didn't let go. They held us firm.

Think of those good, strong hands now! They have dominion over empires and over "every name that is named." The nail marks in His hands are now tokens of glory. With hands extended in benediction over all His fol-lowers, He whispers His promises: "Peace I leave with you, My peace I give unto you: not as the world giveth, give I unto you. Let not your heart be troubled, neither let it be afraid" (John 14:27 KJV). Again: "I am with you always."

Lord, keep Your good, strong hands under me, over me, and around me to support, protect, and strengthen me. Amen.

Carl W. Berner Sr./Aug. 17, 1975

Dealing with the
Great Intruder

When Jesus had received the vinegar, He said,
"It is finished." John 19:30 RSV

*D*eath is the great intruder on life. It does not wait for people to finish what they are doing but snatches them in the midst of their life.

They die in offices at their desks, in shops at their machines, in markets at their counters, in fields at their plows. Mothers die while they are busy bringing up young children. Teenagers die in the bud of life before they finish school—before they have a chance to get started.

Death is always an interruption; it puts a period in the middle of a sentence of an unfinished book. It may break off the story near the beginning, in the middle, or toward the end. But even if it comes on the last page of the last chapter, it is always a disturbing conclusion.

There is only one exception to that rule—the Living One who did not allow death to interrupt what He was doing, the one who made death wait until He was done with His work, the one who could say just before He died: "It is finished." Jesus Christ said that on Calvary's cross.

He said it for you and me so we might be free from the fear of death and find eternal life in Him. Believe it and rejoice!

Lord Jesus Christ, we thank You for overcoming death and for giving us the life in You that knows no end. Amen.

Frederick C. Hinz/Oct. 5, 1986

NONE IS TOO BAD

Here is a trustworthy saying that deserves full acceptance: Christ Jesus came into the world to save sinners—of whom I am the worst.
1 Timothy 1:15

*J*esus came to save all kinds of sinners, even the really bad ones. He dealt not only with "good" people, but with thieves, crooked politicians, prostitutes, and social outcasts. St. Paul admitted that he had been a blasphemer, a persecutor, and a violent person—the worst of sinners. But by God's mercy he was led to faith in Jesus, and the great persecutor of the church became the great missionary.

We may have done things for which we hang our head in shame. We may know someone who has led an especially wicked life. God invites such sinners to come to Him, too, and He will restore and renew them and make them valuable workers in His kingdom. We may have squandered much of our life and wasted our talents, but through the atoning blood of Jesus we are fully restored, and God can make us valuable assets in His kingdom.

The prodigal son was not put on probation when he returned to his father. He was received back as a son. For every penitent sinner these are precious words: "This man [Jesus] welcomes sinners and eats with them" (Luke 15:12).

Thank You, dear Savior, for Your forgiving love that embraces every lost sinner, including me. Amen.

Oscar J. Klinkermann/Jan. 11, 1987

WAITING ON THE LORD

Wait for the LORD; be strong, and let your
heart take courage; yea, wait for the LORD!
Psalm 27:14 RSV

We live in a world of the "instant." We stand in front
of a microwave and count the seconds. We get
upset if it takes too long to hear a dial tone. We expect our
television sets to have immediate noise and picture. We
are a generation that does not like to wait.

Yet we did not have to wait with the Old Testament
people for the coming of the Messiah. We have come to
know, through the Word of God, that the prophecies have
been fulfilled in Jesus. God's Son has come to a lost world.
He has made things right between us and God on the
cross of Calvary. No, we do not have to wait for our salvation—it is fulfilled, it is ours, and it is now.

But when God lets us wait for answers to prayer, we
frequently panic. We want God to adhere to our
timetable. If His will doesn't fit ours, we may be tempted
to move on without Him.

Scripture instructs us to "wait for the Lord." While we
wait, we are to be confident that He is already answering
and taking care of our needs. Let us commit ourselves
today to waiting confidently for our Lord, who has not
forgotten us and never will.

*Lord God, help us to wait confidently for Your
answers to our prayers. In Jesus' name we pray.
Amen.*

Gary and Christine Dehnke/May 5, 1988

FORGIVENESS

*Son, be of good cheer; thy sins be forgiven
thee. Matthew 9:2 KJV*

*J*esus spoke these words to a paralytic man who had been brought to Him for healing. Perhaps the man felt that God was punishing him in this way because of his sins. Whatever it was, Jesus knew that more than physical healing was needed. The man was sorely troubled in spirit.

Jesus therefore addressed His first words to the man's inner need. He said, "Son, be of good cheer; thy sins be forgiven thee." Then, to demonstrate to the grumbling skeptics around Him that He indeed had power on earth to forgive sins, He showed this divine power in a visible way. He said to the paralytic, "Arise, take up thy bed, and go unto thine house. And he arose and departed to his house" (Matthew 9:6–7 KJV).

Jesus sees the sins that separate us from God. He says to us, "Be of good cheer; thy sins be forgiven thee." He has this power as the Son of God, and has given this authority to His church: "Receive the Holy Spirit. If you forgive the sins of any, they are forgiven" (John 20:23 RSV). Whether we ponder this word of forgiveness in the quiet of our room or hear it pronounced by a minister in church, it is the same living Christ who stands behind this grand assurance. Let us hear it with a believing heart, trust His Word, then be of good cheer.

Receive us, O God, for Jesus' sake, and deliver us from all evil of body and soul. Amen.

Robert Howard Clausen/May 4, 1962

CHRISTIANS PRAY

The Spirit ... maketh intercession for us.
Romans 8:26 KJV

*P*aul said: "We know not what we should pray for as we ought." If Paul felt that way, we need not be ashamed to confess that we often find ourselves in the same dilemma. Life becomes more perplexing every day. Evils we never dreamed of years ago we now find on our very doorsteps. Problems that seemed so simple, looked at from a distance, baffle us when they become our own. In our perplexity we turn to God and often find ourselves stammering.

Paul says that the Spirit "helpeth our infirmities," making intercession for the saints according to the will of God.

At times our hearts are heavy, and we sob our way to God. At times fear besets us and, unable to move our lips, we tremble on our knees. Or tragedy strikes, and we just look up and scream. Here Paul says that we have a Helper in the person of the Holy Spirit. He takes our misshapen thoughts and molds them into perfect form. He takes our sobs and cries and screams of agony and composes a symphony—all of which He presents to God on our behalf as a perfect prayer wholly acceptable to God.

O God, I thank You for Your Holy Spirit. His presence gives me strength; His guidance gives me assurance; His intercession gives me utter confidence; for Jesus' sake. Amen.

Clemonce Sabourin/Sept. 13, 1970

The Best Is Yet to Come

For as in Adam all die, so also in Christ shall
all be made alive. *1 Corinthians 15:22 RSV*

*D*eath is our last and great enemy. There are no exceptions. Every person lives with the certainty of this event. We detest, we dread the idea that we are born only to dissolve into the earth, never to live again in this world.

Death was never God's intention for us, the crown of His creation. He created us to live with Him everlastingly. Only disobedience and rebellion against the Creator brought the curse of death. Death is a natural product or fruit of sin, just as apples are a natural result of a growing apple tree. There are no scientific cures for death, now or ever. Because humans became sinners, death has become part and parcel of our existence. We can never escape the grave.

Only Jesus, the Son of God, has the cure for this disease. That cure is Easter, the death of death. Jesus entered the chamber of death and—if you please—threw away the key. He placed Himself under the unbreakable bonds of death, then did the impossible. He destroyed the power of death and returned to life. Furthermore, He guarantees to His followers the same victory. Everlasting life, not death, is our destiny. Heaven is real!

Jesus, hear our joyous thanks for everlasting life. Amen.

George R. Kraus/May 27, 1973

149

The Living God

Lo, I am with you always, to the close of the age. *Matthew 28:20 RSV*

*J*esus spoke the words of our text just prior to His glorious ascension into heaven. The message in these words is extremely important for our spiritual well-being. Many in our world consider Christ in terms of the saying, "Out of sight, out of mind." For them the Christian teaching of God's omnipresence is lost. Also lost is the Christian assurance that Christ is truly with us in all we do.

Even believing Christians are susceptible to forgetting that Christ has promised to be with them always. They remember the great words and actions of God in the past; but they may fail to see God just as surely acting and speaking in our world. God did not abdicate or pass out of existence with the last chapter in the Bible. The Word of His Gospel is pointed directly to us today. The living God speaks in the Gospel. He is with us to "the close of the age."

We are invited today to experience personally the presence of God in Word and sacraments. He will not let us down. The living God will take hold of us. Through the Gospel, with its eternal power, the Holy Spirit will grip us. This is Christ's promise. All this is ours—today!

Dear Lord Jesus, we thank You for having promised to remain with us. Enable us to live in this confidence, knowing that wherever we are gathered in Your name, even if only two or three of us, You are in our midst. Amen.

Daniel P. Aho/May 3, 1974

150

Deny Yourself

*If any man would come after Me, let him deny
himself and take up his cross and follow Me.*
Mark 8:34 RSV

*H*ow out of step with present-day thinking do these words of our Savior seem to be! Today we are told to assert ourselves, to love ourselves, to do what feels good to us. In contrast, Christ tells us, "Deny yourself."

Our criterion for determining what we are to do and why is not what *we* want or like but what *Christ* wants. The standard is not what pleases us but what pleases Him. He even asks those of us who would follow Him that we be willing to carry a cross just as He did. Because He carried the cross and died on it, Christ's sacrifice delivered us from sin and death. By asking us to carry a cross, He is asking us to be ready to suffer and to sacrifice for His sake.

It may seem that there is little joy and happiness in following Jesus Christ. But we need only to look around us in the world to see how short-lived joy is for those who live for themselves. When we follow Christ, we soon learn that true joy is found in losing ourselves in the service of others in His name. In fact, He tells us that it is in the losing of our life for His sake that we find it.

Jesus, help us die to self and become alive to You so we may willingly take up our cross and follow You. Amen.

Stephen G. Mazak Jr./Sept. 25, 1985

151

OUR DWELLING PLACE

Lord, Thou hast been our dwelling place in all generations. Psalm 90:1 KJV

*H*ave you ever seen a great rock casting its shadow on a river flowing past its base? That picture symbolizes the things that change and those that do not. The river is restless, moving constantly. The rock is permanent, remaining always the same. So it is with our God as described in Psalm 90.

Here Moses expresses one of the fundamental truths of our faith. He speaks of the eternal existence of God; of the dependence all creatures have on Him; and of our personal relationship to Him as our dwelling place in all generations.

For 40 long years Moses and the Israelites had been weary wanderers in the wilderness. How blessed for them to know that there was a refuge, a home, in *God!* What Moses found, we too may find.

Home is a place of safety. Nothing can harm us in the shelter of Christ's everlasting arms. The traveler gladly returns home from the fatigue and peril of the journey. It is home to which the prodigal returns in the penitent hour.

The way back to our eternal home is no longer blocked by the avenging angel with the flaming sword. It stands open forever to all who through Jesus Christ find in God the eternal dwelling place of their souls. Jesus' pierced hands have opened the door.

"Our God, our help in ages past, Our hope for years to come; Our shelter from the stormy blast, And our eternal home." Amen.

Gerhard E. Nitz/Feb. 3, 1965

No Room for Fear

*When the doors were shut where the disciples
were assembled for fear of the Jews, came Jesus
and stood in the midst, and saith unto them,
Peace be unto you. John 20:19 KJV*

*T*he path from the open tomb is one void of fear. Yet on that first Easter there was much fear. The disciples were so afraid that they gathered behind closed doors.

The disciples had no business behind locked doors. Jesus had told them He would rise from the dead. They should have been at the grave waiting to meet Him with joy. Instead they settled for a day of dread that lasted until the Lord appeared to them that evening.

Faith in Christ casts out fear. Unless we accept and trust the words and promises of Jesus, we will find ourselves in the same fearful condition as the disciples. Jesus rose from the dead that we might be released from fear and live in hope.

Are we living behind the locked doors of fear? We can come out into the open with the certainty of sin forgiven and with the assurance of salvation and life eternal. There is no fear when we walk through life with Christ, our Savior.

Lord Jesus, Your resurrection has banished fear and filled us with hope. For this we praise and thank You. Amen.

Walter C. Loeber/April 11, 1990

153

GOD'S INVITATION
AND HIS PROMISE

Cast thy burden upon the LORD, and He shall
sustain thee. Psalm 55:22 KJV

*T*his invitation and promise we find in many other vers-
es of the Bible. Some of the most meaningful of all
God's assurances were spoken by our Lord Jesus. He invited:
"Come unto Me, all ye that labour and are heavy laden, and
I will give you rest" (Matthew 11:28 KJV). He promised:
"Ask, and it shall be given you; seek, and ye shall find; knock,
and it shall be opened unto you" (Matthew 7:7 KJV).

Also our Lord's actions emphasized the certainty of
God's invitation and His promise to burdened people.
Blind Bartimaeus and the centurion whose servant was
sick, the bride and groom at Cana, the Syrophoenician
woman, the lepers and the palsied—all experienced the
love of the compassionate Lord. The same love, invitation, and promise are extended also to us.

Our greatest burden is our sin. Do we dare to feel that the
holy God who hates sin invites us to place this burden on
Him? Yes, because He sent His Son, the great burden bearer, into the world for this very purpose. "[God] made Him
to be sin for us, who knew no sin; that we might be made the
righteousness of God in Him" (2 Corinthians 5:21 KJV).

What a wonderful passage to say aloud each day: "Cast
thy burden upon the Lord, and He shall sustain thee"! To
such a gracious God we want to pledge anew our loyal
devotion tomorrow.

Lord, unburden and sustain! Amen.

Robert Schroeter/March 21, 1959

154

No Fickle Finger

*Then He said to Thomas, "Put your finger
here, and see My hands; and put out your
hand, and place it in My side; do not be faithless, but believing." John 20:27 RSV*

One of the most famous paintings in the world is Michelangelo's "Creation" on the ceiling of the Sistine Chapel in Rome. Many of us have a mental image of the one section where the finger of God is touching the finger of Adam. It was Michelangelo's way to show God imparting power and life to His new creature.

Here exactly the opposite seems to be happening. Thomas must reach out his finger to touch his Lord—not God's power, but apparent weakness: the wounds of Jesus.

Yet the resurrected Savior, despite His wounds, is not weak. Jesus knows that God's power has prevailed over death, the last enemy of humans. He is the risen Christ. Because He lives, His followers will live also.

Thus, when Thomas hears Jesus' invitation to touch, he realizes that he is to be impacted by the very might of God. He is being reached by the power of God to overcome the sin of unbelief. In the place of death, he is to enjoy life. Doubt is to yield to strong conviction as Christ's disciple. That is the gift of the risen Lord.

O Lord Jesus, help us in this day not to be faithless but believing. Amen.

Richard T. Hinz/June 22, 1984

BETRAYAL OF LOVE

Love never ends. *1 Corinthians 13:8 RSV*

*L*ove is patient and kind, but we are impatient and thoughtless. Love is not jealous or boastful, but we are. Love does not insist on its own way, but we do. Love is not irritable or resentful, but we constantly make excuses for such behavior on our part. Love "does not gloat over other men's sins, but delights in the truth" (New English Bible), while we do the opposite. We also put limits on how much we will face, believe, hope, or endure.

We confess that we have betrayed the way of life entrusted to us by Jesus when He said, "Love one another" (John 13:34 RSV). The key to change, however, does not lie in being forced to love despite ourselves. It is found in the last part of Jesus' command about love. He said that we should love "even as I have loved you."

That is what Good Friday was all about. He loved us, the unlovable, to the end, just as He said He would. Remember the prayer He said that day? "Father, forgive them!" His love secured for us the forgiveness we need, and now today and every day can be different as we say, "I am loved. I have been forgiven by God. I shall forgive."

We love and praise You, O Jesus. This world has never seen a love as beautiful as Yours. Amen.

Vernon R. Schreiber/April 12, 1974

ASK FOR THE BEST GIFT OF ALL

*Ask, and you will receive, that your joy may be
full. John 16:24 RSV*

Children often ask their parents for things, for various gifts. But in critical situations—when they are sick or become fearful in the night—they don't ask for *gifts* but for the *givers,* for their fathers or mothers.

Jesus makes mention of the various good and essential gifts parents give the children they love. You wouldn't give your child a stone for bread or a scorpion for an egg. How much more will the heavenly Father give the giver, the Holy Spirit, to them who ask for Him!

It is infantile to ask only for the *things* from God's hand. It is a rare wisdom that desires the giver Himself as the most precious gift one can ask. Forgiveness, peace of mind, hope for the future, faith for the present, love for all occasions—these are fine and desirable gifts. But how much better to ask God for the Holy Spirit, who through Christ freely gives us all things! Rather than depend on piecemeal distribution of favors we may or may not think of requesting, we would be wise to desire the giver Himself! The greatest blessing of Pentecost is the Holy Spirit, who volunteers to be our gift—along with His treasure of gifts: "love, joy, peace, patience, kindness, goodness, faithfulness, gentleness, self-control" (Galatians 5:22–23 RSV).

*Holy Spirit, thank You for offering Yourself to us.
Amen.*

Jaroslav J. Vajda/May 29, 1977

NEVER ALONE

*I am continually with You; You hold me by
my right hand. You will guide me with Your
counsel, and afterward receive me to glory.*
Psalm 73:23–24 NKJV

*A*n aged Scottish woman who lived alone was asked,
"What do you do with all your time?"
"Well," she said, "I take my hymnbook and sing a few
songs of praise to God. Then I get my Bible and let the
Lord speak to me. When I get tired of reading and
singing, I just sit still and let the Lord love me."

Loving people—that's our Lord's specialty. "Fear not,"
He says, "for I have redeemed you; I have called you by
name, you are Mine. When you pass through the waters I
will be with you; and through the rivers, they shall not
overwhelm you. ... For I am the LORD your God" (Isaiah
43:1–3 RSV).

If you have trouble believing that you are dear and precious to God, ask yourself, "Whom am I doubting?"

The Lord Jesus wants our life to be full of joy, lilt and
luster, peace and hope. He died on the cross to win these
blessings for us. To His believing and beloved followers,
He gave this promise, "I am with you always."

We never enter an empty room or car or home when
we believe in Him. He is always there to love us and help
us.

*Lord, there is always cheer when You are near.
Amen.*

Carl W. Berner Sr./May 13, 1983

In Christ—Source of Joy

Rather rejoice because your names are written
in heaven. *Luke 10:20 KJV*

Jesus had sent the 70 disciples out by twos to proclaim
the Gospel of the kingdom. We can imagine their joy
at the opportunity to serve their beloved Lord. We can
appreciate their concern in undertaking the task before
them. Jesus had made clear that He was sending them out
as "lambs among wolves." He had given instructions concerning their conduct when people refused to accept them.
Comfort, but also the fact that they would expect unpleasantness, could be found in His words, "He that despiseth
you despiseth Me" (Luke 10:16 KJV). They went out.

Now they return rejoicing. Many people had listened and
believed. The sick had been healed. And, wonder of wonders, even evil spirits had been cast out in the name of Jesus.

At this point Jesus teaches an important lesson. In
effect He says, "I know. I was with you all the time. I never
send you out alone. Be assured that in the future nothing
can happen to you in My service that is not in accord with
My wisdom and My love for you. However, do not center
your joy in the successes you can see, in accomplishments
or results. Rather rejoice because your names are written
in heaven."

For us today the lesson is equally important. The only
reliable source of joy is this—He has written our names in
heaven.

*Lord, secure in us the joy of living as heirs of
heaven. Amen.*

Robert Schroeter/April 8, 1959

CALLING THE WEAK

My grace is sufficient for thee:
for My strength is made perfect in weakness.
2 Corinthians 12:9 KJV

*T*he amazing thing about God's power is that it makes itself felt in and through people and things we regard as weak. God's idea of strength is different from ours. What impresses you about the power of nature? Is it an earthquake or a hurricane? God often shows His power within His world by sending up blades of grass so weak that cattle can trample them down.

Or consider people. For sheer power among people you may think of Caesar or Genghis Khan. Still, to picture God's power at work in this world with greater force, you can study the portrait of a frail, helpless woman in a long, black dress, the mother of the painter James Whistler. All through the Bible we read that God gets things done through men and women who by themselves would never reach first base.

Jesus Christ, with the world still in His heart, isn't asking us for strength. That's something we need to comprehend. The Christian call for service has never gone to giants who stroll around with their arms folded. The call goes to people just like ourselves—weak, frail, and sinful. Christ gives us the strength to carry out His will and work.

Dear Savior, Your hands can turn our weakness into power strong enough to win the world for You. Amen.

Arnold G. Kuntz/March 5, 1974

160

The Greatness of His Power

*That ye may know what is … the exceeding
greatness of His power toward us who believe.
Ephesians 1:18–20 KJV*

God exercises His power to achieve His saving purposes. It is always at work—effective, masterful, and
available to us who believe. The most dazzling display of
that power occurred when He raised Jesus from the dead.
That is the power we can count on; that is the force that
is at the service of faith. Its energy turned the tide of history on Easter. By it God has destroyed death and brought
life and immortality to light through the Gospel.

Sometimes we Christians are accused of living in a
dream world, of being empty-headed fanatics, of fostering
a vain idealism, of having visions that ignore the hard facts
of life.

There was once a beautiful dreamer and sublime ideal-
ist whose tortured, wounded body lay still in Joseph's
grave. Perhaps the conclusion then was that this Jesus was
too unreal and impractical for a world such as ours and
was certainly destined to end up this way. But Easter
exposed that folly, and the power of God blasted that blasphemy. We are weaklings only when we in disbelief turn
off the power. We can now glory in Him who is "able to
do exceeding abundantly above all that we ask or think,
according to the power that worketh in us" (Ephesians
3:20 KJV).

*When we are weak today, Lord, be strong in us.
Amen.*

Martin L. Koehneke/Sept. 15, 1974

161

RSVP—Please Reply!

Everything is ready; come. Matthew 22:4 RSV

Look what came in the mail: a beautiful wedding invitation! It is an honor to have our presence requested. We are pleased to be invited. But we do not always accept the invitation.

Our Lord gave us a standing invitation to come to the banquet He has prepared. He keeps offering us His redeeming grace, the Father's love, and the fellowship of His Spirit. How privileged we are to be invited to taste and see that the Lord is good—good to us personally!

We accept our Lord's invitation when we take Him at His Gospel word. This we do every time we with mind, heart, and spirit say yes to the Good News. This we do with every inner surge of joy at some word of God's forgiving grace. We do it when our response to our Good Shepherd's voice is, "Lord, I believe." This is how we eat the living bread and drink of the water of life.

But let us beware of patting ourselves on the back because we responded to the invitation. Not only was the invitation pure grace, but the Holy Spirit's kindness in moving our hearts to accept it by faith was a pure gift, pure grace. The banquet, the invitation, and the heart to accept it are all God's doing.

"Just as I am ... O Lamb of God, I come." Amen.

F. Samuel Janzow/June 19, 1977

162

Betrayal of the Cross

I decided to know nothing among you
except Jesus Christ and Him crucified.
1 Corinthians 2:2 RSV

I belong to Paul." "I belong to Apollos." "I belong to
Cephas." "I belong to a greater and wiser teacher than
you. That makes me better than you." In such expressions, many Corinthians were revealing that a proud and
boastful spirit was taking hold of their hearts.

No doubt they still used words about the cross of
Christ, but in Paul's view this was not enough. It was the
cross—not Paul, not Apollos, not Cephas—that had
determined who they were: redeemed children of God.
The power of God lies in the word of the cross, not in
skills, oratory, or charisma. Had they forgotten this and
thus betrayed the cross?

Have we done the same? The power of God for changing lives lies in the Word of the cross, not in the distin-
guished qualities, talents, or showmanship of a certain
leader. One thing lies at the root of a truly new and lasting relationship with God. It is the act of faith in which we
cast aside all human pretensions and trust not in our own
wisdom but in that strange and mysterious power of God
revealed in Christ Jesus crucified for our sins.

O God, keep us from evaluations that are worldly
and have no place in the Christian community.
Keep our eyes on the cross of Christ. Amen.

Vernon R. Schreiber/April 4, 1974

163

A Serpent in the Wilderness

*As Moses lifted up the serpent in the wilder-
ness, so must the Son of Man be lifted up, that
whoever believes in Him may have eternal life.*
John 3:14–15 RSV

*T*he people of Israel had escaped slavery in Egypt and
had begun the journey to the Promised Land. For a
while they had manna to eat and water to drink every day.
But in the face of shortages they began to murmur against
God, saying to Moses, "Why have you brought us up out
of Egypt to die in this wilderness? For there is no food
and no water, and we loathe this worthless food"
(Numbers 21:5 RSV).

Then the Lord sent fiery serpents to bite them. Many
died. Only then did they repent and pray for deliverance.
Through Moses God instructed them to fix their eyes on
a bronze serpent that Moses had lifted up. When they did
that, they were healed, and they lived.

Jesus compared His own death on the cross to that
incident. Whoever looks now in faith to His sacrifice
receives eternal life. Through Christ's merit on that
cross, all sins are forgiven. Renewed and forgiven, we
start the journey of life again and advance toward our
heavenly home. As we do so, our faith looks up to Jesus,
the Lamb of Calvary. He and He alone is the author and
finisher of our faith.

*Jesus, You have gone before us to the Father's house.
Your cross is our strength and power so we can
follow You. Amen.*

Alvin H. Franzmeier/June 6, 1985

164

No Other God Like Ours

There is no one like You, O LORD, and there is
no God but You. *1 Chronicles 17:20*

*T*he one true God is unique. That is what God's people in the Old Testament asserted at the beginning
of every prayer or worship: "Hear, O Israel: the LORD our
God is one LORD!" (Deuteronomy 6:4 KJV).

To add weight to our claims for our human activities
and accomplishments, we borrow superlatives that rightly
should be reserved for an absolutely perfect God. As we
use phrases such as "the almighty dollar," "the invincible
team," "the immortal bard," we readily admit that no one
should take these exaggerations literally. Yet ascribing any
quality that belongs only to God to anything less devalues
that quality and robs it of its exclusiveness. We must save
our superlatives for the one and only being who deserves
them: the Lord, our God.

From Abraham to Moses, David, Isaiah, Mary,
Thomas, Peter, and Paul and down to us, the text above is
echoed through the corridors of eternity: There is no one
like You, O God! That uniqueness becomes all-important
to us when we discover that the one true God is all-loving
and all-merciful, who forgives us *all* our iniquities by the
sacrifice of His only-begotten Son.

*Holy, triune God, You deserve all our praise and
thanksgiving, all glory and honor, now and forever.
Amen.*

Jaroslav J. Vajda/Feb. 3, 1987

FRIENDS OF JESUS

Ye have not chosen Me, but I have chosen you.
John 15:16 KJV

*Y*ou and I could not go to the White House and invite ourselves to dinner. Most likely we would be told, "You have not been invited; stay out." However, the president could give an invitation to the humblest citizen and make him feel at home.

Jesus, the King of kings and friend of sinners, has invited us most graciously with the kindest invitation ever given: "Come unto Me, all ye that labor and are heavy laden" (Matthew 11:28 KJV). And He gives us the assurance: "Him that cometh to Me I will in no wise cast out" (John 6:37 KJV).

We do not choose Jesus as friend. In fact, we cannot do so because we are dead in trespasses and sins. Jesus must do the choosing; He came into our world to seek and to save the lost. This truth He emphasized in the Upper Room when He said to His disciples and to us: "Ye have not chosen Me, but I have chosen you." Therefore, Paul, amazed at the graciousness of Jesus Christ, exclaims: "By the grace of God I am what I am" (1 Corinthians 15:10 KJV).

So we stand in grace because Jesus on the cross blotted out all our sins. Today He says to you and me: "I have chosen you to be My own." This makes our salvation sure. He died for us while we were yet sinners, called us through the Gospel to be His forevermore.

Lord Jesus, I deeply appreciate Your friendship, which has brought me into the family of God in time and eternity. Amen.

Alfred Doerffler/March 15, 1966

SAINTS IN HIDING

When they saw the boldness of Peter
and John ... they recognized that they
had been with Jesus. *Acts 4:13 RSV*

*H*ow do you recognize a Christian? Can you know a
person is a Christian by the way he looks physically?
Can you recognize a Christian by the superiority of her
mind? Is a person's outward action a sure indication of
inner faith? By what sign can a Christian be recognized?

There is a sense in which a Christian is not recognized
as such by others. The strongest Christian influence in
our world always has been that of the unrecognized—the
saints in hiding. These are people who need no badge.
The mark on them is simply the mark of Christ, the
reflection of His Spirit, the presence of His grace. They
are people who have been "with Jesus."

This is the definition of a saint. The New Testament
gives that name to ordinary men and women who, with all
of their faults and follies, have been united with Christ in
faith and have experienced His power in their own lives.
We are all "called to be saints." This is a task that goes on
in the silent depths of our own hearts. Peter and John
were recognized finally by only one thing. It was not their
appearance or their intelligence or their prestige. It was
that they had been "with Jesus."

*Thank You, Lord, for making us saints of Your
kingdom. Amen.*

John F. Johnson/April 7, 1987

Doubting Life's Purpose

I am come that they might have life,
and that they might have it more abundantly.
John 10:10 KJV

*I*s life worth living? This is a question that is prompted by many causes, that is asked in a large variety of moods. It may be asked by one in the throes of discontent or boredom. It may be asked by one who is plagued by frustration and failure. It may be asked by one who is in terrible pain or who has become a permanent invalid. When this doubt enters our minds, we can be sure that we have lost sight of the high and noble purposes God has for us in our lives.

Christ came to give us the abundant life for all eternity, but also a fuller life here and now in this world. He died for us that we might live eternally in heaven and also purposefully here on earth. If, through faith in Him, we have this life that He gives, how could we ever conclude that our life has lost its purpose?

Our primary purpose in life is always to glorify God. We may be called on to do this through patient endurance and perseverance while bearing our cross. Our purpose is also to share our faith in Christ. These eternal purposes completely overshadow any material, temporal purpose we might have. So long as life serves God, it is worth living.

O God, whether in peace or strife, sorrow or joy, sickness or health, cause us always to glorify Your name in Christ. Amen.

Arnim H. Polster/July 20, 1964

"What God Has Given Me, I Share"

A certain Samaritan ... had compassion on him ... and took care of him. *Luke 10:33–34 KJV*

*T*he inspiring philosophy of Christian stewardship as practiced by the good Samaritan can be summed up in the words, "What God has given me, I share." This certainly is evident in what this man did for the robbers' victim. From the human viewpoint, the Samaritan had done enough by taking the man to an inn. However, he paid his bill and stood by to do even more if it were necessary.

A 5-year-old girl was visiting her aunt. During the course of the visit she climbed on her aunt's knee and whispered, "I am going to give daddy a pair of slippers for his birthday." "Yes," replied the aunt, "and where will you get the money to buy them?" Without a moment's hesitation, the girl replied, "My daddy will give it to me."

The aunt smiled as she thought of the father paying for his own gift, yet she knew he would love his daughter for it. How true this is of all of us in relationship to our heavenly Father! What can we possibly give Him that wasn't His before He gave it to us? Even so, He is pleased to receive our offerings because they show our love for Him. Not only our goods but we ourselves are His; we have been bought with a price—the blood of God's Son.

Lord, keep us ever mindful that all we are and have is a trust from You. Amen.

Lewis E. Eickhoff/Sept. 22, 1969

TELLING HIS STORY

Let no man despise thy youth; but be thou
an example of the believers in word, in conversation, in charity, in spirit, in faith, in purity.
1 Timothy 4:12 KJV

Several thousand Christian young people held a con-
vention in Boston. One evening they had a picnic and
an open-air songfest on the famous Boston Common.
The next morning several sanitation crews and trucks
were sent to clean up—the usual routine after such an
event. The cleanup workers found the place spotless.
These young people were different. They were witnesses
to Christ. They told a story by their conduct as well as by
their word. By just being what they were, without apolo-
gies—Christ's young men and young women—they told a
story of what Christ had done for them.

Christian witness is never forced. It comes naturally. It
waits patiently for the right opportunity, and it takes the
opportunity when it comes. Christian people tell the story
of Christ who gave His all for all of us. They tell the story
in a Christlike way.

Christian witness can be given in a conversation with
someone. It is simple and direct. All our Lord asks is that
all of us tell the story of what He has done and what He is
constantly doing for us. That's His story.

*Lord, help us to witness to the saving name of Jesus
Christ, the world's only Savior. Amen.*

Oswald C. J. Hoffmann/Aug. 16, 1972

God's Paradox

*My grace is sufficient for you, for my power is
made perfect in weakness. 2 Corinthians 12:9*

Some time ago a famous athlete used to sell his exercise program by picturing in his advertisement a 98-pound weakling who had a hard time competing at the beach. After a few sessions, the "weakling" would be transformed and would return to the beach to win the attention of all the women.

From earliest times, people have used power to establish and secure a position in the hierarchical structure of society. Society still gives the impression that power is the one indispensable weapon in a person's arsenal that will assure him or her of success.

God apparently is of a different opinion. He seems to delight in choosing the weak, the humble, the average individual to accomplish His will. Jesus, His Son, was humble, becoming obedient to the point of death, even death on a cross. Jesus picked His disciples from the working class of His time. In their weakness, our Lord manifested His strength. Through them He achieved more than all the powerful figures of history put together. Through you, in the face of disadvantages and disabilities, He can do great things.

*Let me serve You, O Lord, despite my weaknesses.
Your power is made perfect in me. In Jesus' name
I pray. Amen.*

Carlos H. Puig/Jan. 21, 1988

171

WISDOM FROM ABOVE

Flesh and blood hath not revealed it unto thee, but
My Father which is in heaven. *Matthew 16:17 KJV*

*T*he Lord Jesus asked His disciples, "Who do you say
that I am?" Peter answered confidently: "Thou art the
Christ, the Son of the living God" (Matthew 16:16 KJV).
That was an inspired answer that will stand for all time.

Peter was persuaded that Christ was truly the Son of
God, not by a process of reasoning, not by knowledge he
could have gained in the best schools of his day. Rather as
Jesus said, it was revealed to him by the Father in heaven.

Worldly wise people in every age have seen Jesus only
as an illustrious character, a noble personality. He who
taught as none ever has, He who healed the sick, fed the
hungry, and went about doing good, gave the world the
convincing evidence that He must indeed be the Son of
God. This was divinely certified when He rose victoriously from the dead.

The strongest appeal that Christ makes is not to our
intellect or reason but to our hearts, which cry out for the
living God and which so urgently need His pardon, peace,
hope, and security.

Because Christ is truly the Son of God, He is able to
meet the innermost needs of our hearts and lives. He is
our peace with God, our assurance of reconciliation, our
comfort in life's troubles, our hope and certainty for a
blessed eternity in never-ending glory.

Son of the living God, grant that we may ever trust
in You and gratefully serve You as our heaven-sent
Savior and King. Amen.

Edwin L. Wilson/Feb. 4, 1960

OUT ON A LIMB

*He ran on ahead and climbed up into a
sycamore tree to see Him, for He was to pass
that way. Luke 19:4 RSV*

*A*nytime we take a chance or extend ourselves con-
siderably to reach a goal, we are said to be out on
a limb. We could say that about Zacchaeus, the publi-
can. A little fellow, he didn't stand a chance of seeing a
procession go by because everyone seemed to be taller
than he. He threw caution to the wind and decided to
climb a tree. He had to see this Jesus, about whom he had
heard so much. His reward was not a broken collarbone
or arm or leg, but an invitation to dine with the Master
and to be assured of the truth that God loved even him.

We don't face such obstacles. With the eyes of faith we
can see the Lord in our Bibles. We can accept His invitation to come to His Supper. We also can hear His gracious
words, "My son, My daughter, your sins are forgiven!"

No more need to wonder what Jesus is like! He reveals
Himself in the pages of Scripture. He tells us how,
because of Him, His heavenly Father feels about us. For
such a Savior we can go out on a limb anytime.

*Dear Lord, we rejoice in Your revelation of Yourself
and of our heavenly Father in Your Word. Help us
as we study it. Amen.*

Howard G. Allwardt/Oct. 16, 1982

173

Thank You, God!

I thank my God in all my remembrance of you,
always in every prayer of mine for you all making my prayer with joy. *Philippians 1:3–4 RSV*

*P*aul loved the believers in Philippi. He had founded
that church when he met a few faithful Jewish
women alongside a riverbank and told them the Messiah
they were praying for had come. He was Jesus of
Nazareth, whom God sent to death on the cross for the
sins of all humanity and then raised again so all who
believed in Him would be saved.

Paul's time among the new Christians in Philippi was
shortened by persecution, but it was long enough to plant
a beautiful congregation of devoted Christians who also
loved their brother in the faith, the apostle Paul, and continued to reach across the miles to care for him.

What a beautiful picture of pastor and people! How
wonderful if every pastor would remember daily to give
thanks for the members of his congregation; if every
Sunday school teacher could tell his or her class, "I thank
God every day for each of you"; if all parents could say to
their children, "We thank God every day for you with
joy." If children and spouses all did this—wouldn't such
prayers change our world?

Heavenly Father, I need to thank You today for
_____. *Thank You*
for placing them in my life. In Jesus' name. Amen.

Daniel A. Reeb/July 3, 1986

THE WORLD NEXT DOOR

*Him we proclaim, warning every man and teaching
every man in all wisdom, that we may present every
man mature in Christ. Colossians 1:28 RSV*

*T*hrilling accounts of conversions to Christ and baptisms in His name have come to us from New Guinea, Nigeria, India, and elsewhere. Wistfully we regret that we are not somewhere on a missionary team doing great things in the world.

Some of us forget that the world is next door as well as far away. We, too, can be on the missionary team witnessing of Christ to the neighbor, to the person beside whom we work or study, to those who are without God and without hope in our community. This is just as important as the seemingly more romantic activities thousands of miles away. St. Paul found and seized opportunities to proclaim Christ wherever he went. He warned of sin and he taught everyone he met all that he knew about Christ. At this he worked with all the wisdom and strength that Christ gave him. His goal was to help others become mature Christians.

With the rapid transportation and communication of our day, more and more of the world lives next door. What a wonderful time this is for the church to fulfill her mission! What golden opportunities there are for all of us to be witnesses of Christ to the world! How can we remain silent?

*Redeemer of the world, here am I; send me to speak
life and salvation in Your name. Amen.*

Herman A. Etzold/Nov. 22, 1966

Like a Mother Eagle

As an eagle stirreth up her nest, fluttereth over her
young, spreadeth abroad her wings, taketh them, beareth
them on her wings: So the LORD alone did lead him.
Deuteronomy 32:11–12 KJV

Sitting out in the wilderness one day, meditating on
what life was all about, quite ready to adjust himself
to the few responsibilities that his exile called for, Moses
observed a mother eagle with her young. The little birds
were content to watch their mother fly but had not the
slightest intention of trying out their own wings. Then
the great eagle took them out of their nest for training.
The young birds flew. They had to. When they grew
tired, the mother swept below to let them rest on her
strength. Years later Moses saw in his own development as
God's servant that the Lord's ways were wiser than his
own. We too must learn this lesson.

God, like a mother eagle, spills us out of our nest of
self-satisfaction, yet He always puts underneath us His
everlasting arms so we do not perish. As we become upset
because of the rough going, God leads us again and again
to Calvary to let us see that He still loves us and wants us
to grow in faith and grace. God does not carry us to the
skies on flowery beds of ease, but He does want to save us.
So He disciplines us so we may in time have pleasure
forevermore in glory.

*O God, teach us not to resent Your gracious prod-
ding to make us grow in Christian faith and life.
In Jesus' name. Amen.*

Arnold G. Kuntz/Jan. 8, 1989

176

In Christ a Miracle

If any man be in Christ, he is a new creature.
2 Corinthians 5:17 KJV

*I*n these few words, God tells of a miracle and mystery. To "be in Christ," the risen Lord, is a miracle as great as the creation of the world. Here is a mystery as deep as the Holy Trinity or the virgin birth or the real presence of Christ's body and blood in the Sacrament. Our Lord in His talk with Nicodemus referred to the miracle and mystery in somewhat different terms. He spoke of being "born again." When Nicodemus marveled, "How can these things be?" Jesus replied, "The wind bloweth where it listeth, and thou hearest the sound thereof, but canst not tell whence it cometh, and whither it goeth: so is every one that is born of the Spirit" (John 3:8 KJV).

To be in Christ is to believe the Gospel of God's love in sending His only Son to do what no word of God's mouth could do. At Calvary it had to be the Word made flesh dying for the sins of the world. Relying on the crucified and resurrected Lord as the only way and truth and life is to be in Christ. This reliance is the Holy Spirit's accomplishment. "By grace are ye saved through faith: and that not of yourselves: it is the gift of God: not of works, lest any man should boast" (Ephesians 2:8–9 KJV).

I believe in Jesus Christ. These are words of conviction and bold testimony, always to be spoken humbly and with reverent awe, because in us God has accomplished a great miracle and mystery.

Holy Spirit, continue in us the miracle of faith! Amen.

Robert Schroeter/March 30, 1959

177

KINDNESS

Look on Your servant with kindness; save me
in Your constant love. Psalm 31:16 TEV

A world-renowned scientist, inventor, and author was once asked how he would like to be remembered by future generations. Much to the surprise of many, he replied: "I would like to be remembered as a kind and gentle person. That would be a great tribute indeed."

How wise he was! But many would disagree. In a world where people vie for wealth, fame, power, influence, status, and the upper hand, kindness and gentleness are seen as weak and inferior qualities. How tragic!

Jesus, the almighty, all-powerful, and all-loving Son of God, frequently told His followers to be kind, gentle, and meek. More than that, He not only showed them how but also enabled them to be like He was by giving them new life. In the end, He went in gentleness and meekness to the cross. To the world, that was a sign of weakness and defeat. To those who believe in Jesus as their only Lord and Savior, it was the ultimate show of strength and victory.

Are you known as a kind and gentle person? If so, it is a great tribute indeed, both to you and to the Lord Jesus Christ whom you serve.

Lord Jesus Christ, as You were kind to others, help me also to be kind. Amen.

Paul W. Devantier/Aug. 23, 1984

MARRIAGE—THE SWEET GIFT OF GOD

Let marriage be held in honor among all.
Hebrews 13:4 RSV

When Martin Luther married Katie von Bora one June day in 1525, he founded a family that was the ideal of Christian families for centuries. What made this marriage a thing set apart was not that the Luthers had more blessings than others. But they did have a love for God, for each other, and for their work.

In things of this world, the Luthers had little. Luther lived only off his moderate salary as a professor and accepted nothing as pastor of the town church or as writer. In fact, he was so negligent when it came to money that Katie ran a little orchard and a fishpond to buy the children's clothes.

They had minor troubles, to be sure. With sermons, lectures, and manuscripts, Luther was often too tired at night to romp with his children or chat with his wife. All the same, he made it a point to write them when he traveled, to stage pageants for them round the fireplace, to carve wooden whistles, to take them hiking, to train them in the Word of God.

The marriage of Katie and Martin proved a blessed one. Looking back on it years later, Luther could write, "Ah, dear Lord, marriage is not an affair of nature. It is the gift of God, the sweetest and purest state."

O Lord, who blessed the bride and groom at Cana, bless now all who live together in love of You. Amen.

Theodore J. Kleinhans/Oct. 26, 1960

A Question of Where
to Find Jesus

He said to them, "How is it that you sought
Me? Did you not know that I must be in My
Father's house?" *Luke 2:49 RSV*

With the gentle reprimand of today's question, the 12-year-old Jesus reminded His mother, Mary, and Joseph that they should have known where to find Him. Where but in His Father's house, about His Father's business?

That is where we find Him still today—in the Father's house—as together with fellow believers we worship Him with Word and Sacrament, prayer and praise, offering and song. Also in our private reading of His Word or in listening to it as proclaimed over radio and television, Jesus is there, speaking to us. The same is true in our family devotions. God's Word at those times makes of our surroundings a house of God as we worship Him in spirit and in truth.

As we enter summer, there are those who claim they don't need to come to church to find Jesus. They can worship Him just as well, they say, out in the woods or on the lake or in the mountains or by the seashore. Can they? Do they? Let us this summer determine not to forsake "the assembling of ourselves together" (Hebrews 10:25 KJV) for the worship of our Savior God.

Savior, this summer we will not vacate our Father's house. Amen.

Martin J. Schmidt/June 21, 1979

180

Not Spectators Only

*His gifts were that some should be apostles,
some prophets, some evangelists, some pastors
and teachers, to equip the saints, for the work
of ministry, for building up the body of Christ.*
Ephesians 4:11–12 RSV

A coach was asked what role spectator sports played in the physical fitness of a nation. He responded: "None. What you have at a game is 22 football players exercising but needing rest, and 55,000 spectators resting but needing exercise."

All too often that accurately describes how it is in the church. A few people do the work while the rest watch and express their satisfaction or dissatisfaction. St. Paul says it ought not be that way in the church, the body of Christ. There are no spectators. All of us are called to be participants. God the Holy Spirit gives us gifts so we might use them to carry out our ministry as a part of the church.

Using our God-given gifts properly is what the stewardship life is all about. It is not optional. All God's people are stewards by virtue of their Baptism. All God's people have gifts to be used to build up the body of Christ. God brought us into the church. Christ suffered and died that we sinners might have forgiveness and fellowship with God. He brings the redeemed into His fellowship, the church, but not to be spectators! God calls us to participate, to use our gifts for His purposes.

Holy Spirit, thank You for Your gifts to me. Amen.

David W. Hoover/Sept. 24, 1986

181

What God Remembers

He hath remembered His covenant for ever.
Psalm 105:8 KJV

*Y*ou can depend on him. He keeps his promises."
When someone says this about another person, we
agree it is an excellent recommendation. You can depend
on God! He keeps His promises! He remembers the
covenant He made with us and keeps it.

The covenant goes back to the promise that the Seed of
a woman would conquer Satan. This was restated to
Abraham and his children; it was renewed throughout the
history of the Israelite people. We sometimes forget
promises in a matter of days, but in four thousand years
God did not forget. He sent His Son, made of a woman,
made under the Law, to redeem them that were under the
Law, that we might be brothers and sisters of Christ.

When the thief hung on the cross, he was concerned
about one thing only—that his Savior would remember
him. "Lord, remember me when Thou comest into Thy
kingdom" (Luke 23:42 KJV). The Savior promised that
He would, and it was done. God still remembers His
covenant. Through the work of His Spirit, people are
continually claimed to be His children, made heirs of salvation and joint heirs with Christ, and given the inheritance of everlasting life. Our God remembers His
covenant forever; He forgets us never. We can depend on
Him! He keeps His promises!

*Never permit me, O God, to mistrust the covenant that
You have established with me through Christ. Amen.*

Edward C. May/May 24, 1959

182

Remembering His Humanness

And while they still disbelieved for joy, and
wondered, He said to them, "Have you anything here to eat?" They gave Him a piece of
broiled fish, and He took it and ate before
them. *Luke 24:41–43 RSV*

A lifetime of miracles, capped by the resurrection
and ascension—what a God! As we remember the
glorious events of that first Easter and the weeks that followed, it's so easy to stand in awe of the Savior and see
Him only as God—perfect and untouchable, enthroned in
heaven and removed from us.

Yet in Jesus Christ, God Himself came to earth in
human form, that is, as a true human being. Because He
lived in this world as a person like us, Jesus understands
our needs: our daily, ordinary needs for things such as
food and clothing, shelter and companionship.

"Have you anything to eat?" "I thirst," "Could you not
watch with Me one hour?"—these are the words of a
human being. He grew weary and slept in the face of a
storm. His feet got dirty and tired from walking. He was
grateful for the woman who wet His feet with her tears.
He was mocked and scorned. He suffered and died. He
understands our problems because He's been through it
all—for us! What a person! What a God!

*We are so grateful, dear Lord, that we can come to
You in prayer, knowing that You understand our
fears and needs. Amen.*

Marlys Taege/April 11, 1983

SPIRITUAL RESOURCES

God is faithful, and He will not let you be
tempted beyond your strength, but with the
temptation will also provide the way of escape,
that you may be able to endure it.
1 Corinthians 10:13 RSV

*T*he Gospel affirms not only that God has delivered His people from sin through the death and resurrection of Christ, but also that God stays with us, protects us, and defends us in times of trouble and temptation.

For this reason, the new life we enjoy as God's children is a life "in Christ." Our resource in moments of spiritual and emotional peril is the Savior who has gone to the cross in our stead. He comes to us today in the Word of the Gospel that runs as a theme throughout the entire Bible. He draws us back to the life-giving waters of our Baptism, where we died to sin once and for all. He calls us to the table of His Supper, where we are nourished by His true body and blood, given and shed for the forgiveness of your sins and mine.

Our own strength in the face of temptation and trial will be of little spiritual help. With our timid and faltering faith we can neither save nor protect ourselves. But the strength that our faithful God puts at our disposal in Word and Sacrament will never fail. It won't fail because God is faithful and His Word sure.

Almighty Father, keep us mindful of Your protection as our only strength and resource in times of trial. Amen.

David A. Lumpp/Sept. 21, 1984

THE JUDGE LIVES

*Beloved, never avenge yourselves, but leave it
to the wrath of God. Romans 12:19 RSV*

O ur Redeemer lives! He lives to save, to bless, to
silence fears, to wipe away our tears, to make ready
our place with Him, and to bring us safely there. He also
lives to judge! Jesus has promised that He will return to
judge the living and the dead. When He comes, "we shall
all stand before the judgment seat of God" (Romans 14:10
RSV). Those who trust that Jesus was judged and sen-
tenced in their place will be invited into life. Those who
refuse God's mercy in Christ will be judged on their own
merits—and be found wanting. In all cases, He will settle
accounts and right all wrongs. The judge lives.

Sometimes it seems as if might has possibly replaced
right in this world. "We can take only so much," we say,
"then we must settle accounts with people and pay them
back as they deserve." If there is no judge and no impending judgment, then, of course, we would be correct to
hold court now and get even.

However, God gives us a better solution: Leave it to
His wrath. Instead of using our time and energy to be
judge and jury, Christ, who rose again, frees us to live cre-
atively and forgivingly. Let us leave the judging to Him.

*Lord, we are neither good nor wise enough to sit in
Your seat. We thank You that You are the judge.
Amen.*

David V. Koch/April 25, 1975

THE CHURCH IN YOUR HOUSE

Paul, a prisoner for Christ Jesus …
to Philemon our beloved fellow worker …
and the church in your house. *Philemon 1–2 RSV*

O ne of the shortest books in the Bible is a letter from the apostle Paul to the owner of a runaway slave. Paul had introduced both the owner and the slave to Christ. Paul begins his letter with this salutation: "Paul to Philemon … and the church in your house." The apostle's words were intended also for the group of Christians that gathered regularly in the home of Philemon for worship and study.

Few of us today may literally have a church in our house, but this phrase should be true in a certain sense of every Christian home. In such a home, the members are bound together not only by family ties but also by their membership in the church, the body of Christ. Here Christ's love shines through in the daily incidents of life— patience in hectic moments, sympathy in times of disappointment, forgiveness for sins committed.

The thought of such a home once led a hymn writer to pen these words: "O blessed home where man and wife Together lead a godly life, By deeds their faith confessing! There many a happy day is spent, There Jesus gladly will consent To tarry with His blessing."

Dear Lord Jesus, help each of us to make our house a church filled with Your love and forgiveness. Amen.

Samuel H. Nafzger/Oct. 6, 1988

186

WHEN YOU NEED HIM THE MOST

Jesus put forth His hand, and touched him, saying,
"I will; be thou clean." And immediately
his leprosy was cleansed. *Matthew 8:3 KJV*

*T*he story is told about a little girl who had a very beautiful doll collection. A woman, looking at the dolls, asked the little girl, "Which doll is your favorite?" The little girl brought her the most pathetic-looking doll the woman had ever seen. Its face was cracked, an arm was missing, and the nose was broken off. "Why do you love this one the most?" the woman asked. The little girl replied, "Because it needs me the most. If I didn't love this doll, nobody else would."

Christ is like that. He loves us the most when we need Him the most. He showed that during his earthly ministry. People were afraid of lepers. But Jesus touched the leper and healed him. Jesus, true God and true man, has power to heal. He loves us at all times. But He is closest to us when we need Him the most. That poor leper was in real trouble, and Jesus touched him.

When we are beaten and battered and broken by the storms of life, Jesus comes to us. He grants grace and guidance; He brings the greatest gift of all—eternal salvation won for us when His body was broken on the cross.

Dear Lord Jesus, we thank You for Your gift of love. Help us bring it to others when they need it the most. Amen.

Victor F. Halboth Jr./Aug. 19, 1981

187

Faith or Feeling?

If our heart condemn us, God is greater
than our heart, and knoweth all things.
1 John 3:20 KJV

A middle-aged woman recently wrote to us about a problem: "I was saved 17 years ago, but I am beginning to doubt my salvation ... I just don't *feel* saved anymore!"

Her mistake lay in attaching her faith to the wrong object. We are not to put our faith in our feelings! Our feelings change from day to day. We may feel saved one moment and lost the next. Nor are we to put our faith in our faith, as though *faith* were some kind of good work that God will reward with the blessing of salvation.

No! We are to put our faith only in Christ and His Word. Jesus Christ is the same yesterday, today, and forever. Our feelings are fickle. Our moods are constantly changing. Our anguished heart may tell us we are lost. But—God be praised!—He is greater than our heart and knows all things. He knows (and He will never forget!) that Christ paid the penalty of our transgressions and has bought for us the robe of perfect righteousness. When God looks at you and me, He sees not us, but Jesus Christ, His Son, and His spotless robe of righteousness that covers us completely. That will remain forever true regardless of our moods or feelings. "On Christ, the solid rock, I stand."

Lord God, heavenly Father, increase my faith in Jesus Christ, my Savior from sin. Amen.

Herman W. Gockel/July 27, 1976

188

MY BROTHER'S KEEPER

Bear ye one another's burdens, and so fulfill
the law of Christ. *Galatians 6:2 KJV*

*I*t was Cain who first asked, "Am I my brother's keeper?" In his case, the question itself was a lie. He already
had murdered his brother, and he was trying foolishly to
hide his guilt from God.

For so many, Cain's question is really this statement: "I
am not my brother's keeper! I have enough problems of
my own. Everyone for himself!"

That's not the way the Bible speaks. "Look not every
man on his own things, but every man also on the things
of others" (Philippians 2:4 KJV). Again: "Bear one another's burdens." The central truth of our faith is that Christ
bore all of our burdens. Our Lord was not stopped by the
shame or pain of the cross but willingly became our substitute. He not only watched and wept; He bore our sins
in His body on the tree.

Now He calls us to love even as we have been loved; to
forgive those who sin against us; to speak the Word of
comfort and strength to the discouraged; to extend the
hand of fellowship to the lonely, the deed of love to those
in need; to weep with those who weep and rejoice with
those who rejoice; and to give the Word of Life to those
in darkness. So we are Christ's disciples because we love
Him and one another.

*Lord Jesus, help us to follow in Your footsteps and to
share Your love with all people. Amen.*

August T. Mennicke/May 4, 1984

Birth of a Family

There were added that day about
three thousand souls. *Acts 2:41 RSV*

*T*he first child born to a newly married couple signi-
fies the start of another family. Usually children
come in ones, occasionally twos or threes, and only on
rarest occasions does a mother bring forth quadruplets or
quintuplets. The start of the New Testament family came
in much larger numbers. With Pentecost as its birthday, it
grew in one astonishing day to a family of three thousand.

God created the New Testament Christian family in a
very special way. He poured out His Holy Spirit in a
miraculously visible manner. The spectators, when they
viewed the apostles, saw what looked like tongues of fire
on their heads. They also heard them speak foreign lan-
guages. Above all, they heard the Gospel message proclaimed with unusual eloquence and power. Before the
day was over, a small nucleus of disciples had become a
large congregation.

Over the centuries God has continued to add children
to this family in such numbers that one can only guess at
the total. Furthermore, having brought it into being, He
sustains it. He provides food and protection so the family
flourishes. How we marvel at and adore God, the Father
of this blessed family!

*O God, we praise You for establishing the family of
the Christian church and for making us members of
it. Amen.*

W. Th. Janzow/May 21, 1972

A DESPISED HERITAGE

Lo, sons are a heritage from the LORD, the
fruit of the womb a reward. *Psalm 127:3 RSV*

*T*he psalmist asserts that children are a heritage from
the Lord. In plain English this means that children
are God's precious gifts. This sentiment is contradicted in
our society not only by the shocking cases of child abuse
reported by the media, but also by the tragic practice of
abortion. For many people, children are a despised heritage.

When God created Adam and Eve, He pronounced a
blessing on them that they should have children. In reality this made them partners with God in the continuing
creation process. It truly is awesome to be part of God's
creative activity as parents who bring into being children
whose life has significance in this world and in eternity.

Jesus made it clear that children are important to God.
They should be no less precious to parents, who should
welcome them as a heritage from God and should be
responsible for their well-being in every dimension of
their lives. Children should be blessed with a happy home
life, with the opportunity for healthy growth, and with
Christian upbringing so they remain faithful to Christ,
into whom they have been baptized.

O God, thank You for the gift of children. Amen.

Carl A. Gaertner/Nov. 13, 1978

191

HIS OFFER OF FREEDOM

If the Son makes you free, you will be free
indeed. *John 8:36 RSV*

*F*ree indeed," said the Son of God, referring to His
gift of spiritual freedom. At that particular time His
listeners were boasting of their political freedom. "We
have never been in bondage to any man," they proudly
said. "That is good," answered Jesus in effect. "Civil liberty is a priceless blessing, but more valuable still is the
freedom of the soul, to be freed from sin's enslavement.
That is being *free indeed.*"

Certainly, national holidays such as this call to mind
our heritage of civil liberties. "Posterity," wrote John
Adams, America's second president, "you will never know
how much it cost the present generation to preserve freedom. I hope you will make good use of it." The price in
toil, blood, and tears has been tremendous. But with all
this—dare we forget how much more it cost our Lord to
make us free indeed, free from sin's oppression, free from
gnawing guilt, free to enter into His presence and to enjoy
the glorious liberty of the children of God?

This freedom, dearly bought, is offered to all. Do we
accept it in faith? Then, even while suffering under some
tyranny or imprisoned in some sickroom, we may breathe
in relief and approach the beloved author of our liberties
with the grateful cry:

*Lord Jesus, when I am free within my heart And in
my soul am free, Angels alone that soar above Enjoy
such liberty. Amen.*

Alvin E. Wagner/July 4, 1960

192

God's Cookout

*On this mountain the LORD Almighty will
prepare a feast of rich food for all peoples. Isaiah 25:6*

Cookouts are very popular in America these days.
Almost every backyard has some sort of grill. Isaiah
25 describes heaven as a cookout on a mountain, with
God spreading out a wondrous feast. The description of
choice meats sounds inviting, but only if you are hungry.
Many don't have time for God's cookout. They are busy
tending to their jobs, getting promotions, paying bills,
and going on vacations. They just don't have time for
heaven. Is that your problem? Full of hamburger, one
doesn't have room for even the tastiest steak. Full of ourselves, we may not be hungry for God and His love.

When we live only to satisfy our whims, we discover
that everything tastes flat. Even the finest wine and filet
mignon fail to satisfy. Spacious swimming pools and
growing bank accounts do not satisfy. Selfishness is sin,
and the wages of sin is death. Empty, we admit our hunger
for God.

And He fills us. He sent His Son to fast 40 days in the
wilderness and to drink the bitter cup of suffering by
dying on the cross. By His death, Jesus invites us to attend
God's great cookout in heaven, freely and without charge.
He not only invites us but encourages us to invite others
as well.

Think about these things the next time you gather with
your family for a cookout.

Lord, help me to hunger for You. Amen.

Stephen J. Carter/July 7, 1988

193

Theirs Is Nicer

But if we have food and clothing, with these
we shall be content. *1 Timothy 6:8 RSV*

*I*n some campgrounds, campsites are assigned when
you arrive. The camper has no choice. Some sites have
spectacular views or are in secluded areas. Others are
crowded together or face trash bins or other unpleasant
sights.

It's tempting to grumble that "theirs is nicer," even
though mountain beauty fills the surrounding horizon.
Often on life's trail we overlook the blessings we have,
magnify our irritations, and desire what others possess.

The Lord has provided richly for us. Food and clothing are all we need, writes St. Paul. We have these and so
much more. Still better, we have forgiveness because of
the suffering and death of Jesus. He paid for our sins of
complaining and coveting. How beautifully His blessings
surround us!

In lifting our thoughts to these blessings, we recognize
that the Lord has acted with love and wisdom to place us
where we are. He made us His children in Christ. We can
accept and be thankful that He has blessed us, especially
in Jesus, even if we don't always get the campsite with a
view.

*Lord, thank You for all You have given us, especial-
ly for the gift of Jesus. Help us to be content. Amen.*

Theo. E. Allwardt Sr./Aug. 2, 1987

You'll Be Better Off

I tell you the truth: It is for your good that
I am going away. Unless I go away,
The Counselor will not come to you;
but if I go, I will send Him to you. *John 16:7*

*T*he time was growing near. Jesus' departure from His disciples was at hand. Soon He must die, giving His life for the sins of the world so those who believe in Him might not perish but have eternal life. "It is for your good that I am going away," Jesus says.

How can that be? How can it be for the disciples' good that Jesus would leave? But so it turned out. He accomplished the work of redeeming the world, then rose from the dead. And He ascended into heaven, where He now rules over the universe by authority given to Him by the Father. All this He did for our good. In His love He did not leave us comfortless when He went to heaven. He gave us the gift of the Holy Spirit.

Jesus is no longer with us in His visible presence. But He is still with us in His Word. His Holy Spirit is with us all the time. And the Spirit gives us all of Jesus' blessings—faith, forgiveness of sins, eternal life. We certainly are better off as we experience the work of the Holy Spirit through God's Word and sacraments. The Spirit is Christ's great gift to us.

Dear Lord Jesus, I thank You for the gift of Your Holy Spirit in my life. May all come to know You through His work. Amen.

Richard A. Mazak/May 22, 1986

195

WHERE ARE YOU?

And the LORD God called unto Adam, and said
unto him, Where art thou? *Genesis 3:9 KJV*

*D*o you really think God couldn't find Adam in the
garden? Is that why He called out, "Where are
you?" Or could it be that God knew exactly where Adam
was crouching in shame and fear. If this is correct—and our
understanding of God's full knowledge assures us that it
is—then this simple question must have a broader meaning.

God knew where Adam was. But did *Adam* know where
Adam was? Did Adam sense the separation his sin had
caused? God was asking, "Where are you—now?"

This, the first question God asks in Scripture, is still
with us. God daily asks each of us, "Where are *you*?" What
is your relationship to Him? What is your relationship to
His truth and love? Where are you?

No matter where we are, we always remember where
God is. He is at our right hand with a ready supply of love,
mercy, forgiveness, and power from on high. That presence surrounded Adam on the day he first confronted this
all-important question of life.

While Adam puzzled over the question—and God's
purpose behind it—God continued in His love for Adam.
In love, He still reaches out for today's Adams—you and
me.

*O precious Lord, help us understand where we are
and surround us with the continuing assurance of
Your love. Amen.*

Charles S. Mueller Sr./March 5, 1968

OUR SUCCESS

I have fought the good fight,
I have finished the race, I have kept the faith.
2 Timothy 4:7 RSV

*H*ow does one define "success"? If the parents of a Hebrew boy named Saul could have seen him at the end of his life, would they have judged him a success? They had planned a great career for him: rabbi; teacher of the Law; a man loved, honored, and respected by his people. Yet he died a jailbird, condemned and despised by his own people.

What did Paul himself say about it? Hear his words: "I have fought the good fight, I have finished the race, I have kept the faith." Success! Right down the line—success!

That is, to say the least, a peculiar success story! So how does one define "success"? Was St. Paul, executed as a criminal, a success? Yes, because he realized the purpose of his existence. Only God, who has given us the purpose of our existence, can tell us what that purpose is. We were meant to live eternally with God. If we miss that destiny, no matter what wealth, honor, or fame we have achieved, we are a failure.

Across the years, there comes to us this voice from the first century, summing up a successful life: "The life I now live in the flesh I live by faith in the Son of God, who loved me and gave Himself for me" (Galatians 2:20 RSV).

Lord, by Your mercy and grace keep us in the faith so we, like Paul, may be accounted a success. Amen.

Henry C. Duwe/Feb. 20, 1971

Saved by Grace

These many years do I serve thee ... yet thou
never gavest me a kid, that I might make merry
with my friends. *Luke 15:29 KJV*

*A*t first everything looks good about the older brother. He had not demanded his inheritance; he had
not left home; he had done everything his father had
asked of him. But when his brother was accepted back into
the family, it was too much. He pouted and wouldn't come
into the house. When approached, he scolded his father.

People who have been Christians all their lives sometimes have a hard time accepting others into the church,
the family of God. "You mean somebody who comes to
Christ on his deathbed will be saved and be treated just
like me in heaven?" Or "God ought to appreciate all I am
and have done for Him all my life. He ought to treat me
better than the last-minute converts."

That's self-righteousness, the same nasty stuff we see in
the older brother. Christians live by grace alone. If I feel
that God owes me something for my obedience, I am asking Him to treat me on the basis of merit, not of grace.
What a terrible plight I am in if ever God treats me the
way I deserve! The Christian's greatest joy is to live for
and with God. No rewards are expected or needed.

*Lord, let me appreciate what it means to be Your
child. Amen.*

Louis W. Grother/July 26, 1972

198

Our Burden Made Light

Cast your burden on the LORD, and He will
sustain you; He will never permit the righteous
to be moved. *Psalm 55:22 RSV*

*H*er name was Frieda. She was 94 years old. Still
actively involved in her church, this Christian
woman had an outlook on life that was truly remarkable.
When asked how she was able to maintain such an active
schedule in her 94th year, Frieda simply replied that she
was determined to cast all her care on God, knowing that
He would give her the strength required.

There are many Friedas in the world and in the church.
They are veterans of the cross who are not worried about
the pains and aches of the aging process. They put one
foot in front of the other and go forward in faith.

Frieda trusted God to care for her, and He did not fail.
She knew Jesus as her personal Lord and Savior. She knew
the power of the Holy Spirit, who through Holy Baptism
and the Word had called her to be a child of God.

A true hero of the faith, Frieda's example of trust and
devotion was an inspiration to many.

When we become discouraged by the problems of life,
we can look to Jesus, knowing that He is able to sustain us
and give us strength.

*Help us, dear Lord, to trust in You and to cast our
cares on You, knowing that You will sustain us.
Amen.*

Henry C. Lubben/April 8, 1986

PROMISE TO THE FEARFUL

It is I; be not afraid. Matthew 14:27 KJV

*T*he disciples sailed to Capernaum ahead of the Lord. It was already dark, and they were quite a distance from the shore. Suddenly a strong wind came upon them. The waves rose high against the boat. The turbulent sea threatened their safety. Then there appeared what seemed to be a ghost. What an experience to be "between the devil and the deep sea!" They heard the familiar, calming voice of their Lord: "It is I; be not afraid."

God's people go through the storms of life. Trials and tribulations come their way. Quite a few become overwhelmed. Some become weak from fear. Then comes the Lord to their rescue because He does not forsake His own. His abiding presence calms and comforts them. He strengthens their faith. He saves them.

The Lord's disciples have learned that behind all the dark, threatening clouds of the impending storms of life and the tragedies that come their way, they have the assurance that their Lord is close by—a ready help to ease and calm their fears! As we, too, go through the storms of life, let us remember that our dear Lord is always near, ready to hold us above water! We hear Him say, "It is I; be not afraid."

Lord Jesus, we thank You for Your abiding presence and Your promise to calm all our fears. Amen.

Alvaro A. Carino/July 14, 1978

200

WE NEED TO PRAY

Praying always ... in the Spirit.
Ephesians 6:18 KJV

*A*braham Lincoln once said, "I have been driven many times to my knees by the overwhelming conviction that I had nowhere else to go. My own wisdom and that of all around me seemed insufficient for the day." Are we conscious of our need of prayer—and not only in times of crisis and difficulty? We can pray at all times. In the commonplace, in the general run of things, we depend on God and need His guidance.

Prayer means communion with God, not just asking for things in time of emergency. We are urged to be thankful, and we can pray with thanksgiving for the beauty of the earth, for His gracious providence and preservation, for our Christian faith and salvation.

At the same time there is a definite place for petition in our prayers. We are to pray for spiritual progress, for a deeper appreciation of our redemption through Christ, for the spiritual well-being of relatives and friends, of all people.

We are to pray for the worldwide program of the church and for the personal readiness and willingness to support it. We are not to be overanxious about material blessings, but even so we are enjoined to pray for them: "Give us this day our daily bread."

Do we pray as we ought? Lord, teach us to pray.

Merciful Father, in all situations help us seek the guidance, wisdom, and strength we need; through Jesus Christ, our Savior and King. Amen.

Edwin L. Wilson/Feb. 12, 1960

201

The Mark of Stability

My heart is fixed, O God, my heart is fixed:
I will sing and give praise. *Psalm 57:7 KJV*

*T*he things of this life in which people trust are shaky, to say the least. More and more, it seems, isolated events trigger worldwide anxiety and unrest in the heart of every individual. In such times, whose counsels are trustworthy? Whose wisdom is really wise? Satan and all his evil forces would bend the Word of God and turn our ears to other voices. But thanks be to God, they shall not prevail. Read Psalm 57 and see.

David lived in treacherous times, yet he showed the mark of stability. His heart was fixed on God, his Redeemer. Even on the darkest days, David could sing and give praise.

God would have us do the same. On the eve of His crucifixion for the sins of the world, our Lord sang in the Upper Room. Paul and Silas sang hymns in prison. Paul says we too can be "rooted and built up in Him, and established in the faith … abounding therein with thanksgiving" (Colossians 2:7 KJV). This stability is ours, a gift of God's grace in Jesus Christ our Lord, as Paul writes: "Our Lord Jesus Christ Himself, and God, even our Father … comfort your hearts, and establish you in every good word and work" (2 Thessalonians 2:16–17 KJV).

O Lord, keep us steadfast in Your Word, grant us joy, and help us to sing Your praise. Amen.

Paul M. Heerboth/July 26, 1974

A QUESTION OF CONSCIENCE

*How then can I do this great wickedness,
and sin against God? Genesis 39:9 RSV*

Joseph asked this question in answer to his master's wife as she constantly tried to tempt him to be intimate with her. In his question he does more than spurn her advances. He does more than say no—even a very firm no. He gives her a glimpse into his conscience, a conscience well aware of his position of responsibility in that household, a conscience deeply aware of the evil reality of sin, a conscience, above all, most loyal to his God and sensitively concerned about offending Him by sinning.

How do we react when faced with temptation? Do we find it difficult to resist but easy to give in? Are we quick to respond with unhesitating testimony to our Christian reason for saying no? Or do we quietly go along with the crowd or with the pressure of the moment because we are ashamed to speak up for God?

May God forgive us for Jesus' sake! May He give us boldness through His Word to do what is pleasing in His sight for the sake of Him—Jesus Christ our Lord—who gave His life to make us pleasing in the sight of God!

O God, give us a conscience that resists temptation and boldness of heart and lips to state the reason. Amen.

Martin J. Schmidt/June 4, 1979

CONTENTMENT IN GOD

Godliness with contentment is great gain.
1 Timothy 6:6 KJV

Some of us are afraid of godliness. Life is so full. Vacations and sports, gardens and books, friends and music. In contrast to this, we set "godliness." It seems to narrow the vast range of life and diminish all its bright color. How wrong an impression!

We don't need to separate our lives into two parts—the "everyday" and the "spiritual." Life is not to be divided.

Look at Christ. He was neither a stuffy, straight-laced Puritan nor a frightened recluse. He strode over the open hills and lived with robust men. Children flocked to Him. He was eager to feed the hungry. When the pious condemned, He reminded them of their own sin.

Christ's goal was not merely to reform men, to make them kind and decent. He came to save. His saving love stabs to the heart of our sin. To lift us, God puts us low. To give us sight, He first must blind. To give new life, He must shatter the old life. Godliness begins with Christ's victory on the cross. There Christ broke the power of evil that separated us from Him. Through faith in our Savior, the Holy Spirit fills our heart with true godliness—piety and loving reverence toward God—and with sincere contentment with the material goods and the position in life that God has granted to us.

O God of love, we bless You for Your many gifts; bless us with godliness and contentment. Amen.

David S. Schuller/Aug. 20, 1959

The Grace of God in Truth

Of this you have heard before in the Word of the truth, the
Gospel which has come to you, as indeed in the whole world
it is bearing fruit and growing—so among yourselves, from
the day you heard and understood the grace of God in truth.
Colossians 1:5–6 RSV

*F*rom the first day when those early Christians heard
the Word of the truth of the Gospel, they knew the
grace of God in truth. The Lord smiles on us when we
really deserve His frown. Though we have no claim on
His goodness by what we are or what we have done, God
is still kind and patient, long-suffering, and of great
mercy. It seems unbelievable, but it is true. Wherever this
Gospel goes, it produces Christian character.

The New Testament is full of talk about the power of
God's grace to change people and their whole outlook on
life: It tells us that "the grace of God has appeared for the
salvation of all men, training us to renounce irreligion and
worldly passions, and to live sober, upright, and godly
lives in this world, awaiting our blessed hope, the appearing of the glory of our great God and Savior Jesus Christ,
who gave Himself for us to redeem us from all iniquity
and to purify for Himself a people of His own who are
zealous for good deeds" (Titus 2:11–14 RSV).

The grace of God works. It works powerfully and pro-
gressively in all who have heard the Good News of forgiveness and life in Christ Jesus.

*Lord Jesus Christ, lead us to know the goodness and grace
of God in all truth. Help us to live by that grace. Amen.*

Oswald C. J. Hoffmann/June 7, 1966

THE VICTORY OF FAITH

This is the victory that overcometh the world,
even our faith. *1 John 5:4 KJV*

*L*ife is a constant struggle, but Christian faith makes us more than conquerors. This faith is that confident trust that Jesus' sacrifice on Calvary has removed all sin, made peace through His blood, and guarantees salvation in the glories of heaven.

The world in which we live challenges this Christian faith. It is an enticing world, which offers us riches, success, and the pleasures of sin. The world tells us that to eat, to drink, to be merry is the chief purpose of life. It tries to make us believe that fattened oxen and filled barns have greater value than peace with God and the hope of heaven.

This same world is bitterly disappointing. Too many of us know this to be true as failure, sickness, sorrow, heartaches, and tears come into our day. Even the world-wise become world-weary. Amid these disappointments our Christian faith clings to Christ and finds in Him peace, hope, and assurance. We cannot perish.

This faith is not of our making. The Holy Spirit calls us by the Gospel into this faith and keeps us there. This victorious faith makes us loyal even in days of adversity. Knowing that God turns everything to our eternal good, we need not be afraid. Underneath are God's everlasting arms, around us the pierced hands of Jesus. This spells victory and triumph.

Gracious Father in Christ, make us more than conquerors over every situation of life. Amen.

Carl H. Thomas/April 25, 1959

206

Useless Stuff

But what things were gain to me, those
I counted loss for Christ. Philippians 3:7 KJV

*I*f ever there lived a man who, on the basis of personal merit, could inherit heaven, it was the apostle Paul. He could boast of righteousness, of ceremony, of ancestry, of orthodoxy, and of zeal. But he wrapped it all together and labeled it "useless stuff." Why? He met Jesus and was captivated by Him!

In Christ Paul found everything he had tried to find in his former religious life and could not. Plagued by a restless conscience, he tried to silence it by fanaticism and persecution of the Christians.

Then he met Jesus, and the folly of his past efforts became clear. Now he knew what it meant to be at peace with God, to have the voice of conscience silenced because of sins forgiven.

Millions have had the same experience since Paul's day. They, too, have gladly let go the "useless stuff" for the "excellency of the knowledge of Christ [their] Lord" (Philippians 3:8 KJV).

How grateful we should be that heaven is the gift of grace! If heaven were based on merit, there would be so much spiritual snobbery as to make living there insufferable. Imagine someone singing, "To me, who lived a good life, who kept the Law, who had a good conscience, who had good ancestors, who did lots of church work, to me be glory!"

The only song the entrants to heaven can sing is, "To Him that loved us and washed us from our sin."

We praise You, Jesus, for our redemption. Amen.

Elmer C. Kieninger/June 15, 1960

207

Joy in Christian Living

Sin will have no dominion over you,
since you are not under law but under grace.
Romans 6:14 RSV

Joy in Christian living seems paradoxical, not only to nonbelievers but also to many Christians. What a pity! This shows a poor understanding of our text. Unfortunately, many Christians think and live as though they are under the compulsion and threat of God's Law. Their Christian living is geared to a set of rigid rules and regulations. They strive to be good because they are terribly afraid to be bad. Fear drives them in life. No one can find joy in this way.

How wonderful it is to live under God's grace! This means we live in the full freedom of forgiveness. The motivating power in our lives is God's love in Christ. In this love we happily live a God-pleasing life. Living victoriously under God's grace, we find that sin loses its power and attraction. In God's grace we turn away from evil and become happy slaves for righteousness.

Now we understand what Jesus means when He says: "If you keep My commandments, you will abide in My love ... that My joy may be in you, and that your joy may be full" (John 15:10–11 RSV). This is exciting, joyous living for Christians under God's redeeming grace.

Lord God, grant us joy in living righteous lives for Jesus' sake. Amen.

Carl A. Gaertner/March 15, 1972

No Desire for the Lord's Supper?

*Do this in remembrance of Me. ... Do this, as
often as you drink it, in remembrance of Me.
1 Corinthians 11:24–25 RSV*

A young man who had not attended Holy
Communion for a long time admitted that he had
no desire to go. By now he had become quite used to not
going. He had once learned to receive the Sacrament frequently, but later he just got away from it.

We know that the Lord first gave His body and blood to
His disciples in this Holy Supper on the night on which He
was betrayed. He then told them: "Take, eat; this is My
body. ... Drink of it, all of you; for this is My blood"
(Matthew 26:26–38 RSV). He had a very special blessing in
mind for them. In every need they would have the effective
memory before them of their Lord and Savior Jesus Christ
giving His body into death for their sins and shedding His
blood for their forgiveness. Always they would need this
special Supper in which the Lord gave them His body and
blood. Not using this holy meal, we lose its benefits. How
can we willfully despise this heavenly food and drink?

We are aware of our own sins. We recognize our need
for the Lord's grace and forgiveness. Why not accept our
Lord's invitation to His table and among our chief problems lay before Him our own indifference? The Holy Spirit
will give us new appreciation of our Lord's gracious blessings. So we pray to Him, "Lamb of God, I come, I come!"

*Lord, fill us with new longing for Your grace and
favor. Amen.*

Alfred Carl Seltz/Aug. 8, 1976

209

LIFE, NOT STRIFE

Any one who hates his brother is a murderer,
... no murderer has eternal life abiding in him.
1 John 3:15 RSV

Our society has become the master of "things." Most problems, it seems, can be solved in our technologically advanced world if we put our mind to it. We have gadgets for everything.

One problem, however, defies our ingenuity—our relations with other people. We spend millions of dollars and hours of time on labor problems, child-parent relationships, lawsuits, and arguments over the back fence. A young man comes to verbal blows with his roommate and may find that one of his most persistent problems is how to get along with other people.

Hatred towards others, quarreling with them, is murder, God says. That is strong language, perhaps so strong that we do not think it needs to be taken seriously. God warns us in this text and in other passages that He is the Creator of all. Hating God's creation is a sin as serious as murder. You cannot hate God and love others, nor can you love God and hate others. Eternal life is at stake.

Christ died for all—even for those who hate us. He died so our sins and shortcomings, as well as those with whom we rub elbows, may be forgiven. He loved so we, too, can love.

"Love divine, all love excelling, ... Fix in us thy humble dwelling."Amen.

Dorothy Rosin/Sept. 27, 1976

210

"Try Jesus"

O taste and see that the LORD is good:
blessed is the man that trusteth in Him.
Psalm 34:8 KJV

*I*t was a Christian family. A little girl was standing next to her grief-stricken mother, whose face was stained with tears over the sudden loss of a loved one. Putting her arm tenderly around her mother, the little one said with all the simplicity of her childlike faith: "Mommy, why don't you try Jesus?"

Could any words have been more fitting? How often, when a person has been surrounded by problems and perplexities, have we heard him say: "I've tried *everything*—but nothing helped"? How often have you and I thought or said the very same thing: "I've tried everything, but …"?

Everything but Jesus! Yet it is He who stands at every crisis point of our life! He stands with open arms and says: "Come! Come to Me! I will give you the comfort, the hope, the peace that you are seeking." King David once exclaimed: "O taste and see that the LORD is good: blessed is the man that trusteth in Him." Nor are we to turn to Jesus as our last resort. In every changing scene of life, we are to remember: He "is a very present help in trouble" (Psalm 46:1 KJV). Try Him! You will not be disappointed.

Lord Jesus, when every earthly prop gives way, You still are all my hope and stay. Amen.

Herman W. Gockel/July 21, 1980

211

Listen as the Good Shepherd Speaks!

My sheep hear My voice. John 10:27 RSV

A young boy who had been blind from birth underwent surgery that the doctors were confident would give him vision for the first time in his life. You can imagine the excitement of his mother as she waited for the bandages to be removed. How would her son react the first time he saw her? The bandages came off and the boy could indeed see. But when he looked at the woman at the side of his bed, there was no smile, no sign of recognition. It was only when his mother spoke that he smiled and the tears of joy flowed.

You see, he had never seen his mother, but he had learned to love and trust her voice. That's the way it is with Jesus and His sheep. We have not seen, but we believe. We live by faith, not by sight. We, too, love and trust the voice of our Good Shepherd.

"My sheep hear My voice," Jesus says. And we know that is a voice we can trust. The voice that says, "Come to Me" and "Believe in Me" does not hold out an empty promise. Heaven and earth will pass away, but not His Word. What He says is based on what He did on the cross and at the empty tomb. As His sheep, let us hear and follow that voice. It will never fail us.

"Lord, open Thou my heart to hear And through Thy Word to me draw near." Amen.

August T. Mennicke/May 14, 1984

GOD WITH US

*Gideon said to him, "Pray, sir, if the LORD is
with us, why then has all this befallen us?"*
Judges 6:13 RSV

How do you answer someone like Gideon? "Why
does God allow this? If He is with us, why doesn't
He do something about it?" Notice that the Lord does-
n't get into an argument. He directs Gideon's energies
toward leadership instead of debate. He encourages
Gideon to use God's strength to help Israel. How can
Gideon do that? "I will be with you," the Lord answers.

That's the point: The Lord is with His people. Jesus
promised the power of the Holy Spirit to those who
believe in Him and are baptized. That power is to be used
for God's people. Jesus offered His life for our eternal
benefit. In thankfulness we dedicate our lives to serve
Him and His people.

Gideon was not brave or even optimistic. He'd rather
debate God's justice than fight. Yet God chose him for this
work and pushed him forward.

God still acts that way today. He chooses us to help
others against their enemies and ours: sin and Satan. If we
whine, "How can I do it?" we hear God's answer to
Gideon: "I will be with you." That is the key that unlocks
the courage within us, pushes us forward, and ends all
debate.

*Lord Jesus, show us how to serve You today. Give us
the courage to face our enemies, trusting firmly in
Your power to prevail. Amen.*

Gary and Christine Dehnke/May 14, 1988

Does God Care?

What is man that Thou art mindful of him,
and the son of man that Thou dost care
for him? Psalm 8:4 RSV

*T*he frontier of space travel has lifted the eyes of people everywhere to the heavens. We look up into its seemingly endless expanse. Our minds travel quickly from one galaxy to another through this awesome beyond. Its vastness and complexity stand in sharp contrast to the small and simple being that each of us is.

Somehow the heavens seem much colder and more distant now than they did centuries ago when many thought of them as the protecting tent over a flat earth. To the heart that trembles in doubt and fear, empty words of human reassurance are of little help. A firm answer must come to the one who cries out in despair.

That answer *has* come. God Himself stood in the very midst of our little planet in Jesus Christ. He spoke of the Father's care for the hairs of our head and for the sparrows. He opened the way to God for us and taught us to say, "Our Father, who art in heaven." His life, death, and resurrection are God's own great yes to our question, "Does He care?"

We look to the vast heavens and wonder if God is mindful of us at all. We look to the cross, and we know that He is.

Heavenly Father in Christ Jesus, who has never forgotten us, grant that we may be ever mindful of You. Amen.

Richard J. Gotsch/July 12, 1968

Peter — The Coward

Lord, I am ready to go with You to prison
and to death. Luke 22:33 RSV

*B*oastful Peter really meant it. If a cross could have been set up then and there in that Upper Room, he would have gladly died for Jesus! In that sacred atmosphere, where the Lord's Supper had just been instituted, where they had heard the table talk of Jesus—there was inspiration and encouragement for the most timid Christian. Unfortunately our moments of elation and enthusiasm do not always coincide with those moments when we are called to be martyrs!

So Peter's false confidence was his undoing. It resulted in fainthearted cowardice. Before the rooster crowed twice, he had denied his Lord three times. Certainly no one could have suspected him of being a follower of the Christ after they heard the cursing and the foul fisherman's oaths!

I ask myself: Am I always loyal to my Lord? Or do I, too, deny the Lord that bought me? Do I just drift along in life like my godless neighbors, blending myself into the general worldly landscape for fear of running counter to something in it?

I remember the words of Paul: "Let any one who thinks that he stands take heed lest he fall" (1 Corinthians 10:12 RSV). Apart from Christ I can do nothing—but I can do all things through Christ, who strengthens me.

"When Thou see'st me waver, With a look recall
Nor for fear or favor Suffer me to fall." Amen.

David A. Preisinger/Nov. 20, 1962

215

Redeemed, Restored, Forgiven

Go and tell My brethren to go to Galilee,
and there they will see Me. *Matthew 28:10 RSV*

*I*n preparation for a meeting with His disciples, Jesus referred to them as His "brethren." The warmth of that designation is supported by His stated desire to be with them in Galilee.

Consider the behavior of the disciples. They slept during His agony in the garden. They fled when they sensed danger despite their promises of faithfulness. Peter denied again and again that he even knew Jesus. Their only support was from afar. They were a disappointment.

The disciples—and we too—have the credentials of the prodigal son. Though a father and a brother are at home, the prodigal's earlier rebellion and weakness allow at best the status of a hired hand, as he himself requested. But just as the father welcomed and restored the prodigal to sonship with festive rejoicing, so Jesus forgave and restored His disciples.

We are dear to God for Jesus' sake. His death and resurrection served to redeem us from slavery to sin. In Him we are forgiven everything. Our penitence leads to full restoration. We enjoy the status of sons and daughters of the heavenly Father because of our brother, our Savior.

Though we are not worthy to be called Your children, we praise You, Father, for Your boundless mercy. Amen.

Ray F. Martens/April 10, 1985

WHEN JESUS COMES

He went into a city called Nain.
Luke 7:11 KJV

*T*he only claim to fame that Nain has and the only reason its name is remembered is that one day Jesus came to that town. He came with His mercy and help, and something wonderful happened: He raised the dead son of a widow to life and brought joy to that mother's heart.

Jesus came to a city of Samaria, and many of the people, hearing His words of life, believed in Him and confessed, "This is indeed the Christ, the Savior of the world" (John 4:42 KJV). He came to Bethany and blessed the home of Mary, Martha, and Lazarus with His gracious presence. He came to Jericho and restored sight to a blind man and brought salvation to the home and family of a tax collector.

No city is too small, no home too humble, and no person too insignificant for Jesus to visit with His love and blessing. He comes to our city, our community, and our home. He comes wherever people need Him. He comes in all kinds of seasons because He is the man for all seasons. He comes, He sees, and He acts, as He did when He came to Nain. Whatever the situation or need may be, He comes to do us good and to leave a blessing so we can say, "God has visited His people."

Lord Jesus, come to our city, our home, and our hearts with Your saving love and Your healing power. Amen.

Felix H. Kretzschmar/Nov. 28, 1977

217

You Won't Run Dry

*The jar of flour was not used up and the jug of
oil did not run dry, in keeping with the word of
the LORD spoken by Elijah. 1 Kings 17:16*

*B*ut Pastor, what if I reach 65 and I don't have anything left?" The voice was panicked. "I only have 20
years to accumulate security."

Twenty years or 60 years will not quiet the fear of anyone whose security is in the size of their nest egg. To be
sure, some people will say, "Soul, be at ease." But Jesus
called that man a fool. Security is simply not in having a
bank account that will not run dry.

Elijah knew this and wanted the widow to know it too.
He helped her by telling her to take her last oil and flour
for a breadcake and give it to him. He knew that as long
as she had some oil and flour, she would be afraid of running out. Once it was gone, she couldn't fear that any
longer. With it gone, she'd have only God left to trust.

Only God? Herein lies the beautiful key to disposing of
fear in our lives. Giving up our trust in oil or in nest eggs
can free us from the fear of losing them and move our
hearts to God alone, who in Christ Jesus made us His
children. He's worthy of our trust too. When we by the
power of His Spirit believe this, neither His love nor our
spirits run dry.

Move me to trust only in You, dear Savior. Amen.

Norbert C. Oesch/Sept. 15, 1988

218

Come, Lord Jesus, Be Our Guest

Behold, I stand at the door, and knock: if any
man hear My voice, and open the door, I will
come in to him, and will sup with him, and he
with Me. *Revelation 3:20 KJV*

*T*he children were glad when Aunt Jenny visited
because she brought gifts. Her gifts were neither
candy nor money but presents specially chosen for each
one and perhaps specially made.

Our Lord constantly comes to abide with us, more so
than a visiting relative or friend. He is our Savior, and He
comes with all kinds of gifts. As the heavenly physician,
He knows the failings of each of us. "He knoweth our
frame," says the psalmist. "He remembereth that we are
dust" (Psalm 103:14 KJV).

Christ, our heavenly guest, comes not to curse, but to
bless. He comes not to destroy, but to save us from sin. He
gives all we have. His love may not always be evident, but
all His gifts come from His love. In Him we have all things.

Our Lord comes continually through the means of
grace and abides in our hearts. He comes into our hearts
with His words of life, whether it is the Law telling us to
obey Him and to correct what is wrong or His precious
Gospel of mercy. With His bags of treasures, He opens to
us life, salvation, hope, joy, and forgiveness. He comes to
sup with us.

*Lord Jesus, You opened the door and entered my
heart at my Baptism. Abide with me always. Neither
leave nor forsake me all the days of my life. Amen.*

George W. Bornemann/Dec. 11, 1988

Sharing Is Accountable

So each of us shall give account of himself
to God. Romans 14:12 RSV

*A*s his composition was being played to an enthusias-
tic audience, the young composer paid no attention
to the audience reaction. His eyes were fixed intently on
his teacher who was sitting near him. The only thing that
mattered to the composer was how his teacher felt about
the composition.

Our whole life is a performance; what matters most is
what our Lord thinks about it.

We'll find out. The Bible clearly and often declares that
Christ will return and will judge the stewardship of our
life. Only God knows when that will be. The account
book of our life must therefore always be ready for audit.

Frightening? It should not be, though we cannot
escape thoughts of regret that we could and should have
done better. But the very faith that motivates us to serve
Christ in love is the faith that brings us to Christ's judgment dressed in His own perfection. The evil in our life
Christ will have thrown behind His back. It will be gone
forever. But the service we rendered in our sharing, He
will remember and commend.

*Gracious Savior, bless our stewardship efforts and
cover our failures with Your forgiving love. Amen.*

Armin C. Oldsen/May 31, 1981

220

WE LEARN OF HIM

Never man spake like this Man. John 7:46 KJV

C hrist is the unrivaled teacher. He spoke with authority, wisdom, and power. His opponents could not answer His questions, meet His arguments, or deny the truth of His teaching. So they conspired to silence by death the great teacher they could not successfully oppose and would not follow.

Yet Christ today lives and speaks with a force that grows with the centuries. All other teachers and all other systems of ethics and philosophy pale into insignificance before the personality and power of our divine teacher. St. Augustine said: "Plato has many beautiful thoughts, but nowhere does he have such words as these, 'Come unto Me, all ye that labor and are heavy laden, and I will give you rest.' " Christ brings pardon and peace to our hearts.

Christ teaches us the truth concerning the real value of the unseen. In the mad race for money, pleasure, and power it is good to recall His challenging question, "For what is a man profited, if he shall gain the whole world, and lose his own soul?" (Matthew 16:26 KJV).

Christ teaches us concerning things to come. Before the door of death, human reason stands speechless and afraid. Then the great teacher and Savior speaks in tones of infinite tenderness: "Let not your heart be troubled. ... In My Father's house are many mansions. ... I go to prepare a place for you" (John 14:1–2 KJV). "Learn of Me ... and ye shall find rest unto your souls" (Matthew 11:29 KJV).

Guide us, O Lord, in the way of eternal truth. Amen.

Edwin L. Wilson/Feb. 21, 1960

HIS LAW AND HIS LOVE

I have written briefly to you, exhorting and
declaring that this is the true grace of God;
stand fast in it. 1 Peter 5:12 RSV

We need to get back to the Ten Commandments."
"Our pastors don't preach enough Law."
Comments such as these are sometimes heard from members and also from church leaders.

When things seem to go wrong, rules often are offered as the cure. Civil laws can change outward behavior when they are accompanied by restraints and incentives, but such laws do not change the heart. That applies also to the Ten Commandments.

God's Law, when taken halfheartedly, leads to self-righteous pride. When taken seriously, it leads to despair. The Law, when allowed to work fully, kills all hope. It cannot save. That is why the Christian looks to the Gospel for hope and renewal.

As far as goodness and good works go, no matter how good we are, God will not love us any more. No matter how bad we are, He will not love us any less. We cannot influence God's love toward us. He loves us because He is love. That is supremely demonstrated in the gift of His Son, our Savior, Jesus Christ. All who believe in Him are loved of God and are saved.

Dear Father, keep me in Your grace. Help me to express my thanks by sharing the good news of Jesus with others. Amen.

C. Leo Symmank/July 17, 1987

GOD'S CARE INCLUDES YOU

"Let the children come to Me, and do not hinder them; for to such belongs the kingdom of heaven." Matthew 19:14 RSV

God's care includes people of all ages—those in Pampers and not yet crawling, those in Levis and crawling over everything, even those using walkers who crawl over nothing.

People are the excluders and discriminators, not God. People like to say, "You're too young"; "You're too old"; "You're not smart enough"; "You're not good enough." People want to put limits on things, especially things such as forgiveness and love. People want to know how far they have to go and when they can stop.

God's care includes, not excludes. When infants were brought to Him, Jesus didn't say, "I'm too busy." In contrast to the all-too-human response of the disciples, who wished to exclude, Jesus included them.

Now if infants barely crawling belong to the kingdom, so can children of all ages. If God does not exclude babies because they cannot reason for themselves, neither will He exclude you and me when we perhaps reason too much. Even as the Son of God gave His life for all, so He bids all to come to Him, young and old. He wants them all to be members of His kingdom.

Thank You, dear Savior, for permitting all children to come to You and to become members of the kingdom of heaven. Amen.

Norbert C. Oesch/July 13, 1985

223

The Most Common Sin

Woe unto you ... hypocrites!
Matthew 23:13 KJV

A hypocrite is a person who pretends, particularly one who pretends to be a better person than he or she really is. The Pharisees were such pretenders, and Jesus denounced them in the strongest language He ever used.

Because we ourselves are sinners, we cannot fully appreciate the contempt and indignation of the sinless Christ over this particular sin; but Christians should certainly take warning and be on guard against it. Even the world despises a hypocrite.

Yet hypocrisy may well be the most common sin, even among Christians. We cannot and should not judge others. Judgment belongs to God; but we can and should examine and judge our own lives so we may know our sins and repent of them.

It is so easy for a Christian to fall into the sin of hypocrisy. When we come to church without the spirit of worship, when we pray thoughtlessly, when we serve merely because we are asked to serve, when we sing praises to God and our heart is not in our song—are we not guilty of pretending? God knows—and He will judge.

Thank God that He will judge in mercy for Jesus' sake! For our Lord atoned also for the sin of hypocrisy when He died to save us from the wrath of God.

"Just as I am, without one plea But that Thy blood was shed for me And that Thou bidd'st me come to Thee, O Lamb of God, I come." Amen.

Henry F. Wind/March 13, 1959

224

MANY GIFTS, ONE SPIRIT

There are varieties of gifts, but the same
Spirit; and there are varieties of service, but
the same Lord. 1 Corinthians 12:4–5 RSV

God did not give us a monotonous creation. He made the world fascinating by means of a vast variety of objects and living creatures. Consider all the shapes, sizes, colors, and sounds! In all this variety everything is coordinated and interdependent.

The same is so in God's church. His new creation is not drab and colorless. There is sameness: All members are forgiven sinners by faith in the Savior. Beyond that, however, there are varieties of gifts and services. All kinds of people in the church have received the Spirit's gifts. Each is equipped to do his or her thing in Christ's body. Some in brilliant performance shine like sparkling diamonds, while others are busy in their little corner, unnoticed like old shoes. But all serve with the Spirit's gifts for the common good.

This truly is great. There is no room for jealousy. We with all this variety belong together. We all are redeemed with Christ's precious blood. Our use of the Spirit's gifts really makes the church shine and sparkle in this sinful world as we humbly and faithfully serve the Lord with thankful hearts.

Holy Spirit, let us be faithful in serving. Amen.

Carl A. Gaertner/March 24, 1972

SOMEBODY CARES

*"Which of these ... proved neighbor
to the man ...?" He said, "The one who
showed mercy on him." Luke 10:36–37 RSV*

*D*riven to the top of the Brooklyn Bridge by despair, the 21-year-old man shouted, "I need help! Nobody cares!" But someone did care. Bridge traffic was halted for an hour while a minister talked him down and police officers risked their lives to assist him on the cable catwalk.

How sad it is that some people live under a crushing load of troubles—some of their own making and others thrust on them by circumstances beyond control. Not everyone announces their plight in such a spectacular way. Often people just bear their sorrow in desperate silence. They appear to be unfriendly, antisocial, hard-to-be-near people. They need to know the love of Jesus. If people are sure God loves them, no burden is too much to bear. But they also need the help of people. The Good Samaritan didn't just comfort the wounded man with the message that God loved him and would take care of him. He himself demonstrated God's love and became part of the answer to the cry for help.

There is many a Brooklyn Bridge and Jericho Road in life. We can be alert to recognize our neighbor's needs. Someone may be whispering today, "I need help! Nobody cares!" Do we hear this?

Thank You, Lord, for caring enough to send Jesus to rescue us from perishing. Help us show others Your mercy. Amen.

Alma Kern/Feb. 20, 1975

A DEADLY FALL

You are dust, and to dust you shall return.
Genesis 3:19 RSV

*M*an was God's "crown of creation," His prize among all creatures, the one who was to have rulership over all of God's world. Like a beautiful refrain, Scripture repeats "God saw that it was good" at the end of each of the first five days of creation. But on the sixth day, when the Creator made man, God said: "Behold, it was *very* good!" The crown of creation was pronounced divinely perfect.

But the crown of creation invited a deadly fall. A subtle, beguiling serpent caused man's dissatisfaction with perfection. His coveting of equality with God led him to this deadly fall.

The fall was from the lofty plateau of holiness and life to the depths of disobedience and death. It was a drastic descent from the delights of paradise to the torments of sin's prison. Paradise was lost, and death became the frightening "prize." Deceived and irrational man, what an inequitable exchange!

But, God be praised, barely had sin begun in one garden when God had a Savior in mind in the second garden. In Joseph's lovely garden, Jesus rested, having in our place overcome sin, Satan, and death. His merit restored us to heaven's perfection.

Blessed Lord, lead us by faith from sin to salvation, from disobedience to obedience, from death to life. Amen.

Bernard H. Arkebauer/Aug. 7, 1982

It's Got to Be Good

We know that all things work together for
good to them that love God. Romans 8:28 KJV

These are words that lift our spirits and send them
soaring. Each word is significant. "We *know*." Paul
does not say we think or wish or hope or pray, but "we
know." It is a glad, glorious, stubborn fact—this divine
guiding and governing of the universe for our temporal
and eternal profit and blessing.

"*All things* work together for good." These are all-inclu-
sive words; nothing is left out. The joys, the sorrows, the
ups, the downs, the failures, the successes, the victories, the
defeats—in everything God is active for our good.

"*To them that love God.*" But maybe we don't love Him
enough—deeply and constantly and passionately enough.
Is that why things seldom work out? Of course not! It is
not our weak and wavering love to God that counts and
matters. It is His strong and everlasting love to us, a love
that moved Him to send His only Son to Calvary to
redeem us from the dark dominion of Satan and hell.

It is that great, godly love that turns evil into good,
defeat into victory, and sorrow into joy. This love works
always for our good. So let us rejoice!

*How good it is to believe, Lord, that nothing hap-
pens that is not part of Your great, good plan for us.
Help us remember that under Your guidance all
things, whether good or evil, work together for our
good. Amen.*

Herbert E. Hohenstein/Nov. 14, 1974

Grateful Hearts

So Jonah was exceeding glad of the gourd.
Jonah 4:6 KJV

A supermarket had its grand opening. A little girl ran home with a free sack of candy. Mother asked anxiously, "You didn't ask for it, did you?"

"Oh, no," replied the youngster. "All you have to do is stand close by. The man knows what you want."

In the same way, God neither forgets His own nor disregards their troubles. Jonah needed a shade tree. It was given to him, and he was saved from the scorching sun. Wherever there is the burning sun of calamity, there is also the gourd of some helping circumstance. A destroying angel routs a besieging army; manna feeds millions in the desert; an earthquake opens prison doors; sufficient grace is given to make a thorn in the flesh endurable. Sometimes we get what we ask for, but we always receive what we need.

"Jonah was exceeding glad of the gourd." And well he might be! But seemingly he rejoiced in the shade of the tree and forgot God, who had prepared it.

There is no greater danger today than that of not recognizing God's hand in nature and history. Is it not true that often we do not trace our best blessings to their heavenly origin? All of our earthly goods, even those for which we labor with skill and sweat, are the gifts of God. Happy is one who finds every blessing sweetened by the thought "God gave me this."

Oh, give thanks to the Lord, for He is good, for His mercy endures forever. Amen.

Stratford Eynon/March 26, 1960

WHAT ABOUT SALVATION?

He called for a light ... and brought them out,
and said, Sirs, what must I do to be saved?
Acts 16:29–30 KJV

*T*he warden had gone to sleep confident that Paul, Silas, and the other prisoners were securely imprisoned. The chains were tight; the doors secure. Guards were posted. Such knowledge makes jailers sleep soundly. Then came that awful noise. Rushing into the cell block, he saw all the doors open. *The prisoners have fled!* he thought. In despair he drew his sword, ready to suffer death before dishonor. Then Paul called out, "Don't do that! We're all here." A quick survey proved that Paul spoke the truth.

That is when the jailer asked, "What must I do to be saved?"

Did the question mean, "How can I find salvation?" Or did it mean, as some might think, "What must I do to keep all of you from rushing out?" No matter what the jailer's intent in asking, Paul gave a positive Christian answer: "Believe on the Lord Jesus Christ, and thou shalt be saved" (Acts 16:31 KJV). *Really* saved. In clear, simple language Paul pointed this disturbed man to the cross and to Christ.

That cross still stands, offering to one and all God's final, full, and free solution to the question, "What must I do to be saved?" Bearing in His body the sins of all people, Christ earned for us forgiveness. Believe on Him.

What a friend we have in Jesus, our Savior! Lead us, Lord, to ever find salvation in His name and work. Amen.

Charles S. Mueller Sr./March 12, 1968

230

Sharing Sacrificially

Your lamb shall be without blemish.
Exodus 12:5 RSV

Children were playing in the backyard with an old replica of Noah's ark and all the animals in miniature. They remembered that Noah sacrificed some of the animals on the altar as a thank offering for his deliverance from the flood. So they built a small fire and sacrificed defective toys—a camel that had no legs and a giraffe that had lost its neck. Just like children! Let's be honest—much like us!

We like to help along a good cause, yet we often hesitate to do our best. We'll help, we'll give, as long as the sacrifice is not too great. God knows His people have always been like that. When He gave the Israelites instructions about the animals they were to sacrifice, He stated He did not want anything second-rate. Sacrificing was not to be degraded by getting rid of a blemished animal—one that was blind, or crippled, or deformed in any way. He wanted the best.

Why shouldn't He? God did not send to earth an old angel with broken wings or a bent halo to represent Him. He sent that which was most precious to Him, His only Son. And He sent Him to the altar, to the cross on which Christ died for us. Should not we do our best?

When we share with You, our loving and generous Lord, help us to be at our best. Amen.

Armin C. Oldsen/May 23, 1981

231

REMEMBER YOUR BAPTISM

They came to some water, and the eunuch
said, "See, here is water! What is to prevent
my being baptized?" Acts 8:37 RSV

*T*ake me to the water to be baptized" is part of a
spiritual that slaves used during the services of Holy
Baptism. It may have been sung as they made their journey to a creek or river for Baptism.

The spiritual reminds us of the statement made by the
Ethiopian eunuch after he had been instructed by Philip.
Passing a body of water, he said: "See, here is water. Why
can't I be baptized?" Philip baptized him. The eunuch
probably never forgot that day. His Baptism was a constant reminder that he was a child of God.

As we read these words, we remember our Baptism—
the day that we received the "washing of regeneration and
renewal of the Holy Spirit." In fact, Martin Luther urges
us to remember our Baptism every day. He says that upon
arising each morning, we can make the sign of the cross
and remind ourselves of who we are as a result of our
Baptism.

When we were baptized, our sins were washed away,
but that is not all that happened. Our Baptism is also our
identification with Jesus. We were baptized into the name
of the Father and Son and Holy Spirit. We received His
name. We were adopted into His family.

*Father in heaven, at my Baptism You made me
Your dear child. Grant that I may remain faithful
to You. Amen.*

William H. Griffen/Feb. 2, 1986

232

Deep Roots

Blessed is the man who trusts in the Lord. *...*
He is like a tree planted by water, that sends out
its roots by the stream. Jeremiah 17:7–8 RSV

*I*n the Southwest desert the tumbleweed grows large. It
dries up in the summer heat and, breaking away from
its shallow roots, is driven about by the wind. On the
other hand, trees put down deep roots. Years of growth
with good watering give them deep roots that can with-
stand heat and drought. In storms they bend with the
wind.

The psalmist calls the man blessed who delights in
God's Word, comparing him to a fruit-bearing tree
"planted by streams of water."

Planted in the water of our Baptism, our faith puts
down roots close to the stream of God's love and forgiveness. The roots grow deeper through the daily watering of
our faith through the Word of God.

Sometimes we don't feel much like strong trees.
Sometimes we feel more like the tumbleweed. The storms
of life blow us around; we are wearied and withered from
the heat of trial and conflict. That's when we can lean on
our faith in Jesus and bend with the wind. He gives us the
strength to be strong and resilient trees. We are bowed
but not broken because of our well-watered roots.

O Lord, in Your presence I find strength for today
and the deep roots to face the storms of my life.
Amen.

Louise Mueller/July 31, 1984

233

My Past

*Remember ye not the former things, neither
consider the things of old. Isaiah 43:18 KJV*

*B*y means of proverb after proverb, the world tries to
get rid of the past! People say: "What's done is
done!" "Let bygones be bygones!" "Never look back!" But
to no avail. Like Pilgrim in Bunyan's story, I carry on my
back a gigantic sack of all my past, and "I fain would lay
my burden down." My mistakes, my harsh words, my
thoughtlessness, my evil deeds come back to haunt me. Or
else they burrow deep into my mind and soul and there
fester and break out in ugly sins of irritability, short temper, cruelty, lovelessness, and even bodily illnesses and
pains.

There is a way of getting rid of my burden. Pilgrim laid
his sack down at the foot of the cross and walked away a
freed man. I can do the same. I am invited to do so.
"Come unto Me, all ye that labor and are heavy laden, and
I will give you rest," said Jesus (Matthew 11:28 KJV). As
the ancient hymn has it: "My burden in Thy Passion,
Lord, Thou hast borne for me, For it was my transgression Which bro't this woe on Thee." But because He bore
my burden, I can do what the world vainly tries to do:
"Remember ye not the former things, neither consider
the things of old." I hear Him say: "Be of good cheer; thy
sins be forgiven thee" (Matthew 9:2 KJV). What a relief!

*Let me know Thy gracious pardon, Wash me, make
me white as snow. Amen.*

Walter E. Kraemer/Sept. 5, 1968

234

Enough for Everyone

Everyone ate and had enough.
Matthew 14:20 TEV

A lady, born and raised in a cold-water flat in New York City, lived all her life in the same tenement. She had never traveled more than four blocks in any direction. It was a poor neighborhood, and she was among the poorest of the poor.

One summer the Community Settlement House sent her to the seashore on a Fresh Air Fund vacation. Her first sight of the ocean—its rolling waves, its wide expanse—filled her with wonder and awe and prompted her to say, "Thank God! There is enough for everyone."

Enough for everyone—enough fish, enough bread to feed five thousand and many more. There is also enough of God's love, mercy, and forgiveness in Jesus Christ to go around and include everyone. It seems that the more of God's love we use, the more is left to be used. On Calvary forgiveness was wrought, and it is a never-ending, inexhaustible forgiveness. There is enough for everyone! It is there for the asking. Go to the cross and experience God's love anew.

Lord, I know that You love me. You never let me down. Thank You! Amen.

Albert L. Neibacher/Aug. 4, 1988

HIS YOKE IS LIGHT

Take My yoke upon you … you will find
rest for your souls. For My yoke is easy, and
My burden is light. Matthew 11:29–30 RSV

*Y*okes are not comfortable things—for animals or for people. Oxen were hooked up between these wooden frames. Attached to the frame was a yoke bar, which in turn was attached to a plow. Life under a yoke is very difficult.

People were often put in yokes too—kept under yokes of iron or wood. No wonder the yoke quickly became a symbol of subjection and servitude! It breaks the spirit as well as the back.

So also is the yoke of keeping God's Law for our salvation. Life lived in an attempt to win God's favor by keeping the Law only makes it a terrible drag. It, too, breaks the spirit, leaving one subjected to the slavery of sin. No one is justified in God's sight by keeping the Law.

The yoke of Christ is not heavy, however. When by faith we devote ourselves to Christ, our spirits are set free from the guilt of sin, free from the burden of the Law, free to love. His yoke is light because the burden of guilt and sin that once dragged us down has been removed. Christ Himself pulled that burden to the cross. His life and death freed all humanity from the drag of sin and the Law. "Take My yoke upon you … you will find rest for your souls," He says.

Lord, I find rest because I give You my load of sin. Amen.

Norbert C. Oesch/July 8, 1985

WELCOME HOME

It was meet that we should ... be glad; for
this thy brother was dead, and is alive again;
and was lost, and is found. Luke 15:32 KJV

W hat the father had said to his servants, he now repeats to his older son in support of his right to make merry and be glad. It had been a long time since there was any reason to celebrate and be glad in the father's house. This father, who originally had two sons, for quite some time now really had none. The younger had demanded his inheritance and had gone off to squander it on evil companions and pastimes. No cause for joy here—just concern and anxiety! The older was at home working the farm. But it seems communication between him and his father was practically nonexistent. No joy here either!

Now the younger son has returned, sorry and repentant, hoping to make a new start. The father's heart overflows with joy: "It was meet that we should make merry." We are not told if the older son saw the light, experienced a change in heart, and entered into the spirit of a happy welcome home. We can only hope that it was so.

This much, however, is always true: Because of Christ, our heavenly Father is ever ready to welcome home His returning children. There is joy in heaven over every repentant sinner.

Thousand, thousand thanks shall be, dearest Jesus, unto You for leading us from death to life. Amen.

Raymond C. Hohenstein/Oct. 31, 1969

Don't Break the Habit

They went up to Jerusalem after the custom
of the feast. Luke 2:42 KJV

*J*e just goes to church out of habit." How often
is this charge leveled against the regular church
attendant! While God is displeased with mechanical
worship, much can be said in favor of "going to church
out of habit."

Of Jesus' earthly family, we are told that they went to
Jerusalem every year at the time of the Passover "after the
custom of the feast." Years later when He visited
Nazareth, Jesus attended the local synagogue on the
Sabbath "as His *custom* was." For Him it was the most nat-
ural thing to do, and so He did it. It was His custom.

We can break good habits such as regular church atten-
dance only at great spiritual peril. Once such habits are
broken, they will be replaced by the habits of nonatten-
dance, nonfellowship, nonparticipation, and a dwindling
source of spiritual nourishment. In that direction, ultimately, lies spiritual death.

If we are attending church merely out of habit, so be
it! But let us continue to attend. Meanwhile we pray for
the higher motivation of King David: "Lord, I have
loved the habitation of Thy house, and the place where
Thine honor dwelleth" (Psalm 26:8 KJV). He who hears
God's Word regularly finds that one good habit leads to
another.

Lord, let me never stray from You. Amen.

Herman W. Gockel/Jan. 13, 1975

PRAY FOR OTHERS

You also must help us by prayer.
2 Corinthians 1:11 RSV

*F*or the prayers of our church friends there is no adequate expression of appreciation." So wrote a grateful mother to those who had prayed for the recovery of her son from a serious motorcycle accident. A missionary wrote to people back home, "We can feel your prayers for us and our work."

Intercession, praying for others, is a characteristic of God's people. The prophet Samuel told the rebellious Israelites, "God forbid that I should sin against the Lord in ceasing to pray for you" (1 Samuel 12:23 KJV). Abraham begged God to spare wicked Sodom for the sake of 10 righteous people who might live there. Moses pleaded with the Almighty not to destroy Israel. Jesus is the greatest intercessor. "Father, forgive them; for they know not what they do" (Luke 23:34 KJV) was His prayer for those who would arrest and slay Him. On the night before He died for us, Jesus spoke a long prayer for His apostles and all believers after them. Jesus "always lives to make intercession" for us.

Prayer expresses faith and love. St. Paul indicates that we help others when we pray for them. Jesus told Peter, "I have prayed for you that your faith may not fail" (Luke 22:32 RSV). We, too, can tell others, "I'm praying for you." That may encourage them. Let us say a prayer right now for someone in need!

Heavenly Father, have mercy on ... Amen.

Herbert M. Kern/June 23, 1987

239

Proclaim His Death

Whenever you eat this bread and drink
this cup, you proclaim the Lord's death until
He comes. 1 Corinthians 11:26

Only one who is going to die need make a last will and testament. This is what our Lord does in the Upper Room. Beyond this room there is Gethsemane, then Golgotha. Our Lord goes to the cross for us. In the Sacrament of the Altar He gives us His body to eat and His blood to drink. Therefore Martin Luther advises the Christian, "When you are troubled by your sins do not go to Calvary. At Calvary sin was answered for. But come to the Lord's Supper, for it is here that the forgiveness won at Calvary is bestowed."

Our Lord is the host at His Supper. He invites sinners to be His guests because the content of His testament is the forgiveness of sins. It is not our pious actions, our prayers, our feelings of worthiness or unworthiness that make the Supper what it is but the faithful and effectual Word and work of the Lamb who was slain. That Lamb, without spot or blemish, has carried our sins to the cross. He drained dry the cup of suffering, the cup of God's wrath. Now He gives us, along with His body, another cup to drink. This cup is the new testament in His blood. When we receive the Sacrament, we proclaim Christ's death.

Faithful Lord Jesus, we give You thanks that You have established the Holy Supper for us. Amen.

John T. Pless/Feb. 11, 1989

240

HE KEEPS ASKING

He said to him the third time,
"... Do you love Me?" John 21:17 RSV

*Y*ears ago some homes had the Little Leather Library, which consisted of short pieces of literature in small-size booklets. Among these was an exposition of 1 Corinthians 13 bearing the title "The Greatest Thing in the World." The little book was on the greatest subject—love.

What greater thing is there for a child than the parents' love? Or for a married couple than each other's love? Or for a human being in trouble with God than His forgiving love?

After the crushing realization that he had denied his Lord, what happier news could Peter have heard on Easter morning than that the risen Christ wanted to meet in Galilee with "His disciples *and Peter*"? What a joy to be singled out personally for Jesus' pardoning love!

Does our Lord in His turn have moments of special joy because of us? How about the times when we commit ourselves in love and loyalty to Him? He wants our commitment. Three times He asked Peter, "Do you love Me?" After each response He reassigned Peter to the great privilege and task of caring for the spiritual needs of the members of His flock. He still asks for our love and adds: "If you love Me, you will keep My commandments" (John 14:15 RSV).

Give us, Lord, the love to obey Your will. Amen.

F. Samuel Janzow/June 18, 1977

No Room for Fatigue

Let us not grow weary in well-doing,
for in due season we shall reap,
if we do not lose heart. Galatians 6:9 RSV

So easy to say, so hard to do! We hunger for appreciation. It is not enough for us to know that we did a
good job. We want others to know it and to say so. If they
fail to show appreciation, we often think of quitting.

Is this because the things we do are not worthwhile?
No. Because we were not accomplishing good? No. Well,
why then? The reason is simply that people are not taking
notice.

We need to ask ourselves: "Is the task we are doing a
godly task?" If so, then we should keep on doing it. That
is all that is necessary. Nothing more is needed—no
encouragement, no appreciation, no name in the head-
lines.

Our Lord did not direct His course by the appreciation
index. The closer His crucifixion came, less was the
encouragement He received. Nevertheless He suffered
and died for us because it was "well-doing" for its own
sake. In that action Jesus directs our attention away from
ourselves to Himself. In part that is what it means to rise
from the dead with Him. The starting point is Christ, the
goal is Christ, the power is Christ. He makes the appreciation index undeserving of our serious attention.

*In all our work, Lord Jesus, help us to look not so
much for appreciation from others but to please You.
Amen.*

Paul W. F. Harms/March 7, 1973

Jesus' Love: Source of Our Love

[Jesus] said to His mother, "Woman, behold,
your son!" Then He said to the disciple,
"Behold, your mother!" John 19:26–27 RSV

*H*e sat by his mother's bedside, as he did each Sunday afternoon. Sometimes he read aloud from the Bible—favorite passages that she had often quoted from memory. Sometimes he read from books that she had read to him as a child. More often he sat silently and remembered times they had shared together. She had given much to him: a home filled with love, encouragement when life seemed too difficult, a cautioning hand when he dared too much. She always had been there when he needed a bandage for a scratched knee, when he returned from school each day bubbling over with news, when sadness entered his life at the death of his puppy. From her he had learned the meaning of love, tenderness, and care.

People wondered why he came each week to sit beside this woman who seldom recognized him and said very little. He came because of his love for her. This love was no accident; it was no mere sentiment. His love had its source in the love of Jesus for him and for all people—a love that drove Jesus to the cross to save us all, a love He had extended to His own mother, whom He honored to the end.

Teach us, O Lord Jesus, to honor our mothers as You loved and honored Yours. Amen.

Alston S. Kirk/May 13, 1989

243

STRENGTH IN WEAKNESS

"My grace is sufficient for you, for My power
is made perfect in weakness."
2 Corinthians 12:9 RSV

*T*his assurance of our loving Lord shines like a brilliant diamond displayed on a piece of black velvet. The contrast of the shining gem against the dark background sets it forth in all of its beauty and value.

In our day of adversity, as in Paul's, when we have sought help and have not found it, when we have tried remedies and have not succeeded, when we think we have reached the end of our endurance, then our blessed Savior comes to us with this wonderful assurance. He reminds us that His grace is equal to our every need. His power never falls short; He never lacks knowledge as to what to do. He who loved us even to death is not going to let us down in the severe trials of our life.

In the midst of our weakness, the God in whom we trust has the power to fulfill our need. He will support us in weakness, guide us in our perplexity. According to His loving plan for our life, He will do whatever is needful for our welfare.

We can lean on God in confident faith. He is able to sustain and uphold us. He enables us to bear our burden in life. With Christ we can overcome.

Lord, make my faith strong enough to rely on You. Amen.

Edgar C. Rakow/Jan. 17, 1972

SHARING OUR TIME

*We must work the works of Him who sent Me,
while it is day; night comes, when no one can
work. John 9:4 RSV*

*C*hrist left the eternal glory of heaven and stepped into a harsh world and into the restriction of time. The years He shared visibly with the human family were few, but look at what He accomplished: teaching, preaching, healing, providing, comforting, guiding, and above all, working out our eternal salvation. He wants to share His time with us even now and forever because His promise is, "I am with you always."

God knows we need much of our time for sleep, work, recreation, and countless other activities. Yet God wants us to share some of our time with Him in a special way: worship, prayer, Bible study, and church work. He also wants us to share some of our time with others in a special way, therefore also with Him: visiting the sick and those who need comfort and cheer, helping where we can, showing love.

For every living being time is limited, yet few fully realize that it's true also of their life. To become aware of how far the clock of one's life has run down can be shocking. The best way to keep that shock from becoming aggravated with guilt and regret is to use time wisely, while our life clock is still keeping good time.

O God, we want to spend more time with You. Amen.

Armin C. Oldsen/May 18, 1981

245

LIVING BREAD

I am the living bread which came down from
heaven; if any one eats of this bread,
he will live for ever. John 6:51 RSV

We all like food. Eating is one of the most pleasurable things we do. We all enjoy our favorite dishes. In fact, we are made so the body hungers for food; we are fashioned so we can take in food and digest it, transforming it into flesh and blood. Food gives us nourishment and strength. All the food the body needs grows out of the earth or is at least found on the earth. It is of an earthly kind.

Jesus taught that we also have a spiritual life. This life, too, is made so it requires food. It also must receive nourishment and be strengthened. As the soul is not earthly, it cannot live by anything that is found on the earth. It must have the spiritual food that comes to us from God through His Word.

What is the spiritual food by which we live? We live on Christ and His presence in our lives. When Jesus says that we must eat and drink His flesh and blood to have life, He means that the gift of His body in death and the shedding of His blood on the cross creates and sustains our spiritual life. The only way to a full, nourished life is through faith in Christ.

Loving God, in Jesus You give us bread for our wilderness life and wine for our journey. Amen.

John F. Johnson/April 9, 1987

246

THE GOSPEL HAS NO "IFS"

God was in Christ, reconciling the world unto
Himself, not imputing [not counting] their
trespasses unto them. 2 Corinthians 5:19 KJV

*T*he young pastor was preaching eloquently. He was exhorting his congregation in all earnestness and no doubt in all sincerity: "*If* you will put your trust in Christ, He will save you." He went on to use the word *if* at least three or four times. This makes salvation conditional.

That is not the proper way to present the Christian Gospel. At best, it is misleading. At worst, it can end only in abysmal despair. There is nothing "if" about the way of salvation. The Gospel of Christ does not contain an "if" clause. The Scriptures tell us in a simple, straightforward declarative sentence, "Christ died for our sins." Again: "God was in Christ, reconciling the world unto Himself, not imputing [not counting] their trespasses unto them."

We are not saved *if*. We are saved *because* God in His immeasurable mercy sent His Son into the world to die for your sins and for mine. Our salvation is complete. Christ died. He rose again. We can trust this message. Not "if" but because our Lord has said so.

"Just as I am, Thou wilt receive, Wilt welcome, pardon, cleanse, relieve; Because Thy promise I believe, O Lamb of God, I come, I come." Amen.

Herman W. Gockel/June 5, 1989

Betting against Hell

*About the ninth hour Jesus cried out in a loud
voice, ... "My God, My God, why have You
forsaken Me?" Matthew 27:46*

*H*ell is a place of indescribable torture. Many people do not believe this. They ridicule hell with foolish jokes. Some rationalize that a loving God would never consign His human creations to damnation. Others feel that hell is a 14th-century myth of the church, used to browbeat people into obedience. In essence, these people are betting against the existence of hell.

Christians regard hell as a definite place, as stated clearly in Scripture. Beyond its physical torment, hell suggests a separation from God, which is so much worse. To be cut off from God's love, to be abandoned by Him, to be considered as spiritual orphans—this is a consequence almost too horrible for any person to contemplate.

But the good news is that Jesus descended into hell as our substitute, demonstrating that He had overcome its power. All sinners who believe in Christ as the Savior escape from hell because they have full forgiveness of their sins. We are no longer the enemies of God but redeemed saints. Let us cling to our Savior because in Him alone can we have perfect peace, joy, and everlasting life.

*Holy Spirit, give us strength to live holy lives in
appreciation for Jesus' sacrifice for us. Amen.*

Herbert G. Walther/Aug. 20, 1989

WHAT'S IN A NAME?

They will put My name on the Israelites,
and I will bless them. Numbers 6:27

W hat's in God's name? Where God's name is, there
God Himself is present to bless His people.
Drawing on Psalm 124:8, our church liturgy reminds us:
"Our help is in the name of the LORD, who made heaven
and earth" (RSV). Everything that God has done for us,
He has packed into His name. No wonder that God's Law
forbids us to misuse the Lord's name: "You shall not mis-
use the name of the LORD your God" (Exodus 20:7 RSV).
Instead we are taught to pray "Hallowed be Thy name."

God put His holy name on us in Baptism. To be baptized in the name of the Father and of the Son and of the
Holy Spirit puts our lives "under" His name, under His
"account." Our names are inscribed under God's name in
the book of life.

With God's name, we are given the assurance that He
is indeed with us to bless, sustain, guide, and protect
because in Jesus God has made us His redeemed children.
God's name given to us in Baptism is God's signature on
our foreheads, marking us as His sons and daughters.
Therefore we join David in confessing, "I will bow down
toward Your holy temple and will praise Your name ... for
You have exalted above all things Your name and Your
word" (Psalm 138:2).

*Triune God, I praise You for all the blessings of Your
name given to me in Baptism. Amen.*

John T. Pless/Feb. 6, 1989

WHY WORK?

Let him labour, working with his hands the
thing which is good, that he may have to give
to him that needeth. Ephesians 4:28 KJV

*P*erhaps it is a good thing that the upcoming Labor
Day is a holiday. At least we have a little time to
think some of God's thoughts on why we work honestly
and faithfully. When God made Adam in His image, He
did not create him to be idle. Work is not a curse; it is
Adam's sin and our sins that have "cursed the ground" so
we often eat our bread in sorrow and anxiety.

Our Father in heaven views all our opportunities for
honorable labor as His blessing to us. In our daily work
He is our true employer. He created us with the capacity
for work. He purchased us at Calvary to serve Him in all
we do. He set us apart in Holy Baptism to do our daily
work under the guidance of the Holy Spirit.

We are to work at "the thing which is good, that he
may have to give to him that needeth." Our goal should
never be how much money we can get for ourselves, but
how much we can share with others!

So let us work to supply the needs of our family and relatives, to help the needy in our Christian fellowship, and
to provide for those who are suffering in all the world.
Above all, let us bear witness to Christ who "labored" on
the cross that we might enjoy the fruits of His redemption, even heaven with all its glory.

*Dear Master, take care of me as You have promised,
then help me to take care of others for You. Amen.*

Martin L. Koehneke/Sept. 7, 1964

GOOD AND BAD

Adam ... became the father of a son in his own
likeness, after his image, and named him Seth.
Genesis 5:3 RSV

*T*his is a birth announcement, Old Testament style. It
reports that Adam became a father and called the
little fellow Seth. This was good news for Adam's family,
just as birth announcements today bring joy to relatives
and friends. Every birth reminds us of God's blessing spoken to Adam and Eve and of our partnership with God in
the ongoing creation process. This is good.

Seth's birth announcement, however, contains some
bad news. It tells us that this little boy was in Adam's likeness, after his image. This does not mean that he looked
like Adam, but that he was, like his father, a sinner. He
inherited from his parents a corruption that permeated his
nature. What a tragedy for Seth and for us all! From generation to generation the thinking of our hearts is evil
from infancy. By nature we are dead in trespasses and are
children of wrath. This we need to know if we are to
understand ourselves and our desperate need for help and
deliverance.

Thank God there is help! God in His mercy has supplied the remedy in His Son, the Lamb that has taken
away the sins of the world. He also has given us the Holy
Spirit to quicken us and make us new people in Christ.

*Thank You, Father, for Jesus and the Holy Spirit.
Amen.*

Carl A. Gaertner/Nov. 10, 1978

Once Lost, Now Found

[The woman said,] "Rejoice with me,
for I have found the coin which I had lost."
Luke 15:9 RSV

*W*as that coin lying in a crack in the floor? Had it slipped under the baseboard? Was it under the bed? It was somewhere in the house, but where? Oh, what a search it took to find it! But it was found. And when it was, a great celebration took place. The lost had been found.

Of course the parable is about God and His diligent search. He does not search for coins, however, but for people—for you and me. Wherever we might be hiding, He comes looking. Behind baseboards of fear, within cracks of bitterness, beneath beds of guilt, He comes looking. He pulls up, looks under, turns over whatever is necessary to find us. We are the objects of His search.

Why? Because we are the objects of His love. Our value lies not in how important we are by nature, but in the affection of His heart. His love makes our value so high that He will stop at nothing to find and restore us.

So He came in His Son, Jesus, to seek and save the lost, yes, you and me. And He comes today in Word and Sacrament, and in the concern of fellow believers, to find us each time we get lost. When we are found again, only the angels in heaven surpass us in expressions of joy.

Father, keep on finding me. I want to be Yours forever. Amen.

Norbert C. Oesch/July 22, 1985

DEATH—I FEAR YOU NO MORE

And free those who all their lives were held in
slavery by their fear of death. Hebrews 2:15

I wish you could meet Karen. She has a brain tumor. Three months ago she was told she had two weeks to live. We talked about her death then; we talk about it now, too, because it is soon to come. But the light in her eyes, the joy in her heart, and the smile on her face speak loudly. "Death, I fear you no more!"

Karen trusts the death of Jesus. She knows that He destroyed the one who held the power of death, namely, the devil, when He arose on Easter. It's so basic to the Christian faith that, as some might say, it borders on the ho-hum of spiritual boredom to repeat it—unless you are still held in slavery of the fear of death. Then to see Karen is to be shocked. How could she so calmly look forward to her death and not fear it at all?

It's really not complex. Karen, as well as you and I, can truly believe that Jesus Christ destroyed the power of death by conquering Satan. Now death is only a moment on the way to life—a movement from earth to heaven.

"Death, I fear you no more! Jesus Christ is the Lord of life." Say it out loud. Say it with conviction. It is true!

Thank You, Jesus, for breaking death's power by conquering Satan. Help me to fear death no more. Amen.

Norbert C. Oesch/Sept. 25, 1988

Every Morning — Glory

*In the morning, then ye shall see the glory
of the LORD. Exodus 16:7 KJV*

*L*et's take that literally of each new day that comes our way, every morning that awakens us from sleep. There is a deep sense in which every returning dawn—when night shadows scatter before the sun—is a great moral and spiritual moment in the history of the soul.

In it you can hear, if you have ears for it, the rallying voice of God saying, "Here is a fresh, unspoiled day before you, a brand-new opportunity. Here is a clean page for your book." If earlier pages have been filled with blots and blunders, and the record has been marred by mistakes and errors and inexcusable sins that shame you bitterly when you look back at them, here is this page, untouched and spotless, waiting for the record that your finger is going to write. The past is over and forgiven. This is the moment of another chance.

One great secret for achieving serenity is to commit your way to God not just in some high and decisive moment but every morning. Immediately on awakening say, "God, here for the next 24 hours is my life." This gives the daily miracle of God's grace the opportunity to work in you and through you for another day. Any morning, every morning, the glory of the Lord!

Thank You, God, for giving us another chance today. Bless us in the name of Jesus, our Savior. Amen.

Arnold G. Kuntz/March 11, 1988

HE KNOWS US

Now I know in part; then I shall understand
fully, even as I have been fully understood.
1 Corinthians 13:12 RSV

*T*he purpose of education is to know. Americans are driven by a passion for knowledge of every kind—of cause and effect, original meanings, basic sources, intricate operations, and broad outlines of activities. God has given us the power of reasoning. Neither God nor society will reward us for laziness and indolence. We admire those who are active and alert.

However, we sometimes get the notion that we have the power to know everything. So many of the secrets of nature have been seen through the microscope and the telescope that it seems but a mere matter of time before human beings will know everything about everything.

However, we are reminded in that beautiful chapter, 1 Corinthians 13, that we know only "in part," and it will only be in the hereafter that we will know fully (v. 13). Then our thirst for curiosity will be fully satisfied.

That will be soon enough. Right now it is more important that we are known by God. Because we are His children through our redemption by Christ Jesus, God not only knows us inside out, but He loves us and cares for us. He permits us to know what is good for us. What more do we need to know than that our God "has done all things well" (Mark 7:37 RSV)?

Lord, knowing You is to know all. Amen.

Dorothy Rosin/Sept. 5, 1976

255

CARING FOR THE ONE

"It is not the will of My Father who is in
heaven that one of these little ones should
perish." Matthew 18:14 RSV

*I*t is the will of God to find us whenever and wherever
we have stumbled and strayed. He wants to bring us
back into His fellowship, where there is forgiveness and
new life.

That one whom God seeks out is each of us. At some
time or other each of us goes astray. Our Lord's reference
to the one lost sheep, which He contrasts with the 99, is
His way of showing that God is concerned about claiming
for His own every person whom He has made and
redeemed. This is not to say that the 99 are the good
sheep who are without need. We are all sinners whom
God has restored through Jesus Christ. It is not because
we try to be good or appear to be good that we are Christ's
sheep; it is only because of His call to us, again and again:
"You are Mine!"

The Good Shepherd's flock is the fellowship of forgiv-
en sinners. We are good sheep, not because we found our
way back or never went astray but because He found us.
We are good because He is good. Therein lies our responsibility for one another. Like the Good Shepherd, we
search for the erring one because it is God's will that not
one of us should perish.

*Lord, help us to regard one another as Your sheep.
Amen.*

Ronald C. Starenko/April 23, 1976

256

How Do We Find Ourselves?

When he came to himself ... Luke 15:17 RSV

Germans have a greeting that, translated literally, means "How do you find yourself?" The question concerns itself with the general well-being of people. It is an interesting question for every human being. Just how does one find oneself?

The prodigal son in Christ's parable found himself when he was sitting in a pigsty. He had gone through all his money. The companions he had picked up with his free spending had abandoned him. He was debating whether he should attempt to satisfy his hunger with the husks the pigs were eating. Then "he came to himself." Like the prodigal, we wander off to a far country when we sin. We leave the Father's house and table. We throw away our inheritance as God's children. We try to satisfy our spiritual hunger with the empty husks of do-it-yourself religion. We need to come to ourselves.

After the prodigal son had found himself, he resolved to go home to his father and say, "I have sinned." We can go home with him and admit that we, too, have sinned. The wonderful thing about this is that when we return, we find the Father is waiting. He opens His loving arms. He forgives our sins. He restores us to sonship. He celebrates our return. We truly find ourselves in the Father's house.

Father, apart from You we are lost. Help us to find ourselves and to abide in Your presence forever. Amen.

Philip L. Fiess/June 3, 1972

GOD DESIGNED OUR SALVATION

By grace are ye saved through faith.
Ephesians 2:8 KJV

Sir Christopher Wren designed Windsor Town Hall near London in 1689 with a ceiling supported by pillars. After it was finished, the city fathers ordered more pillars. They believed that the number of pillars Wren had put in would never support the ceiling. Wren did as told.

However, the four added pillars didn't touch the ceiling. It only looked that way from below. The great architect of our salvation, our heavenly Father, knows what it takes for us to be saved. In Holy Scripture He has revealed His saving knowledge, as St. Paul writes: "By grace are ye saved through faith; and that not of yourselves: it is the gift of God: not of works, lest any man should boast" (Ephesians 2:8–9 KJV).

How often do we feel that God's grace in Christ will not support "the ceiling of salvation"? We always want to put in more pillars. We say, "I've always tried to do right" or "I've always done for others what I could." He who looks from above is fully aware that none of these pillars reach up to support the structure of our salvation. He who looks down from above, unfooled by our optical illusions, says through the apostle: "Not by works of righteousness which we have done, but according to His mercy He saved us" (Titus 3:5 KJV).

Thanks, Lord, for blessing us with salvation as a gift. Amen.

Holger G. Cattau/June 26, 1986

Eyes on Christ

[Peter] was afraid and, beginning to sink,
cried out, "Lord, save me!" Matthew 14:30

O ver my desk hangs an old print by the artist Ricardo
Pinx entitled "Lord, Help Me." It depicts Jesus
walking on the water and reaching His hand out to help
Peter, who is sinking.

As long as Peter kept his eyes on Christ, he was able to
walk on the water. But as soon as he looked at the angry
waves crashing around him, he sank. Peter broke eye con-
tact with Jesus, and the waves started to engulf him.

Once we take our eyes off Christ and the cross, we
begin to sink. Life becomes too much for us because the
waters of life are not always as smooth as a mirror.
Troubles and dangers disturb these waters. They become
rough and threatening. We, too, become frightened and
begin to sink, losing sight of the outstretched hand of
Jesus.

When threatened, we can "lift high the cross" and keep
our eyes focused on Christ. He has invested His suffering
and death in us, and He will never let the angry waters of
life swallow us. As we keep our eyes on Christ, we will see
His hand reaching out. The cross is our life raft.

*Lord Jesus, help me as the storm clouds gather and
the waters of life become rough. Amen.*

Albert L. Neibacher/Aug. 26, 1988

259

We Go to the Physician

"They that be whole need not a physician,
but they that are sick." Matthew 9:12 KJV

*A*ll of us should have periodic physical checkups. Although we might feel well and be in good health, wisdom says, "Be sure." With today's modern medicine and medical skill, we go to our physician to determine whether we are in good health.

What is more important, our bodies or our immortal souls? The answer is obvious. Jesus says in the text, directing His remarks to the self-righteous Pharisees who believed they were perfect in God's sight, "They that are whole need not a physician, but they that are sick."

In view of this remark, we should seriously ask ourselves: "Do we need the heavenly Physician?" First, He does what any physician does when we visit, namely, He diagnoses our condition. This Jesus does through the Law because "by the law is the knowledge of sin" (Romans 3:20 KJV). When the Law shows us our sins, which it does because all have come short of God's glory, then we don't need to despair. Instead, we can accept in faith the one, the only, and the sure cure for our spiritual sickness, namely, the righteousness Jesus Himself gained for us as our substitute.

Jesus took those sins on Himself and paid the penalty in full for us. We believe this because "This is a faithful saying, and worthy of all acceptation, that Christ Jesus came into the world to save sinners" (1 Timothy 1:15 KJV).

Lord Jesus, our heavenly Physician, by Your mercy cleanse us from all our sins. Amen.

Lewis E. Eickhoff/June 20, 1963

260

Taking Time Out

He said to them, "Come away by yourselves
to a lonely place, and rest a while."
Mark 6:31 RSV

*I*n sports a coach calls for time-outs to give players a
rest, to correct mistakes, and to slow the momentum
of the opposition.

Time-outs are wise also in everyday life. After the apostles had returned from a preaching mission, Jesus told them to rest a while, to take time out. Our body and mind need periodic relaxation to function effectively. So does our spirit.

We take spiritual time-outs by focusing on God. Sundays are prime time for worshiping God. Bible study is another way to revitalize our spiritual system. We need spiritual breaks throughout the day. We need to remind ourselves: "God is with me. He loves me. He will give me strength."

Like athletes, we take time out to correct mistakes. We ask God to pardon our sins for the sake of Jesus, who shed His precious blood for us.

Time-outs slow down the momentum of our spiritual opposition. We are constantly exposed to evil influences. In time-outs we ask God's Spirit to empower us to resist evil and to be part of God's people in His world.

Holy Spirit, move us to take regular spiritual time-outs so we may praise You and be more helpful to those around us. Amen.

Herbert M. Kern/June 6, 1987

A Crown in Layaway

*Henceforth there is laid up for me the crown
of righteousness, which the Lord ... will award
to me on that Day. 2 Timothy 4:8 RSV*

*M*any stores have a policy of permitting a customer to place items in layaway. The store will place an item in layaway for a certain period of time. The customer pays only a small amount of the purchase price. When the full amount is paid, the item is taken out of layaway and becomes the property of the customer.

St. Paul speaks about a crown of righteousness being laid up for him and awaiting his arrival in heaven. At that time God would give him the crown of eternal life.

We, too, have a crown in "layaway." But we did not pay for our crown. In fact, we did nothing to deserve the crown; on the contrary, we do not deserve to receive this crown at all. It is a gift to us.

Payment was made for the crown by Jesus Christ. He did not pay in money. He paid with His holy, precious blood and with His innocent suffering and death. The crown has been stamped "Paid in full," and it is there awaiting our arrival. On the day of our death God will take it out of layaway and hand it to us. We look forward to this day with joyful anticipation.

O God, help us to be ever mindful of Your just judgment so we may be stirred up to holy living here and by faith dwell with You in heaven. Amen.

William H. Griffen/Feb. 22, 1986

Part-Time Christianity

Be ye doers of the Word, and not hearers only.
James 1:22 KJV

A great musician was in the habit of playing his violin as he made his way homeward through the streets of the city. A woman who enjoyed his music met his wife one day and said, "It must be wonderful to be married to a man like that."

"Yes," answered the wife, "except that he hangs up his violin when he reaches home."

How about us? Do we hang up our Christianity once we reach home after work or after school or after the club meeting? Do we hang up our consideration and courtesy, our even temper and cheerfulness, thus making it difficult for our family members to understand how our friends and acquaintances can speak so highly of us?

The Christian life is not something we can turn off and on according to our mood. The Christian life is a 24-hour-a-day proposition. It is to be just as evident at home as at church. A consistent Christian life is possible when we subject ourselves to Jesus Christ, look to Him as our God and Savior, and let Him live in our lives. Believing in the saving grace of God, we will "live soberly, righteously, and godly, in this present world" (Titus 2:12 KJV).

Lord God, prompt me to live like a Christian each day, all day. In Jesus' name. Amen.

Milton J. Nauss/Aug. 28, 1962

So You Want More Money!

The love of money is the root of all evil.
1 Timothy 6:10 KJV

We are inclined to evaluate people today in terms of what they have, rather than in terms of what they are. Everything about us must proclaim to the world our success. The size of our home announces our importance. Our clothes indicate our status. The horsepower of our cars becomes an extension of our own personality and power.

People will evaluate us in terms of what they see. This is why most of us want more money and what money represents: success, popularity, accomplishment, power. We want to make our position secure; we want to impress and influence others.

Is this wrong? In today's reading Paul helps us reach an answer: "But they that will be rich fall into temptation ... for the love of money is the root of all evil." The emphasis here is not on the evil of possessions or money. In each case Paul's concern is with the *desire* to be rich, the *love* of money. This love is like a weed; slowly it chokes out other desires. It blinds our judgment. We evaluate people and experiences by a warped standard.

This whole process cuts us off from God. It is vicious because wealth may swell our human pride to the point where we feel no need for God. But we need God's cleansing. We need His power to live in a world of possessions—and to love *Him*!

Shed Your divine light on the earth's wealth that we may see it for what it truly is. Amen.

David S. Schuller/Aug. 19, 1959

No Difference?

*There is no difference: for all have sinned, and
come short of the glory of God; being justified
freely by His grace through the redemption
that is in Christ Jesus. Romans 3:22–24 KJV*

We humans are different in many ways. We differ in
appearance, in physical strength, and in skills. We
have different fingerprints and different voices. We have
different feelings and emotions and more. In short, we are
individuals, and it can truly be said: "There is nobody just
like you."

In a very special way, we also must say of the human
race that there is no difference. This refers to our sinful
condition and the means God used for our common
redemption. In plain and simple language, the apostle
Paul tells us that all have sinned and come short of the
glory of God. There are no exceptions, not even one
(Romans 3:12). St. John is just as explicit: "If we say that
we have no sin we deceive ourselves, and the truth is not
in us" (1 John 1:8 KJV).

No one can buy or earn the way into heaven. It can be
obtained only as a free gift by the grace of God through
the redemption that came by Jesus Christ through His
death on the cross. In dispensing His grace, God does not
recognize any difference between Jew or Greek, between
white or black, between male or female. We are all one in
Christ Jesus.

*Lord, I confess my sins and rely only on Your free
grace. Amen.*

William A. Lauterbach/Oct. 17, 1984

THE RIGHT WAY OF ESCAPE

The ungodly shall not stand in the judgment,
nor sinners in the congregation
of the righteous. Psalm 1:5 KJV

*P*eople run away from life. They try to escape from the reality of it all. Some do it by watching television; others by plunging madly into work. Still others dream of getting away to a little desert island all their own. There are all kinds of desert islands—some far away in the South Seas and others in the middle of a crowded city surrounded by millions of people. Some create little islands by drinking themselves into a stupor; others look for them in a dream world of drugs. That's no escape, as anyone who has tried it knows.

There is no escape from God. So there's only one thing to do: Come into the daylight of God's favor and join the company of God's faithful people who don't have to run away because the sins they have confessed can be left in the darkness behind them. By faith in Christ, we come alive and are awake to the world in which we live. We know that Christ is Lord. We have the assurance of forgiveness in Him.

Only God's forgiven people can stand in the congregation of the righteous. They can stand up and lift up their eyes. They are God's men, God's women, God's boys and girls.

Lord, make us see that You alone are God, passing judgment on the world and on all who live in it today. Amen.

Oswald C. J. Hoffmann/Aug. 5, 1972

266

THE NEIGHBOR'S GOOD NAME

Do not speak evil against one another,
brethren. James 4:11 RSV

Gossip is a vile sort of thievery. It robs a person of a most prized possession—one's good name. Wise Solomon: "A good name is rather to be chosen than great riches" (Proverbs 22:1 KJV). Shakespeare: "Who steals my purse, steals trash. But he who filches from me my good name robs me of that which does not enrich him and makes me poor indeed."

In the Eighth Commandment, God has built a fence around our neighbor's good name with the prohibition: "Thou shalt not bear false witness against thy neighbor" (Exodus 20:16 KJV). And James here cautions: "Do not speak evil against one another."

Once evil words have left our lips, they can never be recalled. Gossip is like casting feathers to the winds. They are swept hither and yon, far beyond the reach of the person who cast them. They can never be retrieved. The damage has been done.

We can ask God to help us avoid gossip. The tongue is a two-edged sword that we want to keep sheathed. What is more, we can ask God to help us always to be kind to each other. Then we will not speak evil because kindness precludes evil. Through faith in Christ, our Savior, we receive strength to speak only well of others.

Lord Jesus, keep my tongue from evil and my lips from speaking guile. Enable me to follow You. Amen.

Julius W. Acker/June 23, 1976

Jesus, the Great Physician

"Son, be of good cheer; thy sins be forgiven
thee. ... Arise, take up thy bed, and go unto
thine house." Matthew 9:2, 6 KJV

Several men of faith brought the paralytic to Jesus. Everyone expected Jesus immediately to heal him. However, Jesus knew the sick man's deepest need and therefore said, "Thy sins be forgiven thee." What a burden of sin and guilt was lifted from the man! In healing him, Jesus was true to His mission because He came to seek and to save that which was lost.

Today, too, our greatest need is forgiveness. All have sinned and fallen short of God's glory. How good it is that we can go to God through Christ to receive forgiveness! In His name it is also our privilege, through Word and Sacrament, to say to penitent sinners, "Your sins are forgiven for the sake of Christ."

In our story, the Pharisees accused Jesus of blasphemy, saying, "Who else but God can forgive sins?" Then Jesus showed that He was God when He said to the paralytic, "Arise, take up thy bed, and go unto thine house." To the amazement of everyone, the man arose and walked home.

Because Jesus is our Great Physician, we turn to Him for healing when we are sick. In addition, like Jesus, we show the genuineness of our faith by works of Christian love.

Lord, help us to share Your love with others. Amen.

Henry J. Eggold/Jan. 23, 1977

Do Not Erase!

Take heed lest you forget the LORD your God.
Deuteronomy 8:11 RSV

When Albert Einstein was teaching at Princeton University, he filled the blackboard with complicated equations. At the close of the period, he put instructions for the janitor on the board. Across everything he wrote one word: *erase*. But in one corner, above the simple equation 2 + 2 = 4, he wrote: *Do not erase!*

The significance of Einstein's request seems to be clear. Although we delve into complexities and mysteries, we should never lose sight of simple, foundational truths. That has application in many areas of our life, including our faith life.

Many people are searching desperately to find themselves and their place in a life that seems to have no supportive meaning or purpose. Even Christians may sometimes be plagued with the problem.

Under the influence of the complications and diversions of modern life, we can focus on the simple truths of our Christian faith. We live with the awareness of our amazing God, who created and loves us, who gave His Son to die for our sins, and who asks of us loving service in our stewardship of life.

Loving Father, teach us to find joy in serving You so we do not become unduly concerned about unimportant matters. Amen.

Armin C. Oldsen/May 1, 1981

The Christian Is Holy

Be ye holy in all manner of conversation.
1 Peter 1:15 KJV

God is holy. He is the absolutely pure and Holy One. In Him is no sin or stain at all. Human beings, by contrast, are totally evil, completely unholy. The holy God, because He is also the God of love, bridged that gap by becoming one of us. Jesus' redeeming work, the manger and the cross and all that lies between, spells out the price that He paid to bring us back to God. The holy God has laid His hand on us and claimed us as His own. This grace and mercy of God is the theme of our constant song.

But the joy walks hand in hand with responsibility. The holy God, whose own we are, wants us to be holy. Holy means marked off, separated, withdrawn from ordinary use, dedicated to the service of God. Christians, then, are involved in an obligation to be and to do what is in accord with the character of the Lord, our God. We are committed to a steady effort to express in our lives the evidence that the holy God has chosen us to be His own.

Our lives have much that is routine—sleep, get up, go to school, do the washing and ironing, run the factory machine or a tractor, pound a keyboard, sell the merchandise. Does this become humdrum? Then let us try viewing all our conduct as a daily opportunity to reflect the holiness of God, who has called us to be holy.

O holy and living God, help our daily living to be marked by holiness. Amen.

Ewald J. Otto/Oct. 17, 1959

September 21

GOD'S WATCHFUL EYE

Behold, the eye of the LORD is upon them that
fear Him, upon them that hope in His mercy.
Psalm 33:18 KJV

*M*any years ago the King of England visited
Norwich to lay the foundation stone of a new hospital. Thousands of school children greeted him and sang
for him. After the king had passed the crowd of children,
the teacher saw a little girl crying. She asked, "Why are
you crying? Didn't you see the king?"

Sobbing, the little girl replied, "Yes, but the king didn't
see me!"

How different it is with the Lord, our King! While we
do not see Him, He sees us. "The eye of the LORD is upon
them that fear Him, upon them that hope in His mercy."

God knows those who are His. He has claimed us as
His own through the redemption that is in Christ Jesus.
We belong to Him as His dear children, and He watches
over us.

The Lord's eye on us is a *loving* eye. He sees us as those
whom He has loved with an everlasting love, a redeeming
love. His eye on us is a *merciful* eye. He knows our needs
and well provides for us. His eye on us is a *protecting* eye.
He defends us against all danger.

His eye is on the sparrow. Not one of them will fall to
the ground without God's knowledge and will. Surely,
then, His eye is on us!

*Lord Jesus, look on us in Your mercy and save us.
Amen.*

Elmer O. Luessenhop/May 3, 1969

271

FREE TO PRAY

Christ Jesus our Lord: in whom we have boldness and access with confidence by the faith of
Him. Wherefore I desire that ye faint not at
my tribulations for you, which is your glory.
Ephesians 3:11–13 KJV

What happens when we pray? For one thing, it means that we dare to step into the very presence of God and His holy angels and talk the language of our heart to His heart. Surely it takes a lot of nerve to walk up to God, with all those angels watching and listening!

No, it's not a matter of nerve, but a matter of faith to believe that God our Father wants it that way. Because Jesus is our Lord and is not ashamed of us, we can pray unashamedly and boldly. Jesus paved the way for us.

Jesus has given us the great freedoms of speech, status, and feeling. We can talk to our Father about anything. In Christ Jesus we are His children—by His choice, not ours. We are members of God's household, of His family. Our boldness is not brashness. Instead of wondering whether we have the right to come into His presence, we can be reminded that we have the freedom to do so. This is one of the great privileges God extends to us. We come because He says "Come." We miss much when we do not come. He misses us when we fail to come.

Father, thank You for making us Your children in Christ. Help us to pray boldly and confidently. Amen.

Martin L. Koehneke/Sept. 26, 1974

PEACE OF MIND OR GOD'S PEACE?

Peace I leave with you, My peace
I give unto you. John 14:27 KJV

*N*otice the difference. The peace of God is a gift, not an achievement. Peace of mind is something one can find—must find—if one is to have it. But you can't find the peace of God. It finds you.

The cross brings God's peace. Most Christians recognize the biblical claim that on Calvary Jesus established not just a truce but an alliance between God and us. St. Paul explains it: "You ... have been brought near [to God] in the blood of Christ. For He is our peace" (Ephesians 2:13–14 RSV). In Christ we have a peace that the world cannot give or even understand.

The peace of God that passes understanding rests on the forgiveness of sins. A person who has peace of mind based on personal goodness and competence does not want to talk about sins because it would disturb that peace. God's peace is not only the opposite of peace of mind, it is the end of it. It abandons all satisfaction with the way *we* are managing. It is the end of contentment with oneself and one's good works. It lets go of its grip and settles into the arms of God. Peace of mind disappears at the point where God's peace steps in.

May the peace of God that passes understanding keep our hearts and minds in Christ!

In the midst of turmoil grant us Your peace, O Lord. And being at peace with You, let us be peacemakers on earth. Amen.

Arnold G. Kuntz/March 24, 1974

273

We Can Be Like God

"Be perfect, therefore, as your heavenly Father
is perfect." Matthew 5:48

*I*n the first temptation coming to the first human
beings, Satan convinced Adam and Eve that if they
took control of their own lives, they would be like God.
Tragically, they forgot that they were already as much like
God as any creature could be. Cutting themselves off
from God, they lost the image of God and paradise with
it.

Actually, God wants us to be like Him. Urgently and
lovingly, He coaxes us to be like Him: holy, righteous, loving, and merciful. He wants us to be like His beloved Son,
Jesus Christ, to live and walk with Him so closely that we
begin to think like Him, act like Him, and work with Him
in building His kingdom. When people see us, we want
them to be attracted to the one who gave us the spirit of
regeneration, to be moved by our reflection of God to
glorify our Father in heaven.

By His life, death, and resurrection, Jesus Christ
destroys our old mutinous nature. By Baptism and faith
we are given a "new self, created to be like God in true
righteousness and holiness" (Ephesians 4:24). Some day
we shall be completely restored to that lost image and to
paradise.

*Keep on conforming us, Holy Spirit, to the image of
God by making us more like Christ, our Savior.
Amen.*

Jaroslav J. Vajda/Feb. 9, 1987

PICKED FOR A PURPOSE

To the praise of the glory of His grace, where-
in He hath made us accepted in the Beloved.
In whom we have redemption through His
blood, the forgiveness of sins, according to the
riches of His grace. Ephesians 1:6–7 KJV

When the Holy Spirit calls, gathers, enlightens, and sets His Christian church apart from the world, He does so with a purpose—and to give purpose to our lives.

Lives lived "to the praise of the glory of His grace" are full of purpose for those who live them and full of consequence for those affected by them. Since we have been made acceptable to God in that beloved one, His Son, we accept each other in the family of God and in the world of humanity on these new terms. The voice from heaven that said at Jesus' Baptism and again at His transfiguration "This is My beloved Son, in whom I am well pleased" (Matthew 3:17 KJV) speaks to us just as plainly and reminds us all that God says the same about us and all our fellow Christians.

God has satisfied our deep human need for acceptance. He accepts us with the same good pleasure that He accepted His Son Jesus Christ. This is the way we can accept each other who love the beloved: as brothers and sisters, as equals. This is the way we can reach out to people who are not aware of His love. We who are "graced" can be gracious to all.

Help us to accept each other as You have accepted us. Amen.

Martin L. Koehneke/Sept. 6, 1974

275

A SENSE OF WONDER

The things which have now been announced
to you … things into which angels long
to look. 1 Peter 1:12 RSV

*P*eter had a knack for putting things in a delightful way. He sees angels peeking over God's shoulder to catch a glimpse of the salvation He prepared for all the world. He envisions prophets scratching their heads trying to get a grasp of what God was doing through that Spirit working in them. He describes a profound sense of wonder in those who got only glimpses of what God was up to.

What about our sense of wonder? Is it still there? Have we ever really had it? Astronauts have gone back and forth to the moon. They have lived in space for months. We turn a knob and view an event taking place on the other side of the globe. All this without batting an eye. It is so commonplace. There is little wonder. All we do is shrug and reply, "So what else is new?"

But without a sense of wonder the world is drab and dull. Life is unexciting. That explains the boredom many feel. Can we regain wonder? That depends on whether we recognize the importance of the Good News preached to us. It makes us new. It gives us hope. It offers peace. It brings joy. We do well to take a closer look. A sense of wonder will surely follow.

Father, help me recognize what Your Good News means to me, and restore my sense of wonder. Amen.

Henry R. Schriever/May 3, 1976

Making the Secular Sacred

Whatsoever ye do in word or deed,
do all in the name of the Lord Jesus.
Colossians 3:17 KJV

A scrubwoman, wringing her wet rag over a bucket of water, was once approached by an active church member and asked: "And what work do *you* do for the Lord?" Her answer was simple and direct. "All of it," she replied.

There was perhaps more good theology in those three short words than in any other answer she could have given. In her mind, *all* of her work was being done for the Lord. While it was true that *some* of her tasks were more directly in His service, she nevertheless felt that no matter what the specific task may be, she was always in His employ. She had been saved to serve.

We may learn a lesson from her. The danger today is that we draw too sharp a line between the sacred and the secular—that we consider "church work" sacred and floor scrubbing secular. When we perform our daily tasks "in the name of the Lord Jesus," the secular becomes sacred—it becomes a service of worship to Him who with His blood bought us to be His very own, that we might live under Him in His kingdom and serve Him.

"And then for work to do for Thee, Which shall so sweet a service be That angels well might envy me, Christ Crucified, I come." Amen.

Herman W. Gockel/Oct. 22, 1987

The Oil of Gladness

Thou hast loved righteousness and hated
lawlessness; therefore God, Thy God, has
anointed Thee with the oil of gladness beyond
Thy comrades. Hebrews 1:9 RSV

*A*n old man carried a small oil can with him wherever he went. If he opened a door that squeaked, he oiled the hinges; he oiled the latches of gates that were hard to open. In this way he spent his final years, lubricating wherever he went and making it easier for others to open doors. He meant to be of service.

The lives of many people creak and grate harshly as they continue from day to day. With them nothing is right. They need lubricating with the oil of gladness, compassion, and kindness.

What a blessing to be among God's chosen ones in Christ who have experienced the kindness of God. He sent the Savior, Jesus Christ, anointing Him with the oil of gladness, the Holy Spirit. Through Him the harshness and bitterness is removed from our lives. He enables us to put on kindness as we administer the divine lubricant of His Word to discordant lives.

We may touch other individuals only once or twice, but let us thank God we can touch them with the Gospel as the oil of gladness and forgiving love in Christ Jesus, making sin-rusted lives smooth and joyous.

O God, give us "the oil of gladness" that we may be
a balm of healing to others. Amen.

Frederick C. Hinz/Oct. 29, 1986

ANGELS — HIS MIGHTY ONES

Bless the LORD, O you His angels, you mighty
ones who do His Word, hearkening to the
voice of His Word. Psalm 103:20 RSV

*T*oday is St. Michael and All Angels Day. On this day
we think especially about God's angels, who serve as
His messengers and "do His Word." God has used angels
in the past to announce good news to His world. An angel
told Mary she would become the mother of the promised
Savior. Angels announced to the shepherds the Savior had
been born. An angel told the women at the tomb Christ
had risen and was alive.

Angels also have brought protection and help from
God. An angel protected Daniel from vicious lions. An
angel brought comfort and encouragement to Christ in
the Garden of Gethsemane. An angel brought deliverance
from prison to Peter.

God's angels continue to carry out His will and to help
His people in ways that are not always obvious to our
physical sight. Yet we know that angels are present and
active in serving us, the heirs of salvation. They are interested in our welfare. The good news of our salvation,
writes St. Peter, is something "into which angels long to
look" (1 Peter 1:12 RSV). As a final service, angels will
carry the souls of dying Christians to Abraham's bosom,
or heaven, as Jesus tells us.

*Father, continue to bless us through the ministry of
Your angels, the mighty ones who do Your will.
Amen.*

Stephen G. Mazak Jr./Sept. 29, 1985

Our Father in Christ

For us there is one God, the Father, from
whom are all things and for whom we exist.
1 Corinthians 8:6 RSV

*P*erhaps the greatest but least appreciated privilege given to Christians is the opportunity to address God as "Father." Jesus Himself taught His disciples to address God with an intimacy and familiarity that was very startling to the people of His time.

In one sense, God is our Father simply because He created us. But the basis for calling God "our Father" is that we "are all the children of God by faith in Christ Jesus" (Galatians 3:26 RSV).

We were prodigal sons and daughters who had squandered our inheritance, yet God called us back to Himself. He gave His Son, Jesus Christ, as a ransom to buy us back from our slavery to sin. He has restored us to His family in Holy Baptism, and He clothes us with the perfect righteousness of Jesus Himself. He continues to shower us with His gifts, and He promises that for Jesus' sake we shall inherit everlasting life in the Father's heavenly mansions.

In the context of our redemption and of our adoption by Him, we call on our Father with confidence and boldness, sure in our relationship and certain of His blessings.

Gracious God, we give thanks that through Your Son we can call You "Father." Continue to show us Your favor and mercy. Amen.

David A. Lumpp/Sept. 19, 1984

280

Sure of Our Salvation

*This is the promise that He hath promised us,
even eternal life. 1 John 2:25 KJV*

God wants us to be sure of our salvation. A person in spiritual struggle, driven by doubt and despair, said to a pastor, "I just can't come to the assurance of my salvation." The wise pastor asked: "Whom are you doubting?" This is the way John would answer those who are not sure.

We can be as sure as the unbreakable promises of God. He has promised the gift of eternal life to all who put their trust for salvation in Christ. We can bank on the promises of God without taking a chance. We cannot be sure of our eternal life because we feel it, because we want it, and certainly not because we deserve it. We can be sure of eternal life only because God promised it to all who confess their sin and in faith accept the cleansing through the sacrifice of the Savior.

In Baptism every Christian is anointed with the Holy Spirit, who brings us into the holy Christian church to enjoy the salvation that Christ purchased on the cross. By faith we are clothed in Christ's righteousness, and if we abide in Him, we will never be ashamed before Him at His coming at the end of time. We abide in Him when we remain clothed in His righteousness and walk in His love. Christ will in the Day of Judgment honor the righteousness that He Himself has given.

O dear Lord, help me to abide in faith and love that I may never be ashamed. Amen.

Carl W. Berner Sr./Oct. 11, 1962

281

DISCIPLINED CHILDREN

Blessed is the man whom Thou chastenest,
O LORD, and teachest him out of Thy Law.
Psalm 94:12 KJV

*T*he God who has chosen us to live and reign with Him forever is, above all else, a loving God. Because He loves us, He wants to make something of us.

A father does not show love for a child by allowing the child to do anything he or she pleases. Most very young children would like to eat too much candy, to get too little sleep, and to see what kind of pretty fire they can make with matches.

It goes against our pride to admit it, but in spiritual matters we are all very small children. We need a Father's correction. This does not mean that we enjoy such correction. In fact, like the small children that we are, we often react by throwing temper tantrums or accusing Him of not loving us or threatening to run away from Him.

But there is one great difference between our heavenly Father and our earthly parents. Sometimes parents punish us unjustly, and sometimes they punish us in anger rather than in love. But our heavenly Father never chastens us unjustly, and His chastening is always prompted by love.

The older we become, the more grateful we are for fathers and mothers who did not spoil us. His chastening is an assurance of His love for us.

O loving Father, teach me Your way, if necessary through pain. Amen.

John Strietelmeier/April 21, 1959

THE FORGIVEN FORGIVE

*Lord, how oft shall my brother sin against me,
and I forgive him? Till seven times?*
Matthew 18:21 KJV

*I*t's so hard to forgive. It's so much easier to nurse a grudge and to seek revenge. Peter thought if you forgave someone seven times, that was about enough.

Jesus responded by telling a story. A servant owed his master a large debt. Surprisingly the master forgave him instead of throwing him into prison. Immediately thereafter the servant found a fellow servant who owed him a small debt. Mercilessly he had him cast into prison. When the master heard about it, he withdrew his forgiveness and had the servant imprisoned. The lesson is obvious: "Likewise shall My heavenly Father do also unto you, if ye from your hearts forgive not every one his brother their trespasses" (Matthew 18:35 KJV). Remember that we pray, "Forgive us our trespasses as we forgive those who trespass against us."

We learn to forgive at the foot of the cross where Christ won forgiveness for us all. Now in repentance over our sins we can pray, "Forgive us our trespasses," with the assurance that our prayer will be answered. Having our debt removed, how easy it should be to say to another, "I forgive you because God has forgiven me so much."

Lord God, for the sake of Jesus Christ You forgive us so much every day. Give us forgiving hearts toward others. Amen.

Henry J. Eggold/Jan. 26, 1977

WILL YOU GO AWAY?

Simon Peter answered Him, "Lord,
to whom shall we go? You have the words
of eternal life." John 6:68 RSV

*I*n reply to Jesus' question, "Will you also go away?" (John 6:67 RSV), when many who had been following Him were drawing back from their discipleship, Peter's response was, "Lord, to whom shall we go? You have the words of eternal life."

Tragically, many of Jesus' contemporaries deserted Him. In our day, too, many people who once called themselves Christians have turned their backs on the Lord. They have become lax in their worship. Or for business or social reasons they have found it inconvenient to live their faith. Or they have been ensnared by cults that lead people away from the saving faith.

By God's grace, however, we have come to know Jesus as the Holy One who has the words of eternal life. Jesus came into the world not only to preach the Gospel, but also that by His suffering and death there might be a Gospel to preach.

Our Lord's words of grace are to us the good news that through faith in Him we have eternal life. With the aid of God's Spirit, who strengthens us through Word and Sacrament, we shall remain in that faith to the end and shall inherit eternal life in heaven.

Lord, let nothing draw me away from Your Word of life. Enable me to increase in faith and in its fruits. Amen.

William J. Hassold/Nov. 17, 1985

CONTRADICTIONS
REDUCED TO HARMONY

For everything there is a season, and a time for
every matter under heaven. Ecclesiastes 3:1 RSV

*T*his text has been interpreted fatalistically, as if it
said: When it is time for something to happen, it
will happen—irresistibly, like birth and death. What will
be, will be! Or, reading on in the verses following the text,
one might think that life is full of diversified, if not contradictory, experiences; something new and different is
always happening. One moment there is something sad,
and we weep. The next moment there is something joyful,
and we laugh. Never a dull moment! Who knows what is
coming next?

From this seeming uncertainty, one might draw the
further conclusion that life is a haphazard swirl of pur-
poseless events.

Sometimes believers see with the sight of experience.
More often their perception is with the eye of faith and
hope. Since under the Spirit's power they have seen how
God could make sense out of the apparent foolishness of
Christ's cross as the remedy for sin, they can live with
seeming contradictions. The sight of faith and hope is
part of the believers' equipment for living the life of trust
in a Lord who can reduce all seeming contradictions to
harmony.

*Almighty Father, help us to realize that You are
in control even when events seem jumbled and
contradictory. Amen.*

H. Armin Moellering/Oct. 5, 1980

You Can Be Sure
About God's Love

*We know that all things work together for
good to them that love God. Romans 8:28 KJV*

*T*hese words from Paul's letter to the Romans are
among the most beautiful in the entire Bible. They
are also the most difficult to say at certain times.

When we are enjoying good health or pleasant experiences, we can say, "See how things all work together for
our good!" Or even after we have found the going rather
rough and have been able to see that it was actually to our
advantage, we can say, "It is true! All things do work
together for the good of them that love God."

The real test of faith comes in the very middle of our
difficulties. Then to say and believe that all things work
together for good is not so easy. But because we are sure
of God's love—the proof of it is seen on Calvary—we also
can be very sure that He will bring all things to work for
our benefit.

Had we stood beside the cross of Jesus and seen His
suffering, we might have asked, "How can any good come
out of such suffering?" Now we know that it was all for us
and that without the cross we could never hope to obtain
the crown of eternal life. "God commendeth His love
toward us ... while we were yet sinners, Christ died for
us" (Romans 5:8 KJV).

*Help us, blessed Master, to ever be sure of Your love.
Above all, grant that our love for You may never
waver. Amen.*

Hartwig M. Schwehn/Aug. 3, 1964

On Eagles' Wings

I bore you on eagles' wings. Exodus 19:4 RSV

Sometimes we are fearful to try our wings in a new area of endeavor. We are frozen with the fear of another failure.

One day a fisherman watched a mother eagle drop a young eaglet into the canyon below. The eaglet plummeted and fluttered. It seemed about to be dashed to its death on the rocks below when out of the sky the father eagle plunged and caught his offspring on his broad back. Then he flew up high and dropped the young one again. This time the mother eagle caught the little one on her back. The routine was repeated until the little eagle learned to fly.

God gives us opportunities to try our wings so we might learn to fly on to greater and higher experiences. Often these flights are adventures together with our Lord in ministry to others. Our Father always watches over us and spreads His wings of protection beneath us.

God, who sent His Son to die for us and to lead us through death to life eternal, will certainly not forsake us on our earthly flights.

Mount up with wings like eagles! The Lord will sustain you.

O Lord, when I grow weary, lift me up on Your wings. Give me the courage and strength I need for today. In Jesus' name. Amen.

C. Leo Symmank/July 26, 1987

Remembering His Miracles

His mother said to the servants,
"Do whatever He tells you." John 2:5 RSV

*W*hy? That's a question children often ask when told to do something. Christ's followers perhaps asked it too when He gave directions before some of His miracles. Why fill huge jars with water when there is no wine? Why cast out the nets when we have fished all day and caught nothing? Why begin sharing five loaves and two fish when there are five thousand to feed? Why put mud on the blind man's eyes?

Why? So the water could become wine, so the nets could be filled with fish, so the bread and fish could be multiplied until there were 12 baskets left over, and so the blind man could see.

We don't always understand His ways either. We too ask why. Why are we to forgive 70 times 7? Why must we love our enemies and pray for those who insult and persecute us?

Why? Because the Lord loves us and knows what is best for us. Because He likes to give good gifts to those who ask Him. Because, like Mary at Cana, we can be sure He will supply our needs. Has God not already given us the best gift of all—eternal life through His Son?

Enable us, dear Savior, always to do whatever You ask of us, and help us to see Your hand at work in our lives. Amen.

Marlys Taege/April 14, 1983

OFF THE TRAIL—LOST!

He calls together his friends and his neighbors,
saying to them, "Rejoice with me,
for I have found my sheep which was lost."
Luke 15:6 RSV

*I*n the mountains an average hiker should never set out cross-country. Some think they can find their own way, but they may end up off the trail—lost! Most find their way back eventually; rescue parties find many, but some are never found.

Some terms for sin are transgression, aberration, going astray. All these can be defined as "getting off the trail." Once we sin, we are off God's trail—lost—with no way back. Each time we sin, we need to be rescued.

Jesus is our rescuer. He left the glory of eternity to enter the wilderness of this world. He searched for us lost sinners by perfectly obeying what we disobeyed and by laying down His life to atone for our sin. This He did to rescue all people.

As the Holy Spirit brings us to faith, this rescue benefits us individually because "by grace you have been saved through faith" (Ephesians 2:8 RSV). Christ's work on Calvary is the basis of our daily forgiveness.

Because He keeps forgiving us through faith, we keep coming back to the trail, trying to follow His will all day long.

Thank You, Lord, for daily forgiveness because of Jesus. Help us follow Your will faithfully today. Amen.

Theo. E. Allwardt Sr./Aug. 18, 1987

289

GOD WITH US IN ALL BEAUTY

O LORD, how manifold are Thy works!
In wisdom hast Thou made them all: the earth
is full of Thy riches. Psalm 104:24 KJV

*A*bout this time of the year many parts of the land witness autumn's glorious change of dress. Elsewhere nature still sprouts new blooms. Everywhere God is at work.

Perhaps not all of us have equal opportunity to view the marvels of God's creation, but the wonder of it is there for all who will seek it. Do we still catch our breath at what God has made? Or are we too busy seeking push-button happiness, marveling only in what we have made? St. Augstine once wisely said that people can be measured by the things they prize.

Now let us speak of the best sight of all. It comes when we pause to think quietly on the Lord's goodness and mercy. Nothing can compare with the discovery of God's beauty through worship. "One thing have I desired of the LORD, that will I seek after; that I may dwell in the house of the LORD all the days of my life, to behold the beauty of the LORD, and to inquire in His temple" (Psalm 27:4 KJV).

God is with us, and we can rejoice in all His works. Above all, our hearts are filled with thanksgiving and praise that He has sent His Son so we might see the glories of heaven eternally.

God of all creation and love, open my eyes that I may rejoice in the beauty of Your holiness and find peace at the foot of the cross of Your Son, my Savior. Amen.

Vernon R. Schreiber/Oct. 10, 1965

290

THE INVITING JESUS

Come to Me, all who labor
and are heavy laden, and I will give you rest.
Matthew 11:28 RSV

*A*longside many streets and highways in South India there are stone slabs resting on stone pillars—all about an average adult's height. They are supports that are placed so people bearing heavy burdens, usually on their heads, to or from the marketplace can slide their loads onto the support, rest a while, then comfortably resume their burden and journey.

Christ is our load support because He relieves us of the burdens of our sin and sorrow—not only for a temporary rest but permanently. "Surely He has borne our griefs and carried our sorrows" (Isaiah 53:4 RSV). He did away with our sin and guilt with His sacrifice on the cross. "With His stripes we are healed" (Isaiah 53:5 RSV).

He also gives *rest*—rest for weary souls in a hectic world, rest from the terrors of sin in a Christ-based peace of conscience, the rest of a soul resting in God. This is the rest in Jesus Christ that remains for the people of God (Hebrews 4:9); it begins in grace here and is perfected in glory in the hereafter.

We are weary and heavy laden, Lord. Give us the peace and rest that surpasses all human understanding. For Jesus' sake. Amen.

Andrew J. Buehner/May 4, 1979

291

God Plants His Power

The Gospel of Christ ... is the power of God
unto salvation to every one that believeth.
Romans 1:16 KJV

When God speaks, things happen. When God said, "Let there be light," light came into being. For God to speak is for God to act. His Word conveys His power.

In these last days He has spoken to us by His Son (Hebrews 1:2). The Word was made flesh and dwelt among us (John 1:14). The all-powerful Word of God came in the person of Jesus Christ. He came to heal and to forgive. He came to wrestle with the devil, to defeat death, and finally to win victory over evil. In the life and death of Jesus Christ, the Word of God accomplished the salvation of the world.

The Word of God, all-powerful to accomplish God's purpose, is still at work in the world. Turning our hearts to faith, the Word of God makes saints out of sinners and gives us a peace that the world cannot give.

Like a tiny seed, the Word of God seems insignificant, but it has great potential. It needs only to be planted and it will grow and produce fruit.

Our task is to be where that seed is planted. Our task is to study the Scriptures—the readable Word; to hear the preaching—the audible Word; to use the sacraments—the visible Word. When God sows His seed, He plants His power in human hearts.

Keep us under Your Word, O Lord, and accomplish in us what pleases You. Amen.

Paul J. Schulze/Feb. 16, 1963

"Nevertheless, at Thy Word"

*"We have toiled all the night, and have taken
nothing; nevertheless, at Thy Word I will let
down the net." Luke 5:5 KJV*

Jesus was asking the disciples to let down their nets to catch fish at the worst possible time and place. What He suggested was totally unreasonable. After all, they knew something about fishing. What Jesus was ordering violated their better judgment.

It may have happened to you that you were doing something this way or that without success. Then some Johnny-come-lately entered the picture and suggested smugly—as if he knew something you didn't—that you do something you've been doing all along. "Let down your nets." What did Jesus think they had been doing for the last eight hours?

Peter said: "We have toiled all the night and have taken nothing." But Peter went on to say: "Nevertheless at Thy Word I will let down the net." It didn't matter to him that the advice was unrealistic, that it went contrary to all his experience as a fisherman. It was the Word of Jesus, the Master. Nothing else counted. "Nevertheless at Thy Word ..." Like Peter, we can do what Jesus tells us. In faith we can reply, "Nevertheless at Thy Word." Then anything—even a miracle—can happen in our lives.

We rejoice, dear Savior, that Your wisdom exceeds ours. We will gladly obey Your Word to us. Amen.

Arnold G. Kuntz/March 11, 1974

WESTWARD HO?

As far as the east is from the west, so
far does He remove our transgressions from us.
Psalm 103:12 RSV

*M*any years ago Horace Greeley advised those who wanted to make something of their lives: "Go west, young men, go west." Not only the young but also older people who had made mistakes in their lives had the opportunity to move out west to start over.

Many of us at some point in our life have had to close the book on the past and start life afresh. The wonderfully astounding truth is that God offers us this chance daily. What about our past? Jeremiah quotes God as saying, "I will remember their sin no more" (Jeremiah 31:34 RSV). The past is buried in God's gracious forgiveness on Calvary, where Jesus died for our sins.

We don't have to go west to start a new life. We can start it right where we live. We can look to the cross with trust in Christ's death for full forgiveness of our sins. We can rise reassured that we live forgiven. We can celebrate our new life in Christ by sharing the good news of God's grace with a friend, and we can express our thanksgiving by caring for someone in need. God, who has put our sins behind Him and buried them in the depth of the sea, will be pleased.

Gracious Lord, remember not my sins but remember me always as one in need of Your forgiving love. Amen.

C. Leo Symmank/July 15, 1987

In the Presence of God

*Before they call I will answer; while they are
still speaking I will hear. Isaiah 65:24*

*T*he beautiful picture Isaiah paints for us in this chapter certainly causes us to rejoice. Those of us who have felt the presence of the Lord in our lives will testify that He does hear us when we come to Him in prayer and that, in keeping with His promise, He does grant the petitions of those who approach Him honestly through the merits of the Lord Jesus.

In His High Priestly Prayer, the Lord Jesus repeats again and again the one phrase that helps us understand the verse quoted above. He prays to the Father that we may be in Him and that He may be in us, just as He is in the Father. Our fellowship with Christ by faith keeps us in communion with Him constantly, and He knows our thoughts even before we express them.

In this we can take comfort because regardless of what troubles us, Christ is always present to hear our cries and is eager to come to our rescue. In our Baptism He gave us His Holy Spirit to live with us so as God's children we may enjoy His blessing and the heavenly Father's constant presence.

We thank You, our Father, for allowing us to live in Your glorious presence, thanks to Christ's merit and mediation. Amen.

Carlos H. Puig/Jan. 14, 1988

The First Letter of Peter

Since therefore Christ suffered in the flesh,
arm yourselves with the same thought.
1 Peter 4:1 RSV

A father was heartbroken with grief over the sudden death of his son. In an emotional outburst, he cried, "Where was God when my son's life was snuffed out?" The pastor looked at him and said, "Right where He was when He gave up His own Son." Our loving God does not excuse us from trouble or suffering. We can expect it. He does give us the strength to endure it. Through faith in the Son who died for us, we can overcome all.

Peter's message throws the light of Christ's suffering on the path of our suffering. "Christ also suffered for you, leaving you an example, that you should follow in His steps" (1 Peter 2:21 RSV). Out of His suffering and death came the victorious resurrection. What is true for Christ is true for His followers. Beyond all our suffering is the assurance of "an inheritance which is imperishable, undefiled, and unfading, kept in heaven for you" (1 Peter 1:4 RSV).

We are in God's hands. We can throw the entire weight of our anxieties on Him. And after we "have suffered a little while, the God of all grace ... will Himself restore, establish, and strengthen" us (1 Peter 5:10 RSV).

Heavenly Father, help us heed the Savior's call to take up His cross and follow Him. Amen.

Walter M. Schoedel/May 23, 1971

296

Do Not Sin When Angry

Be angry but do not sin; do not let the sun go
down on your anger. Ephesians 4:26 RSV

*T*he teacher had reprimanded some children for
becoming angry with one another in a game. Later
in the day the teacher became angry when several pupils
repeatedly caused a disturbance in the classroom. When a
girl noticed that the teacher was angry, she asked why it
was all right for the teacher to be angry but not for the
children. The teacher had considerable explaining to do
until all were satisfied that there is a difference between
anger and anger.

There is a difference! Not all anger is sinful. Jesus was
angry, but did not sin, when He chased the money chang-
ers from the temple. It is possible also for us to be angry
without sinning, but it is not easy. Our motives usually
will determine whether our anger is sinful.

For the most part, however, people sin when they are
angry. Such anger manifests itself quickly in malice and ill
will toward the other person. Thoughts of revenge and
retaliation become dominant, rather than the desire to
forgive and forget. What frightful damage is often done
by sinful anger!

However, whether or not the anger is sinful, a good
rule to observe is, "Do not let the sun go down on your
anger." With Jesus let us pray, "Father, forgive them."

*Forgive us, O Lord, our sins of anger and move us
to forgive those who may be angry with us. For
Jesus' sake. Amen.*

William H. Eifert/July 10, 1963

297

INCLUDED IN CHRIST

You also were included in Christ when you
heard the word of truth. Ephesians 1:13

You could size up the situation in a moment. Nine boys were playing basketball on an outside court. One boy had just walked up. He held a ball in his hand, paused, and watched. It didn't take a genius to see that the look in his eye said, "Please, invite me to play." Would the players notice him? Would they include him, or would he be ignored and excluded?

Being included is of great significance to us. Few things are more painful than exclusion. No doubt this is because God made us to have relationships—with Him and with one another. When we are excluded, something at the core of our being is negatively affected. When we are included, that same part of our life is positively affected. No wonder that God speaks in the Gospel to tell us that we are included—included in Jesus Christ and in His entire plan of salvation.

This has powerful meaning. Even the loneliest one of us is not alone. Even if we feel that we are outcasts, we are not cast out of the fellowship of Christ. We are in. We are included. Nothing changes this truth because it is based on Jesus' act of redemption for us all.

Thank You, dear Father, for including me in the fellowship of Your love in Jesus Christ. Amen.

Norbert C. Oesch/April 7, 1989

CHOSEN TO BE CHOICE

He hath chosen us in Him before the foundation of the world, that we should be holy and
without blame before Him in love.
Ephesians 1:4 KJV

Someone has called this verse "St. Paul's first chapter
of Genesis." It tells us of the beginning of God's new
creation, His church. In it we are reminded that God
chose us in Christ Jesus to be His choice people. We are
not Christians by some strange accident of fate. There is
nothing unprepared or unforeseen in God's dealings with
us. His wisdom toward us and His knowledge about us
are as deep as His grace is wide. His new creation is not
limited by geographical, racial, or cultural boundaries.

God's world is a work of time; His church is a work of
eternity. The world is a system; it has a method and a
plan and therefore a foundation. Before the foundation,
there was *the Founder*. In laying His plans for the world,
the Creator had the purpose of His saving grace clearly
in view. Someday we will inherit fully the kingdom "prepared for us from the foundation of the world." Our salvation in Christ is more secure than the foundation of
the world because it rests on Him, the church's one
foundation.

We are chosen to be choice—different, blameless,
loving—in Christ. We are His very special people.

*Thank You, Lord, for choosing us to be choice.
Amen.*

Martin L. Koehneke/Sept. 4, 1974

299

The Value of Daily Devotion

My soul thirsteth for God. Psalm 42:2 KJV

*T*he Christian life is a continuous life. Each day is God's day. We do not serve Him properly if we confine our worship to one day in the week. We should endeavor, God helping us, to make our whole lives an expression of our love and devotion to Him.

No day can be complete without its period of quiet communion with our Lord. If each day has its temptations, requiring strength to resist them; if each day's blessings present reasons for thanksgiving, then each day also needs its period of devotion.

Our lives are busy. The rush of business, social, and recreational life is tremendous. Even a teen lives in a whirl of activity that makes home more or less a dormitory.

How it must wound our blessed Savior to see people crowd their days with this and that, leaving no time or interest for Him! We can ask the Holy Spirit to help us make room in the crowded schedule of our lives for the risen and exalted Lord and King.

Taking time out of a busy schedule each day for Bible reading and prayer will do much to keep alive in our consciousness the precious assurance of our Redeemer's grace and blessing. In that assurance we find strength to meet the tests and challenges of each day with confidence.

Move us, divine Lord and Savior, to take time each day for meditation on Your Word and prayer. Amen.

Edwin L. Wilson/Feb. 15, 1960

Not Guilty—In Christ

It is the Lord who judges me.
1 Corinthians 4:4 RSV

O n the face of it, the above sentence is frightening when we apply it to ourselves. We know all too well the standard that God sets for us, and we realize even more vividly our perpetual failures and shortcomings. We can fool some of the people all of the time, and perhaps all of the people some of the time, but we can fool God none of the time.

The miracle of the Gospel is that we do not have to. God does not simply dismiss our guilt, instead He transfers our blame to His blameless Son. Writes St. Paul: "For our sake [God] made Him to be sin who knew no sin" (2 Corinthians 5:21 RSV). The Lamb without blemish and without spot is judged guilty and is sacrificed in our place. God judges and condemns Jesus Christ; therefore He can judge and *absolve* us.

Once our relationship to God is secure through the work of His Son—and through the Son's work alone—we can announce the Father's verdict of acquittal through Jesus Christ to others threatened by the prospect of God's eternal judgment. Released from the shackles of sin, we are free for service, witness, and worship.

Gracious Father in heaven, we give thanks for Your mercy in Jesus Christ. Through Him we are innocent, and we look forward to everlasting life with Him. Amen.

David A. Lumpp/Sept. 13, 1984

Bring a Friend to Jesus

They went up on the roof and let him down
with his bed through the tiles into the midst
before Jesus. Luke 5:19 RSV

*T*here is a poem about a man who dies and goes to hell. His remarks are directed to an earthly "friend." They had done everything together, sharing hopes, joys, and sorrows. But the friend had never shared Jesus with this man.

The friends of the paralyzed man cared deeply. They took their hurting friend to the only one who could help him. They could have made excuses: there were too many people; the Master might not have time; and the like. But they took a risk. They went beyond a mere gesture of friendship.

We all have friends. We share tools, rides to work, social events, and meals. But do we care enough to share our faith? Do we bring them, hurting in body and soul, to Jesus, the Savior who died also for them? Do we put aside the excuses so they can share eternal life in heaven with us?

No matter what else we share with a friend, when we neglect to say that Jesus died and rose again, we have neglected to offer true friendship—ours and the Lord's. On the other hand, we know what a friend we have in Jesus; to lead others to Him is to let them share His love.

Dearest Jesus, give us courage to bring our friends to You. Help us to love them enough to desire their salvation. Amen.

Gary and Christine Dehnke/May 7, 1988

THE SILENT TREATMENT

A man finds joy in giving an apt reply—and
how good is a timely word! Proverbs 15:23

A frustrated wife says, "He won't say a word. I come to him with my hurts and disappointments. I need his support, but he clams up and refuses to answer me. He doesn't care about me at all. He just buries his head in the newspaper."

How devastating! Sometimes we nag because we want a reaction from our spouse. No answer. We beg and plead. No answer. We try a complaint. No answer. The silent treatment becomes a weapon to frustrate and repay the other person for verbal abuse. We may feel superior for holding our tongue, but often we stand guilty of lovelessness.

Proverbs states the positive value of speaking at the right time: "A man finds joy in giving an apt reply—and how good is a timely word!" We come face to face with our need for forgiveness and our responsibility to forgive one another. Paul says it so well in our Bible reading: "Be kind and compassionate to one another, forgiving each other, just as in Christ God forgave you" (Ephesians 4:32).

Christ knew when to keep silent before His accusers, but He also knew when to speak words of encouragement, caring, and forgiveness. His death on the cross and glorious resurrection makes us His own and frees us to "find joy in giving an apt reply."

Dear Lord, open my mouth to speak the timely word of compassion for Your sake. Amen.

Stephen J. Carter/July 20, 1988

303

Kind, Tenderhearted, Forgiving

Be kind to one another, tenderhearted, forgiving one another, as God in Christ forgave you.
Ephesians 4:32 RSV

*I*t was a sorry scene that greeted Grandma's eyes when she dropped in for a visit at her daughter's house. Scattered on the kitchen floor lay the shattered remains of a piece of prized china. Mother's voice shrilled at the tearful youngster crawling around trying to rescue the pieces. Grandma stooped to help the child. When the last piece had been gathered, she stood up, looked at her daughter, and said quietly, "It was only a cup." Peace, quiet, and happy smiles were restored like magic.

Keeping things in perspective can be difficult at times, but it is a task we can work on in our personal relations. That holds especially true for us who love God and who live each day in the comforting knowledge of His forgiveness. How often doesn't He look in on sorry scenes of our lives with all their mishaps and misdeeds. How beautiful to hear His quiet "Go in peace; your sin is forgiven you."

Broken china or toys can't always be mended. Broken hearts and lives can be mended when we in penitence bring them to the Savior, who went to Calvary's cross to provide perfect healing.

Lord Jesus, keep me mindful of Your forgiving love so I may be kind, tenderhearted, and forgiving. Amen.

Albert W. Galen/March 2, 1987

GOD'S WORD STANDS

Forever, O LORD, Thy Word is settled
in heaven. Psalm 119:89 KJV

*I*n the days of the French Revolution, enemies of
Christianity said to a peasant, "We will pull down your
church steeples. Then you'll no longer have anything to
remind you of God and your religious superstitions." The
peasant replied calmly, "But you will leave us the stars."

No one can tear down the stars. Neither can anyone
destroy the Bible. Century follows century—there it
stands. Empires rise and fall and are forgotten—there it
stands. Storms of hate swirl around it—there it stands.
Atheists rail against it—there it stands. Profane punsters
poke fun at it—there it stands. Unbelief abandons it—
there it stands. Thunderbolts of wrath strike it—there it
stands. Flames are kindled around it—there it stands.

The Bible is as eternal as its author. God's Word will
not pass away. We can lean our weight on it without risk.
It will never crumble. In the Word we come into the presence of greatness. The Word sweetens life. It is an armor
plate against evil. It feeds the soul and brightens the path.
It sets the spirit ablaze. It is God speaking to us, cleansing
us, holding us, leading us into life eternal.

*Lord, the Scriptures testify of You. Therefore help
me to be a Word lover and Word keeper all my life.
Let Your powerful Word grow in me and bring
forth much fruit. Amen.*

Carl W. Berner Sr./Aug. 24, 1975

ONCE FOR ALL

By a single offering He has perfected for
all time those who are sanctified.
Hebrews 10:14 RSV

Some kinds of damage can be made good. If I break glassware in a store, I can pay the purchase price. If I dent a fender, I can have it restored to its original shape. The more serious the damage, the more I must pay.

Other kinds of damage are beyond restitution. How could one replace a human life? or the affection alienated from one to whom it rightfully belongs? or the life stolen away from God and given over to His enemy? Such damage I did to myself in my relationship to God. I did it when I withheld from God the total loving obedience and the perfect trust I owe to Him. I cannot make it up to God.

But Christ could and did make perfect restitution. He replaced my failures with His perfect righteousness. For the cancellation of all my guilt and penalty, He went to His cross for me. By His action I am restored to what I was meant to be. I have been stamped with the sign of the cross of Christ, who made good for all the damage. Covered by His perfection and sacrifice, I am so perfectly restored that I pass my Creator's inspection and He accepts me into His service.

Thank You, Lord Jesus, for clothing me in the robe of Your righteousness. Amen.

F. Samuel Janzow/June 9, 1977

Meet Andrew

And he brought him to Jesus. John 1:42 KJV

*A*lmost every time Andrew is mentioned in the Bible it is thought necessary to explain he is Simon Peter's brother. It takes a lot of grace year after year to stand in the shadow while the other person gets the praise. But Andrew did not complain.

Andrew was always introducing someone to Jesus! First he introduced Peter. What a pillar Peter became in the early church! Suppose Andrew had not brought him to Jesus.

On another occasion Andrew discovered a lad with a lunch. He might have dismissed the lad as having nothing to offer more than five thousand hungry people. But Andrew had the good sense to introduce the lad to Jesus. What Jesus did with that boy's lunch makes a most thrilling story.

Often we are tempted to bypass boys and girls as having nothing to offer to Jesus. That is a mistake. Jesus can take the most unpromising boys or girls and make them instruments of service.

One day some Greeks wanted to meet Jesus and asked Philip to do the honors. Philip asked Andrew's advice. With a vision that included the whole world in its scope, Andrew introduced them to Jesus! Race, color, and class did not stop him!

Andrew was convinced that Jesus was the Savior of all people, not just a few. When we are truly convinced, we too will introduce any and all to Jesus.

Lord, let me speak for You at every opportunity. Amen.

Elmer C. Kieninger/June 10, 1960

PRACTICE FOR HEAVEN

The four living creatures said, "Amen,"
and the elders fell down and worshiped.
Revelation 5:14

*I*n heaven there will be no meetings of the stewardship committee or evangelism board. Much of what is associated with the life of the church will cease, but the worship of the Lamb will remain for all eternity.

St. John gives us a glimpse of this heavenly liturgy in Revelation. At the heart of that service is the Lamb who was slain. Gathered around the throne of the Lamb we see the whole company of heaven—angels, the four living creatures, the elders, and the saints. All join to glorify our Lord in anthems of perfect praise.

The key word in the worship of the Lamb is *Amen.* The Small Catechism reminds us that this word means "Yes, yes, it shall be so." Our liturgy trains us in the reception of God's promises in faith. In our worship we give God the honor of truthfulness by receiving all that He gives with the hearty *Amen* of faith.

As we gather around God's altar with our fellow believers to receive the Lord's Word and His body and blood, we are indeed "practicing" for the day when we will join the angels at the marriage feast of the Lamb in adding our *Amen* to their eternal song of praise.

Lord Jesus, grant that we may worship You with joy in preparation for our perfect worship in heaven. Amen.

John T. Pless/Feb. 3, 1989

NAMES WRITTEN
IN THE BOOK OF LIFE

At that time your people—everyone whose
name is found written in the book—will be
delivered. Daniel 12:1

*I*t is quite a thrill to read your name in print, at least
when it shows that someone noticed, that you mattered to someone in some way. The greatest human thrill
of all comes from hearing that your name occurs in the
book of life. Daniel 11 describes a time of great trouble.
Daniel 12 announces the deliverance of all whose names
are written in God's book. Our names are written there in
the indelible blood of the Lamb who was slain for us, the
Lamb who has promised to confess our names, as He finds
them in the book of life, before His Father and the angels
(Revelation 3:5). Our names are written there, giving us
eternal reservations at the Lamb's high feast. He blots out
our sins, not our names. He assures us a life that never
ends.

That life is not ours to win or earn. It is not possible to
preserve or retain our names in the book of life by our
own efforts. *He* writes, and it is so. *His* writing makes it so.
His choice of us to be His own insures that the blood of
the Lamb is life-giving blood that will sustain our lives in
the day of trouble and all the way into His eternal presence.

*Thank You, Lord, for writing our names in the
book of life. Let us daily rejoice in the life we have
in Your Son. Amen.*

Robert A. Kolb/Nov. 9, 1988

309

A Humility That Exalts

*Humble yourselves before the Lord and He
will exalt you. James 4:10 RSV*

Sometimes a warring nation is defeated because it tried to wage war on two fronts. Christians are fighting a war not on two but on three fronts. They have to contend with the desires of their sinful flesh, with the world around them, and with Satan, the master strategist. Christians cannot prevail against this triple alliance if they stand alone or rely on their own strength. To do so would be to manifest pride, a fruit of the flesh.

Christians do not fight alone. In his hymn "A Mighty Fortress Is Our God," Martin Luther writes, "But for us fights the Valiant One, Whom God Himself elected. Ask ye, Who is this? Jesus Christ it is." It is the same Valiant One who came into this world to destroy the works of the devil. In this He succeeded when He died on the cross and on the third day rose again.

Pride keeps many from relying completely on Christ. They think it is humiliating. So they go it alone, only to learn that the three fronts are too strong for them. It is much better to put pride aside and look to Jesus for the victory. Those who so humble themselves will be exalted.

*Lord, let me experience victory over sin in my life.
Amen.*

David P Scaer/Oct. 22, 1979

IN PRAISE OF GOD'S GRACE
AND GLORY

To the only wise God be glory
for evermore through Jesus Christ! Amen.
Romans 16:27 RSV

O n Oct. 31, 1517, a young monk and professor at the University of Wittenberg, Martin Luther, nailed his 95 theses to the bulletin board on the door of the Castle Church. In this document he invited his fellow professors to a debate. The Reformation historian, Myconius, wrote that the contents spread throughout Germany in 14 days and in a month throughout all Christendom.

In challenging the indulgence traffic, Luther was convinced that the answer to the problem of sin lay in God's Word. While preparing lectures on the Psalms and on Romans, he discovered God as his merciful Father. The key to the Scriptures was God's promise of forgiveness, to be accepted by faith in the redemptive grace of Jesus Christ. Luther noted that we must be truly humble before God and sincerely penitent to receive God's forgiveness. In his theses he stressed that the Gospel is the real treasure of the church, stating that we "should not rely on the treasury of indulgences, but upon the real treasury of God's wonderful grace, the holy Gospel."

This is what the Reformation message is still all about today. To God be all glory!

Merciful Father, we thank You for the revelation of Your mercy and love for us all in Christ Jesus. Amen.

Milton S. Ernstmeyer/Oct. 31, 1978

SAINTS ALIVE!

Greet every saint in Christ Jesus.
Philippians 4:21 RSV

*I*n his novel *1984* George Orwell warned against the devaluation of words. By clever manipulation a perfectly good word can be so twisted as to convey a meaning quite different from the one the word has.

This devaluation of words may take place not only in politics or economics, but also may affect the way that words are used in the church. For example, people often use the word *saint* to describe a person who is exceptionally good or generous, without reference to that person's relationship to Christ. But the Bible uses this word to describe a person who has been declared holy by faith in Christ and is consecrated or dedicated to the Lord. A saint is a person who has been brought into a living relationship with Christ's death and resurrection.

All who believe in Christ, then, are God's saints. We, as Christians, will seek to produce the fruits of faith in our lives. By these fruits, which show that God is at work in us, we will demonstrate to the world that we are truly God's saints. And, by confession of faith and by our good works, we as saints will be glorifying our Father in heaven.

Grant us, O Lord, that we who are Your saints may dedicate ourselves to live for Your glory. Through Jesus Christ. Amen.

William J. Hassold/Nov. 1, 1985

WHAT SHALL I DO?

[The rich man] thought to [himself],
"What shall I do, for I have nowhere to store
my crops?" Luke 12:17 RSV

*T*he rich man is struggling with a problem, the kind most of us would like to have—having too much. But the *real* problem is making the right decision. So the man decides for bigger barns, more room, larger investments, which will lead to ease and fun! With a smile of anticipation he turns in for the night as on any other night, but this was for the last time.

As carefully as this man had planned, it was all in terms of *me*, *my* possessions, *my* years. Spiritual considerations—God, soul, eternity—were left out.

Decisions—we too must face them: What shall I do with my life, my career, my time, my money? In all our planning, dare we forget what this man forgot? How can we plan, even for a moment, without God? Life is surely more than fine food, fun, and fancy living! Who knows how near death we may be?

Above all, how can we omit from our planning the one who entered our world to make God our reconciled Father, to make life worth living, death worth dying, and eternal life a certainty?

"God of mercy, God of light, In love and mercy infinite, Teach us, as ever in Your sight, To live our lives in You." Amen.

Albert W. Galen/March 7, 1987

313

A Comforter, Indeed!

It is the Spirit Himself bearing witness
with our spirit that we are children of God.
Romans 8:16 RSV

A Christian day school teacher was using the final few moments of Friday afternoon to review the week's work. She asked a first-grader: "Of all the Bible passages we learned this week, which one did you like best?"

After a moment's thought, the little one rose to her feet and with no small amount of pride blurted out: "The one that says: 'Don't worry, I'm going to get the quilt for you.'" Puzzled for a moment, the teacher realized that the child was referring to the passage: "If I depart, I will send [the Comforter] unto you" (John 16:7 KJV).

We may smile, but in one sense the child's use of the word *quilt* was not entirely out of place. In those moments when our accusing conscience will give us no peace, the Holy Spirit, the Comforter, reminds us through the Word that we are covered with the robe of Christ's righteousness. The Spirit soothes our fears. He dries our tears. He covers us and comforts us with the assurance that we are still God's children through Jesus Christ. He is our Comforter, indeed!

Lord, may Your Spirit bear witness with our spirit that You are, indeed, our loving Father through Christ Jesus. Amen.

Herman W. Gockel/Oct. 24, 1987

God's Warmth
for Our Coldness

He sends forth His Word, and melts them;
He makes His wind blow, and the waters flow.
Psalm 147:18 RSV

*T*he weather can make a vacation trip pleasant and memorable or miserable and forgettable. In summertime we prefer cool places, away from the sun's scorching heat. In wintertime we are drawn away from cold and snow to places where the sun shines warmly. It has been said, "As a rule, a man's a fool. When it's hot, he wants it cool. When it's cool, he wants it hot. He's always wanting what it's not."

It's that way on the trip of life too. How often we find ourselves saying: "I don't want … I can't stand … I just won't …" Quite often we are like the weather: hot with anger but cold in our love. Speaking of the last times, Jesus said, "Because wickedness is multiplied, most men's love will grow cold" (Matthew 24:12 RSV).

There is only one thing that can thaw the coldness of a self-serving life: the warming love of God, expressed in the person of Jesus Christ and in the performance of His redeeming work. What is our response? Surely that of the hymn writer: "As Thou hast died for me, Oh, may my love to Thee, Pure, warm, and changeless be, A living fire."

Lord, by the power of Your Spirit melt the ice of my life. With Your loving presence, warm me on life's journey. Amen.

Theodore A. Daniel/Aug. 23, 1979

THE LONG, HARD ROAD

Happy is the man that findeth wisdom and the man
that getteth understanding. Proverbs 3:13 KJV

When our Lord was born in Bethlehem, Wise Men from the East tried to find Him. They found Him because they were wise enough to follow God's directions, wise enough not to be offended at where they found Him, and wise enough to come worship Him.

There is something sudden, startling, and satisfying about the discovery of wisdom. It brings a sense of thrill and relief. To get understanding is equally satisfying, even though we must walk such a long, hard road to get it! Our God teaches us many lessons, and often we are such unwilling students!

To understand His love for us, He teaches us to understand our great need for His love. The more we understand how rebellious we are, the more we understand how reconciling He is. The more we understand our weakness, the more we understand His strength. So He leads us day by day in ways strange to us but clear to Him.

In hours of loneliness we discover how close He can be. On sickbeds we can take time to look up to see His face shine on us. At the death of a Christian we can learn better to know Him and the power of His resurrection. When He rebukes us for our sins, we realize that He is truly the friend of sinners.

Lord, do not become impatient with us, but lead us
on the way to a better understanding of Your great
love in Christ for us. Amen.

Martin L. Koehneke/Sept. 2, 1964

316

The Valley of Decision

LORD, who shall abide in Thy tabernacle?
Psalm 15:1 KJV

*H*ave you ever been faced with a serious problem of right or wrong, a question that tormented your heart? Even an ordinary decision is difficult enough— whom to marry, which job to take, where to live, when to retire, what profession to follow. But if your soul is at stake, the anguish is tenfold.

In the days of the Reformation, Martin Luther was faced with such a problem. Even for this learned professor of theology, the answer was difficult.

Was it not wrong to speak against the church? Was it not wrong to throw off the vows of loyalty he had once taken as a monk? If he attacked the doctrines of the church, was he not attacking God Himself?

For months and years Luther tortured his soul with such questions. Daily he consulted the Scriptures and his conscience. His decision, publicly announced in the city of Worms, set a pattern for every Christian:

"Unless I am persuaded by the Scriptures or by plain reason—I distrust popes and councils because they have often erred and contradicted themselves—my conscience is captive to the Word of God. I cannot and will not revoke anything, for to act against conscience is wrong and dangerous. Here I stand. God help me. Amen."

In temptation and in doubt, O God, be my guide to the truth of Your Son. Amen.

Theodore J. Kleinhans/Oct. 31, 1960

"I Helped Her Cry"

Jesus wept. John 11:35 RSV

*M*ary's doll got broken, and I stopped to help her," a little girl told her mother.

"What did you do? Did you help her mend her doll?" her mother asked.

"Oh, I just helped her cry," her daughter explained.

You, too, can help someone cry—a girl with a broken doll, a boy with a wrecked truck, a divorcee with a fractured marriage, a patient with failing health, a middle-aged person with shattered dreams, an alcoholic who has become the slave of a relentless master. Weeping with those who weep can be therapy for them.

Our empathetic Lord once helped Mary and Martha cry over the broken life of their dead brother, Lazarus. "Jesus wept," we are told in the shortest verse in the Bible.

Not only over fractured things, but also over mended things we can help each other cry "tears of joy." There can be joyous reconciliations with tears if we include estranged brothers, sisters, or other members of the family in approaching Thanksgiving Day dinners and other get-togethers. This is in keeping with the blessed truth that "God was in Christ, reconciling the world unto Himself, not imputing their trespasses [and broken relationships] unto them" (2 Corinthians 5:19 KJV).

Lord, make us sympathetic to one another's problems. Amen.

Elmer E. Maschoff/Nov. 11, 1981

Friends Along the Way

The soul of Jonathan was knit with the soul
of David. 1 Samuel 18:1 KJV

*T*here was a friendship that always will be remembered. There were several things that brought these young men together, but it was their common faith in God that made it the beautiful and unselfish thing that it was. Here were friends who could talk to each other about God; who showed to each other something of the love that God showed to each of them; who committed each other to the care of God; who, as children of God, showed a loving concern for each other. Here were two friends who walked the path of faith together.

Our dearest friend is Jesus, the friend who gave His life for us and who "sticketh closer than a brother" at all times (Proverbs 18:24 KJV). Since we are creatures who need human companionship along the way, we can choose friends who know and love Jesus as we do, friends who also are traveling the way to heaven, friends with whom we can share our Christian faith and hope, friends who will strengthen us in times of temptation and weakness and lift us when we fall, friends who will help and not hinder us along the way to heaven.

Happy the person who has such a friend. If I want that kind of friend, I should be that kind of friend to others. Am I?

Give me, Lord Jesus, friends who will help me on the way to heaven, and help me to be such a friend to others. Amen.

Felix Kretzschmar/Sept. 19, 1963

319

A Question of Humble Awe

When I look at Thy heavens, the work
of Thy fingers, the moon and the stars which
Thou hast established; what is man that Thou
art mindful of him, and the son of man that
Thou cost care for him? Psalm 8:3–4 RSV

*I*f we want to know what David felt as he asked the
above question, all we have to do is look up at the sky
some clear night, preferably in a place away from the distraction of artificial light. So many twinkling stars, so far
away in the deep vastness of space! How tiny and insignificant we feel: mere pinpricks in this seemingly endless
universe! How can the great Creator of it all, busy with
the countless soaring galaxies and each galaxy's number-
less orbiting and rotating star systems, know about us here
on earth? How can He have any time, any concern, for us,
such seemingly small beings?

Yet God does know us, each one of us—knows all about
us! And God cares! As awe-inspiring and humbling as are
the heavens, with sun and moon and stars, we are most
amazed by God's love for us. So great is that love that He
sent His only Son in grand fulfillment of David's Psalm
8—to leave heaven's glories and to spend some time a little lower than the angels, as one of us on this tiny globe,
to die for our sins and to rise again for our salvation.

*O Savior, we stand in humble awe before Your love
for us. Amen.*

Martin J. Schmidt/June 6, 1979

It's Hard to Do the Easy Thing

*My father, if the prophet had commanded you
to do some great thing, would you not have
done it? 2 Kings 5:13 RSV*

Naaman was the victim of leprosy, a ghastly disease. He could look forward only to a steady progression of decaying flesh. Society, unable to accept such disfigurement in its midst, would soon cast him out to wander on the fringes of human habitation. Before long this important public figure would be required to ring a little bell and cry a warning to any chance passerby. Those whom he had called friends would reject him.

Naaman was a desperate man, ready to do anything to halt his terrible disease, including listening to the advice of a servant girl. She recommended a prophet of her homeland. There he found no ready reception. No one came out to probe his flesh, peer into his eyes, take his medical history. "Take a bath!" he was advised. "Take a bath?" Had he wanted to bathe, he could have stayed at home. Except for the servant's pleading, he would have stormed home unhealed.

We at times dismiss some things as too easy and disregard them. Does salvation by grace, without good works, seem too easy? So some think. But it is through Christ, rejected by many, that we are saved.

We look for hard things to do, O Lord Jesus, when You ask us only to believe. Amen.

Alston S. Kirk/May 20, 1989

Lest We Forget

Only take heed ... lest you forget.
Deuteronomy 4:9 RSV

*F*orgetfulness is often more than just a weak memory. It may well be a result of pride. We are inclined to forget what we consider not important enough for us to remember. As we thus pass our own judgment on issues or events, we set ourselves up as superior to what we forget. All the while, forgetfulness also has its proper place.

Some things we must forget, as God also no longer remembers our forgiven sins. To forget our own good deeds, as well as the wrongs others have done to us, is one part of the new life in Christ. Yet at the same time we need to be reminded of what we should remember.

Today is Veterans Day. It is a day for remembering persons, human acts, and events through whom and through which the merciful goodness of God overrode the evil of humanity to grant blessings to many parts of the world. There is much of human failure in the records of the wars in which people serve their countries, much that demands repentance, much of which we cannot be proud. But there is likewise much for which we need to be humbly grateful to God and to those who served us well. We surely pray and work for peace, but when war is unavoidably thrust on us, may God turn it to good.

God of the nations, we thank You for the service of our veterans. We ask You to be with those who now serve. Amen.

Daniel E. Poellot/Nov. 11, 1970

DARK DAYS—LIGHT DAYS

The LORD is my light and my salvation; whom
shall I fear? The LORD is the stronghold of my
life; of whom shall I be afraid? Psalm 27:1 RSV

*R*ead my favorite Scripture," said an aged mother to
her pastor. "It's Psalm 27." Her pastor knew why.
With only one limb, an arm, still usable, she experienced
the usual dark days of trial. Yet for her the opening words
of this psalm of David were especially meaningful because
she was blind. With the psalmist the dear old mother was
saying, "The LORD is my light."

King David, who did much to enlighten the people of
Israel, knew well that his light, like the light of the moon,
was borrowed. It was not his own. His light came from
above, shining through the pages of prophecy to the glorious Christ who fulfilled the prophecies, saying, "I am
the light of the world." So that all would know that
David's light had more than earthly value, he acknowledged the Lord as not only his light but also his salvation.

There is nothing greater than the darkness of sin. Yet
Christ in His death and resurrection overcame spiritual
darkness with the light of salvation. "In Him is no darkness at all." Because of Christ's death and resurrection, we
walk as children of light.

*"O Christ, our true and only Light, Enlighten
those who sit in night." Amen.*

Ihno A. Janssen/April 24, 1982

323

To Know Him Is to Love Him

Draw near to God and He will draw near
to you. James 4:8 RSV

A father visits his freshman son at college. They discover that after 18 years of living together at home, of exchanging gifts and conversing a great deal, they do not really know each other. The investment of all those years on the part of both of them is lost. There is no deep communion between them. If only they had earlier found the way to reach each other's heart!

It takes a lot of communicating to know someone well. Couples can be married for 25 years and still not really know each other. They can learn to know each other by feeling open and receptive to each other about their deepest feelings and longings.

Praying is the revealing of one's heart to God and a searching of God's heart for a response. Or the other way around: It is a searching of God's heart for His will for us, and our response to that loving concern. It is a meeting on a level far beneath the surface formalities.

What a pity if one's relationship to God never gets beyond the formalities of an occasional nod or remark in His direction! But what a richness for our life when we get to know Him intimately as our Father in Jesus Christ, our Savior! It is good instruction that St. James gives us in the above text: "Draw near to God and He will draw near to you."

Precious Friend, draw near to me so I may know
You and Your love for me better each day. Amen.

Jaroslav J. Vajda/May 14, 1977

324

YESTERDAY

Remember Thy Word to Thy servant.
Psalm 119:49 RSV

We usually think of yesterday as the day immediately preceding the one in which we are now living. In terms of time, yesterday always represents the past, whether 24 hours ago or 24 years ago.

All of us live in the past to a degree. That is what makes memory possible. Memory allows us to relive pleasant moments and to recall happy associations. In many ways the recollections of our yesterdays provide us with joys for today and hopes for tomorrow.

Our memories can focus, though, not only on the pleasant but also on unpleasant events of our lives—on mistakes and injustices. Sometimes we dwell too much on the unpleasant experiences of our past. The result can be feelings of insecurity, bitterness, and guilt. Our problem often is that we forget what we should remember, and we remember what we should forget.

God has both a short and a long memory. He remembers us in His grace. He remembers that the redeeming work of His Son was for us. Let us remember that too. God forgives and forgets our past iniquities. "As far as the east is from the west, so far does He remove our transgressions from us" (Psalm 103:12 RSV). Let us forget them too.

Lord God, heavenly Father, help us to forget what we should not remember and to remember what we should not forget. Amen.

Wilbert J. Fields/March 21, 1977

325

Jesus Can Be Bothered

"Suffer the little children to come unto Me,
and forbid them not." Mark 10:14 KJV

O nce the disciples of Jesus thought their Lord should not be bothered by some parents who "brought young children to Him, that He should touch them" (Mark 10:13 KJV). The disciples scolded them for troubling Jesus. Jesus in turn faulted His disciples for giving the impression that He could not be bothered by little children!

In a scene so memorable that few Christians will ever forget it, Jesus "took them up in His arms, put His hands upon them, and blessed them" (Mark 10:16 KJV).

Disciples of the 20th century need our Lord's rebuke if they think it is such a bother to educate His lambs in the best possible way. If we deprive children of the privilege of becoming intimately acquainted with their Savior on the false pretense that we cannot afford to bother Him, He wants it clearly understood that we are the ones who are wrong and that it is we who do not want to be bothered! He wants us to take time to bless His little lambs!

All His children need to understand that Jesus is never too busy to be bothered by them. Have you "bothered Him" in your prayers today? Have you come today to His cross to find forgiveness and peace?

Lord Jesus, forgive me when I get so busy that I cannot be bothered with You. Give me the grace to place You first in my day. Amen.

Martin L. Koehneke/Sept. 6, 1981

CLOTHED IN CHRIST'S RIGHTEOUSNESS

Blessed is he that watcheth and keepeth
his garments, lest he walk naked and they see
his shame. Revelation 16:15 KJV

*T*he God who has chosen us and who seeks to make us blessed is a great King. We do not come swaggering into His presence, wearing any old thing that happens to please us. He has given us a princely robe to wear, and this robe is the only acceptable dress for His children.

This robe is the robe of holiness that becomes ours when we share in the death and resurrection of His Son, Jesus Christ. This we put on in Holy Baptism, in which our old nature is drowned and dies and in which we are created anew after the pattern of Jesus Christ. We miss out on much of the joy of life simply by forgetting what a great thing happened to us when we were baptized.

Sometimes we are tempted to suppose that we can design better garments for ourselves or even that we are so personally attractive that we need no clothing at all. Sometimes the robe seems to be an annoyance or a handicap to certain activities that we would like to engage in, and we are tempted to take it off for a while.

But this robe, and only this robe, makes us pleasing in God's eyes. If we would be truly blessed, we will watch it and keep it and never lay it aside.

O God, who has given me the uniform of a prince of heaven, grant me grace to wear it always gladly and proudly. Amen.

John Strietelmeier/April 14, 1959

Fragile: Handle with Care

Let me know how fleeting my life is!
Psalm 39:4 RSV

*L*ife is short; it is also fragile. It hangs on a breath. That does not make life any less precious. In fact, the very opposite is true. Its preciousness is that despite its brevity and tenderness, life is full of opportunity for glory.

A soap bubble is not a very durable thing. Yet in its moment of existence it is capable of refracting all the colors of the rainbow.

Our Lord's life was like that: It came to an abrupt conclusion. Yet in a short time, He fulfilled much. In His brief days and years, all the glory of God shone through. "In Him," the apostle says, "all the fullness of God was pleased to dwell" (Colossians 1:19 RSV).

We have come to fullness of life in Jesus, God's Son. There can be nothing petty or mean about our living. Although we may be placed in the shadows of life, we can find our joy in doing humble tasks for the love of God. Our humanity is judged not by sheer volume but by the quality of Christlikeness that shines through us.

Our life is frail and fleeting, but the indwelling Christ gives it power and purpose. We say with St. Paul: "I have been crucified with Christ; it is no longer I who live, but Christ who lives in me. ... I live by faith in the Son of God, who loved me and gave Himself for me" (Galatians 2:20 RSV).

Lord, may the small vessel of our life be full of Christ. Amen.

Kenneth Schueler/Jan. 7, 1970

HE CAME AS FORETOLD

In thee shall all families of the earth be blessed.
Genesis 12:3 KJV

A doctor received an emergency call from a home far from town. Not sure of the way to the home, the doctor said, "Put a light in your window, then call your neighbor and ask him to do the same. Have the same word passed from neighbor to neighbor all the way to town." The doctor followed the trail of lights and reached the home.

Christ was born as prophets had foretold. The promises of God in ancient times were a trail of lights that led to Bethlehem and the Savior who was born there. God's promise to Abraham was among the first of those lights. Other lights appeared as God repeated His promises and added more details. All pointed to Christ, born to bring God's love and the blessings of salvation to all the nations of the earth. When Christ appeared among men, Philip said of Him. "We have found Him of whom Moses and the prophets did write" (John 1:45 KJV).

The promises of God find their "yea and amen" in Christ. God never made a promise He couldn't keep or didn't intend to keep. Of Abraham it is written, "He was absolutely sure that God would be able to do what He had promised." Happy the man who has no doubts about Christ as the Savior God promised!

Remove all our doubts, O God, and help us to believe in Christ as the Savior whom You promised. Amen.

Felix H. Kretzschmar/Dec. 3, 1970

329

WHAT THE DEVIL DESIRES

Then the devil comes and takes away the
Word from their hearts that they may not
believe and be saved. Luke 8:12 RSV

Some think of Satan as a mischievous "little imp" whose goal is to get us to commit harmless little sins. Actually he is out to get us to do something much more serious than that. It's a relationship he's out to wreck. It's a fellowship he wants to ruin. He's not merely determined to get a person to commit sins; he wants something greater. He wants us to reject the Father-child relationship between God and us. He wants us to disclaim our adoption into God's family. He wants us to resist the Holy Spirit through whom alone we can know Jesus as our Savior.

That's what he's after. That is what Satan was trying to do to Jesus in the wilderness. He wanted Him to abandon the Father-Son relationship with God and to disobey His Father's will. But Jesus rejected that temptation. He rejected it throughout His ministry. When He died on the cross for our salvation, He overcame Satan once and for all.

That's good news for us. In Christ's obedience and saving death, our place with God is safe and secure. In Jesus' name we too can reject the temptation of Satan.

Holy God, we want You always as our heavenly Father. Never let Satan tear us away from You. Amen.

Paul A. Boecler/Feb. 5, 1976

A Poor Bargain

Thus Esau despised his birthright.
Genesis 25:34 RSV

*E*sau and Jacob were twin brothers. Esau, the firstborn, was ordinarily entitled to the birthright. Jacob, the younger, assured of it by promise, desired the blessing. We cannot justify the means he used to obtain it.

One day Esau came in from a hunting trip. He was half-starved, and he asked his brother for something to eat. Instead of giving his brother food, Jacob struck a hard bargain: "First sell me your birthright." Without hesitating, Esau accepted the bargain for a mess of pottage and thus despised the birthright.

We Christians have a birthright, and it is ours by promise. This birthright is our inheritance incorruptible and undefiled, reserved in heaven for us through the merits of Christ, our Savior.

How Satan tries to rob us of our birthright! He sets up messes of pottage that look very tempting. In times of need he tempts us with recipes on how to get rich quick. In times of discouragement he concocts a dish of worldliness, inviting us to eat, drink, and be merry. We can ask the Holy Spirit to keep us always on guard for anything the devil or this world has to offer. "What does it profit a man, to gain the whole world and forfeit his life?" (Mark 8:36 RSV).

Lord, deliver us from every evil. Amen.

Lewis E. Eickhoff/Sept. 12, 1979

N Is for *Name*

God is known in Judah; His name is honored
in Israel. Psalm 76:1 TEV

What's in a name? Any parent who has chosen a name for a child knows the challenge of that task. Much thought is required.

Parents in ancient Israel had an even harder time than we do today. Traditionally, a name was to tell something about that individual. Naming a child was a chance to express religious convictions or to indicate something about the child's future according to the parents' hopes.

What's in a name? The name of God is more than a name, for example, when we open a liturgical service in His name. We remember our Baptism performed in the name of the Father, Son, and Holy Spirit. In using God's name we once more affirm our faith in Him and acknowledge His presence.

What's in God's name? The psalmist says that to know the name of God is to know God. As Christians, we know God as holy, all-powerful, and, through Christ, the giver of salvation.

For the Christian, God's name is more than a simple three-letter word. It is a name above all names, one that offers assurance of everlasting life. God's name is God Himself.

Triune God, You placed Your name on us in Baptism. Lead us to trust in You always. Amen.

Henry A. and Mary Manz Simon/July 16, 1982

INDISTINCT SIGHT

Now we see in a mirror dimly, but then face
to face. Now I know in part; then I shall
understand fully, even as I have been fully
understood. 1 Corinthians 13:12 RSV

*I*f God knows everything, why did He let sin enter the
world?" This question is often asked. There are other
questions like that one. An honest reply is needed. It is
this: "We don't know the answer." But doesn't that bring
our whole faith into question? Shouldn't we be able to
answer the whys and hows? Why are some people saved
and others damned? Why was Jesus' death necessary to
save the world from sin? Why? Why?

From our point of view from our tiny spot in the vast
universe, with our limited mind and our understanding
twisted by sin, we cannot see all; we cannot grasp all the
answers. There are mysteries to our faith, which point to
the authenticity of our religion. Our God is not cut down
to our size. We do not have a God who is neatly cataloged
by reason.

The Gospel itself, the message of the atoning death of
Christ, is beyond human understanding. It is a mystery
only God Himself perceives. God's acts often leave us perplexed, but where do we get the idea He must leave us
simplified blueprints of His plans for His world? Thank
God for a Lord who is bigger than we are!

*Lord, keep awe and mystery in our faith. Help us
grow in the saving knowledge of Your revealed
truth. Amen.*

George R. Kraus/May 26, 1973

333

The Attitude of Gratitude

O give thanks to the LORD, for He is good;
for His steadfast love endures for ever!
Psalm 107:1 RSV

We human beings find ourselves in quite a fix. Insofar as we are rational beings, we are capable of setting noble goals for ourselves. But because of the weakness of our wills, we sometimes lack the ability to achieve them.

This is true also with respect to the Christian virtues that we seek to cultivate in our lives. We know, for example, that we are to be thankful to God for His abundant blessings to us. We may even sincerely *want* to be grateful. But this is not the same as being thankful.

Genuine gratitude is possible only when there is a change of heart. Thanksgiving begins with seeing ourselves as God sees us, unfaithful and unprofitable servants who deserve nothing but punishment and death.

From this perspective, the unexpected and undeserved goodness of God in sending His Son, our Lord Jesus Christ, to die for us is overwhelming. It transforms us and produces within us an attitude of gratitude that causes us to exclaim from the heart, "O give thanks to the LORD," not only for spiritual blessings but also for physical blessings too numerous to count.

Lord God, send Your Spirit into our hearts and give us an attitude of gratitude. In Jesus' name. Amen.

Samuel H. Nafzger/Oct. 12, 1988

Blessed to Be a Blessing

I will bless you, and make your name great, so
that you will be a blessing. Genesis 12:2 RSV

"Count your blessings!" we are told. Quickly now,
without too much thought, say the ones that come
to your mind.

Did you remember the blessings God gives you in His
love and grace and forgiveness—in making you His? Did
you think of the gift of His Spirit in your life? These alone
are good enough reasons to thank the Lord.

As God's blessings are freely given for the benefit of
His people, they also rub off on others. We are blessed to
be a blessing. "His face [shines] upon us. … that … [His]
saving power [may be known] upon the earth" (Psalm
67:1–2 RSV). To share His love and grace and forgiveness
is the greatest thanks we can give back to God. Other peoples' lives are better, both spiritually and materially,
because they have crossed our path. Is that the way it is?
It should be.

Think about this: If I set my goal to share just one
blessing each day, what a blessing I will be to others!

What blessing can I pass on today? Whom will the
Lord put in my path so I can share a listening ear; some
quiet good manners or considerate action; a happy, sunny
disposition; a witness of my faith?

*Lord, help me to see the opportunity to pass Your
blessing on to someone else today. Amen.*

Louise Mueller/July 13, 1984

THE UNKNOWN HOUR

Of that day and hour knoweth no man, no,
not the angels of heaven, but My Father only.
Matthew 24:36 KJV

When Christ was teaching His disciples privately on
the Mount of Olives, they asked Him, "When
shall these things be? and what shall be the sign of Thy
coming, and of the end of the world?" (Matthew 24:3
KJV). Christ did not expressly answer these questions. A
definite day and the exact moment for the end to appear
are fixed, never to be changed. But these things are to be
found only in the knowledge of the Father.

There has been a long parade of would-be prophets
presumptuous enough to set a time for the appearing of
Christ when He will come to judge. No such time setter
will ever succeed. Christ said that no man, not the angels
of heaven, not even the Son according to His humanity,
but only the Father knows of that day and of that hour. St.
Luke wrote in Acts 1 that Jesus explained to His disciples,
"It is not for you to know the times or the seasons, which
the Father hath put in His own power" (1:7 KJV).

We do not need to know the exact time. Because we
live in faith in Him who gave His life to take our sins
away, we are always ready for Christ's return on that
unknown hour.

Heavenly Father, help us to walk with Jesus day by
day that we may rejoice to see Him when He comes
again. Amen.

Earl E. Weis/Dec. 16, 1982

336

CHRIST IS THE LIGHT

The light shines in the darkness, and the darkness has not overcome it. John 1:5 RSV

*I*n Carlsbad Caverns the lights are turned down to a soft glow to aid the tourists as they view the formations. On one occasion they failed to come back on when the guided tour had ended. A small girl, clutching firmly to her older brother's hand, became frightened and asked him what they should do now. Her brother confidently replied, "Don't worry, there is someone here who can turn the lights on."

When life presents us with many setbacks and the horizon seems dark, "there is someone here who can turn the lights on." It is He who turned them on for Paul in the darkness of a prison, for Job in the darkness of despair, for the thief in the darkness of crucifixion agony.

Jesus Christ turns the light on in the personal darkness that we have because He is the light of the world. He is the light because by His life, death, and resurrection He overcame the darkness of sin. To believe that there will be sunshine in the morning while we are still engulfed in the darkness of a stormy night—this is the essence of hope. It is the kind of hope that springs from a believing heart. Christ makes that hope become a reality.

Lord, illumine our darkness with Your presence. Amen.

Charles Dickson/Oct. 5, 1975

Hard at Work

For this I toil, striving with all the energy
which He mightily inspires within me.
Colossians 1:29 RSV

We dare not tell older people that life in Christ is just a breeze. They know better. We have no right to tell young people that the Christian faith makes no demands on them. They know better. Either faith in Christ makes a difference in our lives, or it is not faith at all.

Being a Christian did not come easily for Paul. He came to faith the hard way. He learned the hard way to love. In the hard way he discovered that God always has the last word.

The power of Christ takes hold of all Christians who yield their life to the Savior in genuine faith. The energy and power of Christ, working as it does always through the Gospel, turned Paul around from the way he had been going and made of him a mature Christian man, able to take the hard knocks of life with gratitude for the constant goodness of God.

We know Christ—do we not? We are forgiven sons and daughters of God by faith in Christ, are we not? The good Word of God that brought us to faith in Christ will do its work in us that we, both young and old, may serve Him loyally with all the energy and power Christ gives.

Lord Jesus Christ, renew our lives with Your energy and power that we may worship You with a full heart and go to work for You with a will. Amen.

Oswald C. J. Hoffmann/Jan. 30, 1976

338

PEACE WITH GOD

Therefore, since we are justified by faith,
we have peace with God through our Lord
Jesus Christ. Romans 5:1 RSV

*T*oday there exists so little peace. How quickly can the inner circle of our homes, the closest association with friends, or peaceful relations in neighborhoods become strained! A lasting peace seems an impossible dream in our domestic, national, and international life.

Within this disturbed setting, however, we now are assured that we can possess a peace that never can be destroyed. It is the peace promised by the prophets, announced by the angels, and preached by the apostles— a peace that we have with God. Nothing can take it from us. In 1522 Martin Luther described it in an Advent sermon: "Behold, this is the peace of the cross, the peace of God, the peace of conscience, Christian peace. This peace makes us calm also externally, makes us satisfied with everyone and unwilling to disturb anyone."

Perhaps our reason cannot comprehend how we can have joy under the cross and peace in the midst of strife, but so it is. Yes, it is a God-given peace that deeply influences our lives and that we can share with others. Everyone should be able to see the peace of God reflected in us. We become His instruments of peace to others.

O God, fill us with all joy and peace in believing. Amen.

Milton S. Ernstmeyer/Oct. 10, 1978

God's Kindness Appeared

When the goodness and loving kindness
of God our Savior appeared, He saved us,
not because of deeds done by us in
righteousness, but in virtue of His own mercy.
Titus 3:4–5 RSV

God came to us in Jesus Christ, and His coming was an act of grace. The almighty Creator took the step down to meet His fallen creatures. Grace is God's idea because this is the way God is. God was not moved by anything He saw in His creatures because not by "deeds done by us in righteousness" are we saved. God came for no other reason than that He loved us without reason.

The grace of God is always God in action. St. Paul wrote to Titus that God's kindness and love toward humanity appeared. People were able to hear and sense and see God's grace when they saw Christ. The human flesh and blood with which Christ clothed Himself at Bethlehem marked Him as a true man, a person subject to hunger and pain and sorrow. The burden of sin that He assumed marked Him as the target for rejection and hate. But the significance of the story of Christ's life and death lies not in what was done to Him but in what He did. The grace of God persevered in the great act of redemption through Christ.

The God who did such great things in Christ is still active among us here and now.

Lord, we thank You for saving us by Your mercy in Christ. Amen.

Oliver R. Harms/Dec. 12, 1978

WHO GAVE UP?

And Abraham drew near, and said, "Wilt thou
also destroy the righteous with the wicked?"
Genesis 18:23 KJV

When Abraham learned that God was going to
destroy Sodom and Gomorrah, he was horrified.
Filled with frustration over what he thought God would
do, Abraham confronted the Lord with the challenge:
"Surely You will not destroy the good with the evil! Spare
the city if fifty righteous are found." God agreed.

And Abraham? His reaction? When he considered
what cesspools of iniquity these cities were, he pressed for
a decrease from 50. First, he asked deliverance if there
would be 45 righteous, then 40, then 30, then 20, and
finally 10. Each time God accepted the bold plea. With
that Abraham was silent. His unspoken judgment was: "If
there are not ten righteous, destroy the place."

Abraham was satisfied; surely there were ten righteous.
But God's justice had to prevail. Through His messengers
He sought to bring out *all* the righteous. In the end not
one righteous person was destroyed.

We have a way of challenging God, using our sense of
right and wrong as the standard of judgment. But God's
view of mercy is much greater than Abraham's or ours.
"God shows His love for us in that while we were yet sinners Christ died for us" (Romans 5:8 RSV).

*Lord, teach us to accept Your standards, knowing
that Your love is greater than ours and Your ways
wiser than ours. Amen.*

Charles S. Mueller Sr./March 23, 1968

341

You Were There!

This is a faithful saying and worthy
of all acceptation, that Christ Jesus came into
the world to save sinners; of whom I am chief.
1 Timothy 1:15 KJV

*I*t is of highest importance that you and I see ourselves as playing essential roles in the Advent/Christmas drama. This is not a drama that we may rehearse for the coming Christmas season, but the mind-boggling drama that took place two thousand years ago in Bethlehem's stable. True, our roles were purely passive, but they were of immeasurable importance. Indeed we were the ones for whom the entire drama took place!

Listen to Paul's words concerning the Christmas miracle: "This is a faithful saying, and worthy of all acceptation, that Christ Jesus came into the world to save sinners, *of whom I am chief.*"

The dramatic event that took place that night in Bethlehem had a cosmic dimension. The Son of God came down to earth with a single purpose: to save sinners such as you and I. We were, indeed, a part of the Christmas drama. Our eternal destiny was wrapped up in that babe cradled in a manger. He had come to save "sinners"—and that is the name you and I had before we had any other. Each of us may well join Martin Luther in his well-known hymn, "From Heaven Above to Earth I Come":

"He will Himself your Savior be, From all your sins to set you free." Amen.

Herman W. Gockel/Dec. 15, 1984

TENDER MERCIES

You will go before the Lord to prepare
His ways. Luke 1:76 RSV

A few years ago the movie *Tender Mercies* became a big hit. It was the story of a destitute and broken man who came to recognize and express his heartfelt thanks for the tender mercies of his newly found family.

John the Baptizer was Christ's forerunner, His prophet, because he came to announce God's wonderful salvation, His tender mercy, to a broken world. He spoke in the name of Christ, announcing the coming of spring after a dark, lonely winter. He announced the tender mercy of God, whose purpose it was "to give light to those who sit in darkness and in the shadow of death" (Luke 1:79 RSV).

We, too, like John, prepare the way of the Lord by announcing His tender mercy. We are the revealer of Christ's immeasurable love—the love that was also the Father's—in His death and resurrection. We call on the brokenhearted to take comfort and to join God's family because in Christ, we are His forgiven sons and daughters. Our warfare has ended, and our iniquity has been pardoned. We have received from the Lord's hand a double measure of His grace, His tender mercy, for every one of our sins (Isaiah 40:1–2). It is a wonderful message we can bring.

Lord, help us to show Your tender mercy in Jesus Christ to those around us. Amen.

Albert L. Garcia/Dec. 12, 1987

CHRISTMAS AND LENT

In Christ God was reconciling the world
to Himself. 2 Corinthians 5:19 RSV

Strange as it may seem, to meet the publisher's dead-line these Christmas devotions are being written in the season of Lent. Is there a connection between Christmas and Good Friday? Indeed there is! Everything in the life of Jesus fits into one great design—the cradle and the cross. The manner in which He came into the world He had made, and the way He left a world that had no room for Him, all point to the one purpose for which He had come. "He was rich, yet for your sakes He became poor, that ye through His poverty might be rich" (2 Corinthians 8:9 KJV).

There is a straight line from Bethlehem to Calvary and the empty tomb. We are in danger of overlooking this connection. We are prone to embrace the sentimentality of Christmas—the "sweet little Jesus boy." We are apt to forget that God "laid on Him the iniquity of us all" (Isaiah 53:6 RSV).

This little Babe brought reconciliation between God and man. In the shadow of His cradle there is always the cross. With that cross, Mary's Child became the world's greatest bridge builder. He spanned the chasm between God and us. It is only as we recognize this that we can prepare our hearts properly for Christmas.

Lord, help me always to see in the Christ of Christmas the Savior who died for my sins. Amen.

Stratford Eynon/Dec. 5, 1972

344

COME INTO MY HEART!

Prepare ye the way of the Lord,
make His paths straight. Matthew 3:3 KJV

*T*he decorations are up in stores and windows, suburban shopping centers, and downtown streets. "Do your Christmas shopping early!" is the call of the season. All this sadly misses the point.

"Repent ye: for the kingdom of heaven is at hand" was the call of John the Baptizer (Matthew 3:2 KJV), who announced the Messiah's coming. John's mission and message was in fulfillment of Isaiah's prophecy, "The voice of him that crieth in the wilderness. Prepare ye the way of the LORD, make straight in the desert a highway for our God" (Isaiah 40:3 KJV). For the Lord to come to us, a highway must be prepared, as it were, into our hearts. Obstacles must be cleared away. Sin, doubt, and unbelief must be removed. For this reason the valleys, plains, and wilderness of Judea echoed with John's cry, "Repent!"

This still constitutes the only adequate preparation for our Lord's coming. Until Christ lives in our hearts by faith, and our hopes rest on the forgiveness of sins, Christmas is phony, shallow sentimentality, and only make-believe.

We must see Bethlehem's manger in the shadows of Golgotha's cross. Jesus means *Savior* because He will save His people from their sins. The only adequate preparation for His coming to us is repentance, faith, and joy in God, our Savior.

"Redeemer, come! I open wide My heart to You; here, Lord, abide!" Amen.

Herman A. Etzold/Nov. 28, 1966

345

WELCOME HOME!

Thy kingdom come. Matthew 6:10 RSV

*D*uring the Christmas season, grandparents and close relatives make special trips from far away to visit our homes. A knock at the door signals their arrival. These visits bring great joy to us and great warmth to our hearts. It would be unthinkable, when we hear the expected knock of our loved ones, to ignore their long-awaited arrival.

Jesus taught us in the Lord's Prayer to welcome our Father's kingdom each day of our lives. In a very real sense we celebrate Advent, the coming of the Lord, each time we pray, "Thy kingdom come." In this special petition, our Lord taught us to pray that we might always expect Him, always be ready to open the door when He knocks. It would be unthinkable not to welcome Him when He calls. He is our long-awaited brother, our precious Savior and welcome guest.

During this Advent season, let us remember that our Lord knocks at our door so we may receive Him. He knocks so we will turn to the Holy Scriptures to find there our message of hope and salvation. He knocks so we may live in the radiance of His love rather than in the gloom of the world. He knocks so we may experience the power of His forgiveness.

Welcome into our homes and heart, Lord Jesus! May Your kingdom come to us today. Amen.

Albert L. Garcia/Dec. 4 1987

346

THE SIGN OF A PROMISE

I set My bow in the cloud, and it shall be a sign of the covenant between Me and the earth. Genesis 9:13 RSV

*J*ust something to show you that I love you."
"Just a sign of our appreciation."
"A token of wedded love and faithfulness."

Each of these quotations describes the human attachment of feelings to an item. The item becomes the visible, touchable sign of a feeling.

God knows our need for a sign as a reminder of what He has told us. In today's Bible reading, He gives Noah the rainbow as a beautiful sign of His promise never again to destroy the entire world with a flood. God bends down to human beings and gives them a visible reminder of His promise and His love.

Throughout the ages, God has given His people signs. He displays them so people can see and understand His love and goodness for them.

At just the right time God sent to the human race the greatest visible, touchable sign of His great love. God's very Word takes on human form in the flesh of Jesus, our Lord and Savior. God shows His love for humanity in a most dramatic way—sending His own Son to take on human form. God keeps His age-old promise, and through this Son the world is made friends with God again.

Dear Jesus, thanks for bending down to my humanity and taking on humanity Yourself to be my Savior. Amen.

Jeanette L. Groth/Aug. 31, 1986

A Sudden Arrival

Behold, I will send My messenger, and he shall prepare
the way before Me: and the Lord, whom ye seek, shall
suddenly come to His temple, even the messenger of the
covenant, whom ye delight in. Malachi 3:1 KJV

*T*he first Christmas came to the world with unusual
suddenness. For centuries people had waited for its
coming. When Christ came in the darkness of the night,
however, His coming was unexpected and sudden.
Heaven interrupted the shepherds in the fields and took
the Wise Men from their studies and shook the cruel
Herod. The promised Lord and Savior came to His temple—the church—with a thrilling suddenness.

In our day we talk and read about Christmas for weeks.
Unfortunately, for many people this dulls their appreciation of the true meaning of Christmas. The Lord doesn't
appear to them—that is, they do not see in Him the only
Savior and Redeemer who, fulfilling a promise, came suddenly in the fullness of time to offer forgiveness to the
world. For some people the true peace and joy of
Christmas will break through when they understand that
Christmas is the birthday of their Savior.

Happy and blessed are the people who prepare their
hearts by placing their faith in the Lord who came in fulfillment of the prophecies and prayers of old! May the coming of Jesus, coming to our hearts now, prepare us, too, for
His second coming and for everlasting Christmas above!

*Come, O Lord Jesus, and enter into our lives with
Your peace. Amen.*

Edwin A. Nerger/Dec. 23, 1959

HAIL, MARY!

"Hail, O favored one, the Lord is with you!"
Luke 1:28 RSV

Some Christians are almost afraid to honor Mary. Because some of their brothers and sisters have gone overboard in giving attention to Jesus' mother, they lean over backward and shy away from any show of respect to the one who was chosen from all other women to bring our Savior into the world.

We don't have to be afraid to admire or look up to Mary. After all, God singled her out for a signal honor. She occupies a unique position among all women. She is mentioned in both the Apostles' Creed and the Nicene Creed.

Even so, hers is a derived glory. Her fame depends on the child she bore. We call her "blessed," not because she was sinless but because her Son was sinless; not because of what she did for God but because of what God did for her.

The Virgin Mother carried the flesh of God's Son near her heart. That privilege will never be duplicated. Yet the same Christ wants to dwell in our hearts through faith.

What God is doing for us is not the same as what He did for Mary. Yet all saints on earth and those in heaven can truly say: "The LORD has done great things for us; we are glad" (Psalm 126:3).

Lord, we join Mary in magnifying You. Amen.

Bertwin L. Frey/Feb. 13, 1972

349

HE WILL COME AGAIN

Ye do show the Lord's death till He come.
1 Corinthians 11:26 KJV

*I*n these days and weeks, we are concerned with our
Lord's first advent, His first coming. For Christians all
of the varied activities and observances of the season serve
to impress on our hearts and minds the fact that our Lord
once "came in blessing."

Implicit in the concept of His first coming is His second coming. He came once; He will come again. We can
never permit our concerns of the moment, even our joyous commemoration of His first coming, to obscure our
realization and keen awareness of His second coming.

Accordingly we regularly eat and drink at the Lord's
Table, thereby showing His death till He come, remind-
ing ourselves that He will return in glory. We daily join St.
John in praying, "Even so, come, Lord Jesus" (Revelation
22:20 KJV). As in the case of Bunyan's Pilgrim, the trum-
pets are all sounding for us on the other side of the chasm
separating time and eternity. With the great apostle we
recognize that we are strangers and foreigners, in the
world but not of the world, awaiting the second coming at
the end of time.

*"So whene'er the signal's given Us from earth to
call away, Borne on angels' wings to heaven, Glad
the summons to obey, May we ever, May we ever
Reign with Christ in endless day!" Amen.*

George J. Beto/Dec. 4, 1961

350

SONGS OF GRATITUDE

Blessed be the Lord God of Israel;
for He hath visited and redeemed His people.
Luke 1:68 KJV

God does not abandon people but remembers and redeems them. He keeps His word. Because God cares, angels and people respond with songs of praise.

God told Zacharias that he would have a son, born to his wife, Elizabeth. When he was able to speak again, he uttered a word of joy: "Blessed be the Lord God of Israel." God had spoken this "by the mouth of His holy prophets" (Luke 1:70 KJV). God kept His word.

God told a young virgin that Jesus would be conceived in her by the Holy Spirit. Mary shared her joy with Elizabeth. She declared, "My soul doth magnify the Lord" (Luke 1:46 KJV). She included words similar to those of Zacharias, saying, "as He spake to our fathers" (Luke 1:55 KJV). Mary knew that God keeps faith.

God's angel told the shepherds about Jesus. The angel chorus praised God, saying, "Glory to God in the highest, and on earth peace, good will toward men" (Luke 2:14 KJV). God gives all that is good through Jesus.

Simeon held Jesus and recognized Him as God's gift, the Messiah. His response was "Lord, now lettest Thou Thy servant depart in peace" (Luke 2:29 KJV). He had seen the salvation that God had prepared. He knew of Christ's mission of love to all.

Lord God, help us to sing our songs of praise; Your love is great; Your Word is sure. Amen.

George W. Bornemann/Dec. 8, 1988

A Glorious Return

Then shall they see the Son of Man coming
in a cloud with power and great glory.
Luke 21:27 KJV

*A*dvent turns our thoughts in two directions: backward to our Lord's first coming into the world at Christmas and forward to His second coming on the Last Day.

Christ will come again in glory. That fact is indicated some five hundred times in the New Testament. It is echoed in the creeds, prayers, and hymns of the church. We mention it when we confess: "From thence He shall come to judge the quick and the dead." Every celebration of the Lord's Supper reminds us of it: "As often as ye eat this bread and drink this cup, ye do show the Lord's death till He come" (1 Corinthians 11:26 KJV).

The fact of Christ's second coming was a mighty force in the lives of the apostles and early Christians. It gave them comfort, courage, inspiration, and hope. They faced hardship, persecution, and death, sustained by the certain hope: "Our Lord is coming again."

He who once came to save men from sin and death will come again to gather to Himself all who have put their trust in Him. That sure hope should have a mighty effect on us. It should keep our hearts set on Christ, make us faithful in our service to Him, arm us in our battle against evil, comfort us in suffering, and cheer us in death.

"Even so, come, Lord Jesus." Amen.

Felix H. Kretzschmar/Dec. 7, 1970

THE GREATEST BIRTH

To us a child is born. Isaiah 9:6 RSV

*T*he greatest birth in history was the birth of Jesus Christ. He was born of a woman, like all other children. But His mother was a virgin. His conception was supernatural, not natural. Our creed says He was conceived by the Holy Ghost, born of the virgin Mary. What a wonderful and awe-inspiring birth that was! The Bible says that in this birth God was manifest in the flesh.

Think of it! When Jesus Christ was born, the Creator took the form and substance of one of His creatures. In a real sense the Master became servant, the Lord became subject, God became man.

Why is this birth so important to us? Not because it is such a fascinating story. Not because the miracle of this birth leaves us amazed. The reason is that it relates to our salvation. When Christ was born, the angels announced peace. Through His atoning work, God and sinners were reconciled. He left His throne so His human creatures need no longer die. His birth was like the rising of the sun. He brought light and healing to the world.

Any birth is a wonderful miracle. The birth of God's Son is the greatest miracle of all time. Let us daily believe and rejoice in the saving wonder of this birth.

Father in heaven, thank You for the birth of Your Son to be our Savior. Amen.

W. Th. Janzow/May 2, 1972

353

THE MIRACLE OF FAITH

And Mary said, Behold the handmaid of the
Lord; be it unto me according to Thy word.
Luke 1:38 KJV

Unbelievers often use the virgin birth of our Lord as a reason for rejecting the Bible as God's revealed Word. They are unwilling to accept the idea that God would break through the laws of nature to accomplish a special purpose. But why should one stumble at the idea of such a miracle? Surely the Creator of "heaven and earth, the sea, and all that in them is" (Exodus 20:11 KJV) can direct a biological process in one of His creatures.

What is incredible about Christmas is that God should decide to become man at all. It is foreign to human reason that sinners are absolved of their wickedness through the sacrifice of the one against whom they have sinned. Yet this is the course of action that God announced to Mary.

It is not surprising that Mary found all this hard to believe. "How shall this be?" she asked Gabriel. But bewilderment yielded to faith. Unable to understand, Mary simply believed. This too is a great miracle. Without it the virgin birth might not have taken place. Without our own miracle of faith, Christmas will not occur in our souls either.

Dear Jesus, we thank You for the miracle of Your birth and for the miracle of faith in our hearts. Keep us in this faith that we may be ready to meet and to greet You at Your coming. Amen.

Frederick E. Trinklein/Dec. 20, 1973

ADVENTURE

To us a Son is given. Isaiah 9:6 RSV

We must acknowledge that nowadays it can be difficult to attempt to celebrate a truly spiritual Advent season. We know that during Advent we are supposed to reflect on the many Old Testament prophecies concerning Christ's coming. We know that Advent is intended to be a season of repentance and reflection. Undoubtedly we all *want* to make the necessary spiritual preparations for Christmas.

So what goes wrong? We may complain, "There's so much distraction, so much noise and confusion and rushing that surrounds this holy season!" Perhaps we find ourselves getting caught up in this confusion and are therefore not really preparing properly for Christmas.

So is that the *real* problem? Is it that the world is too noisy at Christmastime? Or is the problem deeper yet? Perhaps we've allowed our noisy world to deafen our spiritual ears. The prophet Isaiah said, "To us a Son is given." He means what he said. Let us open our spiritual ears once again to this Good News. Christ in His love for us is the center of Advent and Christmas, no matter how much noise the world makes. Take it personally: God loves you! Let Advent become what it should be, a spiritual ADVENTure!

Lord Jesus, thank You for loving us. Amen.

Daniel P. Aho/Dec. 1, 1976

THE ETERNAL RULER

But thou, Bethlehem Ephratah, though thou be
little among the thousands of Judah, yet out of thee
shall He come forth unto Me that is to be ruler in
Israel, whose goings forth have been from of old,
from everlasting. Micah 5:2 KJV

To Bethlehem there came a high honor. Bethlehem was to be the birthplace of royalty—Israel's ruler, the Prince of peace, the Sovereign of creation—born among men, in the form of a man, as the Savior of man.

Long after the other cities of Judah have passed into oblivion, Bethlehem lives in history. Bethlehem remains forever as the place of the incarnation—where God entered history and eternity was fused with time.

Bethlehem is a Hebrew word that means "house of bread." In Bethlehem He was born who is the Bread of Life. This Bread gives nourishment to the soul. Those who eat will live forever. That Bread was broken for the life of the world.

In Bethlehem, "little among the thousands of Judah," the Savior deigned to be born. He sought no pride of birth. He came to Bethlehem, small and obscure, and filled it with His glory.

So, too, He comes to us, humble, unworthy, and weak though we are. With His coming our heart is made glad and our soul revives. In us, as in Bethlehem of old, Christ the Savior is born.

"Cast out our sin and enter in, Be born in us today!" Amen.

Thomas Coates/Dec. 5, 1960

LIVING TOGETHER IN LOVE

*I entreat Euodia and I entreat Syntyche
to agree in the Lord. Philippians 4:2 RSV*

*D*ays immediately preceding Christmas can get pretty hectic. In our homes nerves can be frayed, everybody can be on edge at one time or another. There is still so much to do: cookies to bake, packages to wrap and deliver, shopping to do, carols to be sung, houses to be cleaned. Under such tension Christmas can become a family disaster instead of a time of joy.

What caused Euodia and Syntyche to disagree, Paul doesn't say. What is important is that Paul directs them to the source of agreement when he pleads with them to "agree in the Lord."

Of course, that's where it's all at for all of us. Jesus Himself settled the greatest of all disagreements: our rebellion against God. He did that when He came at Bethlehem that He might eventually go to the cross to die for our sins. This truth should not be overlooked in the hustle and bustle of all our other Christmas preparations.

Not only does Jesus forgive all our disagreements, all our sins, but He gives us the power to live in love and harmony. Even more: When someone in our circle of relationships offends us, we have power to forgive that person in His name.

Lord Jesus, help us to live in peace with one another because You are our Prince of peace and have made us one with God. Amen.

W. Leroy Biesenthal/Dec. 22, 1979

The Word Made Flesh

The Word was made flesh, and dwelt among us, and we beheld His glory. John 1:14 KJV

A nuclear scientist was making an urgent plea for scholarships to be given to American students who would study in foreign lands. Stressing that such scholarships would win for America a much greater measure of understanding abroad, he said significantly: "The best way to send an idea out into the world is to *wrap it up in a person.*"

In a sense infinitely more sublime, that is exactly what the Lord of heaven did on that first Christmas Eve. He had an "idea" He was eager to convey to the whole world: the message of His divine love, the word of pardon, peace, and joy. In His unsearchable wisdom, He took this "idea," which He was so eager to communicate to the human family, wrapped it up in a human form, and laid it into Bethlehem's manger.

That is the eternal significance of Christmas. "The Word [that is, God's Son] was made flesh, and dwelt among us." He is, in truth and in fact, "God come down from heaven"—Immanuel, "God with us." He is God's sweetest Gospel message, wrapped up in a person—a person who lived and died and rose again as a *visible* demonstration of God's unending love for you and me!

Lord Jesus, I thank You for coming into this world to be my Savior. May I always give You love for love. Amen.

Herman W. Gockel/Dec. 21, 1984

MAKING THE MOST OF CHRISTMAS

And the Word was made flesh and dwelt
among us, (and we beheld His glory, the glory
as of the only begotten of the Father,)
full of grace and truth. John 1:14 KJV

Christmas is at the door. On all sides we see men and women making loving preparations. Yet gifts and goodwill do not make for genuine Christmas joy. How do *we* make the most of Christmas?

By centering our thoughts on the Christ Child of Bethlehem. But we must see more than the Babe and the shepherds and the angels. This Babe is "the Word made flesh," very God of very God, the only Son of the eternal God. He came to save sinners.

Therefore, if we want to make the most of Christmas, we must realize that *we* need a Savior, who is to free us from the guilt of sin, cleanse our conscience, and make us new creatures. By nature we are dead in sin. Nothing we do can change this condition. We need a Savior.

To make the most of Christmas, we believe that in this Jesus we have a Savior and come to Him, just as we are, pleading for forgiveness and peace.

To make the most of Christmas we faithfully follow this Jesus. Nothing can be of greater interest to us. He comes first always, even now, as we make endless preparation for Christmas. Without Him, these festive days are meaningless. Are we putting Jesus at the center of our Christmas?

"Oh, come to my heart, Lord Jesus, there's room in my heart for Thee." Amen.

George J. Beto/Dec. 23, 1961

359

BETHLEHEM

But thou, Bethlehem Ephratah …
out of thee shall He come forth unto Me that
is to be ruler in Israel. Micah 5:2 KJV

Some seven hundred years before the birth of Jesus, Micah predicted that the Messiah would be born in Bethlehem of Judah. A sleepy village about six miles south of Jerusalem, its history goes back in Bible story to the days of Jacob. Here that patriarch buried his beloved Rachel. Here Ruth gleaned grain in the fields of Boaz. Here David, her great-grandson, strummed his harp as he watched his father's sheep.

This quiet little town was to become famous because of an unknown virgin, a worried carpenter, an overfilled inn, a dirty stable, a crude manger, a silent night, an angel's song, and a group of worshiping shepherds. All of this was part of God's plan to have David's greater son, Jesus, be born. Certainly a strange place for the Son of God and Savior of all to enter human history!

Here in Bethlehem He, who is the Bread of Life, was born. He nourishes your spiritual life. His body was broken for you on Golgotha's cross. Those who eat this Bread of Life will live forever.

Jesus, your great Redeemer, came humble and poor to save the lowly and the poor in spirit. His coming gladdens and revives your hearts.

Lord Jesus, be born in us today. Amen.

Julius W. Acker/Dec. 15, 1968

360

To Bethlehem

And Joseph also went up from Galilee ...
unto the city of David, which is called
Bethlehem. Luke 2:4 KJV

*T*he offices of travel agencies are crowded these days with people frantically trying to get reservations for a certain destination where they want to spend Christmas. Very few of these people think about the real spiritual destination of our Christmas journey—Bethlehem. Many who do realize the importance of the event that took place in Bethlehem so many centuries ago almost forget about it in the hustle and bustle of their moving around.

All roads these days should lead to Bethlehem. The prophet in ancient times gave the direction when by the Spirit of God he showed people that their journey should lead to Bethlehem, where the Ruler, Jesus the Savior and King, was to be born. The angels of heaven gave these same instructions to the shepherds. The star of the East led the Wise Men and guided them to Bethlehem. Everyone who makes the trip to Bethlehem and finds the Christ Child finds the true peace at Christmas. Knowing this, it is time for us to make reservations for our Christmas trip in faith to Bethlehem to worship the newborn King. The ticket is free, a gift received by our childlike faith. Let us go to Bethlehem!

O Savior born in Bethlehem, we come to You to find true Christmas joy, as we travel in spirit to worship at Your manger bed. Amen.

Edwin A. Nerger/Dec. 21, 1959

361

GOD SENT FORTH HIS SON

When the fullness of time was come,
God sent forth His Son, made of a woman.
Galatians 4:4 KJV

*H*ave you ever fully realized that God took almost four thousand years in which to prepare us for that moment in history when Jesus should be born in Bethlehem? Through prophecies and promises, God directed His people to be ready for the coming of Christ. No wonder then, when the fullness of the time had come, the angel shouted the glad tidings: To you is born a Savior!

How did God send His Son? He was made of a woman. The miracle by which He became a human being is beyond all understanding, but this does not change the truth that the Son of God became man. Here is the fulfillment of Isaiah's prophecy: "A virgin shall conceive, and bear a Son, and shall call His name Immanuel" (Isaiah 7:14 KJV). Here is the fulfillment of the angel Gabriel's words to Mary: "The Holy Ghost shall come upon thee, and the power of the Highest shall overshadow thee: therefore also that Holy Thing which shall be born of thee shall be called the Son of God" (Luke 1:35 KJV).

Although we cannot understand the virgin birth of Christ, we can by grace believe it. God has spoken: "God sent forth His Son, made of a woman." We can trust that Word.

Lord Jesus, we believe that You are the promised Savior, born of a virgin and sent to save the lost. Amen.

Herman C. Scherer/Nov. 7, 1976

How Silently!

There were in the same country shepherds
abiding in the field, keeping watch over their
flock by night. Luke 2:8 KJV

God must love surprises; He certainly has enough of them. One of the Christmas surprises was the quiet way He chose to send His Son. Can you imagine a more unlikely way for the Son of God to come into this world? A weak and helpless baby is born amidst poverty and the discomfort of a barn—and to ordinary parents. Wouldn't it have made more sense to have Him born into a wealthy family that could afford the best of care? Doesn't God know that if you want to make a big splash, you have to have a big pond? Why not Rome, or at least Jerusalem? Certainly not sleepy little Bethlehem! And shepherds! Couldn't the angels have told the Good News to more sophisticated people than poor shepherds?

God's ways certainly are not our ways. His ways usually appear in simplicity and quietness, not in the glare of sophistication. To the poor in spirit and the lowly in heart, God reveals His salvation.

God chose the quiet way. When you are confident of the final outcome, you don't need "Madison Avenue" or a big noise or a big show! "How silently, how silently, the wondrous gift is given! So God imparts to human hearts the blessings of His heaven."

Dearest Jesus, holy Child, come into my heart that I may be a "quiet chamber kept for Thee." Amen.

Stratford Eynon/Dec. 18, 1972

MANGER MESSAGE

She gave birth to her first-born Son ...
and laid Him in a manger. Luke 2:7 RSV

*L*ittle children have a way of making us take notice as they sing their carols and recite their Christmas "pieces." Especially moving is their rendition of "Away in a Manger." We usually understand the phrase "away in a manger" to mean that Jesus was born far away from His heavenly home. On the hay of the manger, "the little Lord Jesus laid down His sweet head."

Let's look ahead some 30 years to the time when our dear Lord indeed "laid down His sweet head" as Roman soldiers nailed His hands and feet to a rough and bloody cross. "But little Lord Jesus no crying He makes," the song continues. How prophetic! As a lamb led to the slaughter, our suffering Savior never once complained as He gave His sinless life in death. May our own response to such greater love echo the words of the carol: "I love Thee, Lord Jesus ..."

He was raised from the dead by His heavenly Father and after 40 days ascended to His heavenly home. Then He sent the Holy Spirit to comfort His disciples and guide them into all truth. That same Holy Spirit leads you and me to join in singing: "Be near me, Lord Jesus, I ask Thee to stay, Close by me forever and love me, I pray."

Dearest Lord Jesus, thank You for coming to our world to save us from the guilt and punishment of our sins. Amen.

Elmer J. Knoernschild/Dec. 23, 1980

364

GLORY TO GOD IN THE HIGHEST!

God sent forth His Son ... that we might
receive adoption as sons. Galatians 4:4–5 RSV

*T*his holy night a child was born. In a faraway land two thousand years ago a young mother delivers a new life from her body and adds her infant Son to the number of humanity. For this the heavens are moved, and God breaks His silence of centuries once again to speak to us in terms of love and grace. For this today the world is stirred, and the voices of uncounted multitudes on earth are raised in prayer and praise. For this—for what?

The child is not a child of earth alone. This is God's Son, not only Mary's Son. He is born, not to take a place in the common destiny of humanity, not just to appear and have His little day and then return again to heaven. There is a glory here that once blazed out into the gloom of the Judean night and that to the end of time will shine into the darkness of the world, which always needs its light.

God became a child of Mary that we might become children of God. He sent forth His Son that He might be our Father. There is no greater thing He could have done. There is no better way to say it. "God sent forth His Son ... that we might receive adoption as sons." This is our faith and our salvation.

Father in Christ Jesus, bless us now as Your beloved children! Amen.

Daniel E. Poellot/Dec. 24, 1965

365

The Wonder of Christmas

Without controversy great is the mystery
of godliness: God was manifest in the flesh.
1 Timothy 3:16 KJV

*I*f there is one sentiment that Christmas should awaken in our hearts, it is the sense of wonder. In the strictest sense of an overworked word, Christmas is indeed something *wonderful*. It brings the wonder of the incarnation. It shows how "great is the mystery of godliness: God is manifest in the flesh."

In our day we have largely lost this sense of wonder. People, unwilling to live by faith, demand proof. They pride themselves on being realists.

But Christmas is a festival of wonder. Its glory lies in the very fact that it surpasses the range of human knowledge, that it transcends the realm of human experience. Its appeal is to faith.

For Christmas shows us a mystery—the mystery of God becoming man; of divinity in humanity; of eternity linked with time. But this mystery is, at the same time, intensely real. In fact, that is just why it is such a wonder! Christmas is no children's tale. It is historic truth. Indeed all history can be read correctly only in the light of Christmas, which shows that human history has a divine purpose and an eternal destiny. In the wonder of Christmas all the ages converge. On this day God was manifest in the flesh.

"Oh, come let us adore Him, Christ the Lord!"
Amen.

Thomas Coates/Dec. 25, 1960

FREE TO FORGIVE

As they were stoning Stephen, he prayed ...
"Lord, do not hold this sin against them."
Acts 7:59–60 RSV

*F*orgiveness is always amazing. It seems incredible that anyone could forgive another, so deeply is the spirit of revenge embedded in us. For that reason Stephen's words amaze us. How could he say, "Lord, do not hold this sin against them" as his accusers become executioners hurling their stones at him? Where did he get this strength, this concern for his enemies?

One thing sustained him. It was his vision. He had seen Jesus "standing at the right hand of God" (Acts 7:55 RSV). He knew that Jesus was Lord; that even the stones would ultimately not hurt him; that the Christ would receive him. This vision gave him courage; it freed him. He no longer needed to be safe and secure. Revenge no longer interested him. Only the future of his executioners occupied his thoughts. So he prayed for them.

What a glorious freedom that must be! How we wish it could be ours! It is ours when we see the vision as clearly as Stephen did. Above all, it *is* ours when, united with our Savior by faith, we receive power to pray His prayer on the cross after Him: "Father, forgive them; for they know not what they do" (Luke 23:34 RSV). Then we also can love our enemies and do good to them.

Lord, help me to see You at God's right hand that I too may be free to forgive. Amen.

Henry R. Schriever/May 14, 1975

367

Bethlehem's Shepherds

The shepherds returned, glorifying
and praising God. Luke 2:20 RSV

A bright light in the midnight sky, a message from
heaven, and a chorus of angels singing the praises
of God. That was the experience of the shepherds on the
fields of Bethlehem. This experience not only touched
them deeply, it roused them to action. When the song was
stilled and the darkness of the night surrounded them
again, they hurried to find the Babe in the manger. There
they paid homage to their Savior and ours, then returned
to their sheep, glorifying and praising God. It was an
experience they never forgot.

Christmas is one of those happy events that, like other
observances, lasts a few days and is gradually forgotten.
Trees wither and songs die away, and soon also this
Christmas, to which we looked forward with eagerness, is
likely to give place to other interests. But is not Christmas
worth keeping a little longer?

Indeed it is. Because we have seen the Babe of
Bethlehem, our life, too, can be a glorifying life. We can
hold on to the wonderful truth that there will always be
light in our darkness. Christmas means love, forgiveness,
joy, and peace. All these we can keep and take with us into
the new year.

*"Glory to God in highest heaven. Who unto us His
Son hath given!" Amen.*

Theophil Schroedel/Dec. 26, 1963

LIVING IN LOVE

And we have known and believed the love
that God hath to us. God is love; and he that
dwelleth in love dwelleth in God,
and God in him. 1 John 4:16 KJV

*T*he past days have been delightful. They have been a real experience that we would like to have continue all through the year. There has been more love and kindness shown than at any other time of the year. So many are saying: "If only it could last!" The apostle of love, St. John, gives the reason for this love at Christmas and also tells us how this love may continue.

All the kindness and goodwill of Christmas, and at any time of the year, finds its true source in God. "God is love." At Christmas we see this visibly demonstrated in all of our worship and celebration. However, we should not only at Christmas time think of the love of God in sending the Savior Jesus into the world to redeem us from our sins. Christmas should be the beginning of a life of love that lasts throughout the year. We who daily remember God's love in Christ to us and let that blessed truth motivate all our actions also will show this love to others in every way. As to our living in love, God will live in us and we in God. Such a life will reach out to touch others with true Christian love. We will be helpful and kind to our neighbor, and above all, we will share with him God's wonderful love in Jesus.

God of love, fill our lives with Your love that we may completely live our life in You and for You. Amen.

Edwin A. Nerger/Dec. 27, 1959

369

HE LIGHTENS OUR DARKNESS

Mine eyes have seen Thy salvation which
Thou hast prepared in the presence
of all peoples, a light for revelation to the
Gentiles, and for glory to Thy people Israel.
Luke 2:30–32 RSV

Candlelight services are specially meaningful during the Christmas season. The worshipers are edified by the splendor of Advent and Christmas candles as they shine in the midst of darkness. These holiday lights represent the light of Christ, who lightens the darkness of our sinful world.

Our experience can be like that of Simeon, who was led by the Holy Spirit to see and hold the Christ Child. Consider his situation and his actions. He was a tired old man. Life's vicissitudes were still affecting him. Led by the Holy Spirit, he approached this seemingly insignificant Child in the temple. By faith he knew that this was the Redeemer, who had come to lighten the darkness of His people and also of the Gentiles. Christ's light was brighter and more significant than the great darkness all around.

This Christmas season that same light is present to lighten our darkness. Whatever our problems, He is our light shining in the darkest of nights. We hope and rejoice in His salvation.

Lighten our darkness, O Lord, and by Your mercy defend us from the dangers of the night. Amen.

Albert L. Garcia/Dec. 23, 1987

To Live or to Die?

For me to live is Christ, and to die is gain.
Philippians 1:21 RSV

A cartoon pictures two saints complete with wings and halos basking in clouds of heavenly bliss. In the caption below, one says to the other, "If it hadn't been for health foods, we could have been up here years ago."

This humor captures in a striking way the mixed feelings with which St. Paul penned the verse quoted above. On the one hand, he writes from his prison cell in Rome to his dear friends in Philippi that he looked forward to an acquittal. This would enable him to continue preaching Christ and serving God's people, and perhaps even to visit them once again. On the other hand, he did not fear a death verdict either because he writes: "My desire is to depart and to be with Christ, for that is far better" (Philippians 1:23 RSV).

Together with the apostle, we Christians also have ambiguous emotions about death. We thank God for the precious gift of life, and we treasure it. But we do not worship it. We reserve that for the one who on the cross has removed the sting of death for us. Therefore, when the hour of our death approaches, we can pray: "Lord, now let your servant depart in peace."

Lord Jesus, help me to celebrate life while it is day and, when the night of life comes, to die in peace. Amen.

Samuel H. Nafzger/Oct. 28, 1988

UNAFRAID

Lord, now lettest Thou Thy servant depart
in peace. Luke 2:29 KJV

*T*he passing of a year brings us face to face with the final truth about life and death. People try to drown out the voice of remembrance with shouts and revelry. But over the din can be heard the words: "Thou hast set our iniquities before Thee, our secret sins in the light of Thy countenance. ... So teach us to number our days, that we may apply our hearts unto wisdom" (Psalm 90:8, 12 KJV).

Simeon, holding the Christ Child, sang, "Lord, now lettest Thou Thy servant depart in peace ... for mine eyes have seen Thy Salvation" (Luke 2:29–30 KJV). For Simeon the one thing needful in life was to see the Lord's Christ and be assured of forgiveness and salvation.

A little girl passing a cemetery one dark and starless night was asked by a passerby: "My child, aren't you afraid to walk by the graveyard at this time of the night?"

She answered, "No, sir. Can you see that light shining just beyond the cemetery?"

"Yes, I see it," he replied.

"That's where my home is," she said. "That's where I'm going."

If we know our Lord and Savior, then we too know where we are going. With Simeon, we are going home to God. For through Him our sins are forgiven. Through Him we have an abundant life here on earth, and through Him we have eternal life in heaven.

"Jesus, lead Thou on till our rest is won." Amen.

Stratford Eynon/Dec. 31, 1966

Jesus Only

They saw no man, save Jesus only.
Matthew 17:8 KJV

*P*eter, James, and John trudged up a mountain path with Jesus and beheld His transfiguration. His face shone like the sun, and His clothes were as white as the light. Moses and Elijah appeared and talked with Him.

This the disciples saw—Jesus in His glory! Is it any wonder that they wanted to remain there? Suddenly, from an overshadowing cloud, there came the voice of God the Father, saying, "This is My beloved Son, in whom I am well pleased; hear ye Him" (Matthew 17:5 KJV). The disciples fell on their faces.

Someone touched them. When they looked up, they saw no one except Jesus only.

Reconfirmed in their faith that Jesus is the Christ, the Son of the living God, these men went down from this mountaintop experience to bear witness of this truth and to spend their lives serving Jesus only.

Trudging up a mountain path with Jesus may not be an easy task, but it may end with a glimpse of Jesus in His glory. Keep walking. "Follow Me," He says.

We can see Jesus in the pages of the Holy Scriptures, in the message from the Christian pulpit, in the blessed sacraments. Here we behold His glory, the glory as of the only-begotten of the Father. Here we find forgiveness and strength and inspiration. Leaving this spot where heaven touches earth, we go back to see and serve Jesus only.

Jesus, let us see You through the eyes of faith. Amen.

Clemonce Sabourin/May 1, 1960

Dust and Ashes

Dust thou art, and unto dust shalt thou return.
Genesis 3:19 KJV

*T*oday is the day of ashes. We call it Ash Wednesday. It marks the beginning of Lent. It marks the beginning of a special time to meditate on the death of Jesus Christ and His resurrection.

When we draw closer to Jesus' cross, we realize more fully that it was our sins that made His death necessary. This should move us to lament our wrongs and to repent.

The Bible tells how sin began when Adam and Eve violated God's plan for their life in the Garden of Eden. As the first sinners were being chased from their happy home, God spoke to Adam and said "unto dust you shall return." In other words, Adam would have to die because of sin.

An early tradition among Christians was that Adam and Eve left the garden on the first "Ash Wednesday." Surely that was a dismal day, a day of death. Christians for many centuries observed Ash Wednesday by putting ashes on their head, a sign that they deserved death for their sins.

While we deserve ashes on our head and death for our sins, Lent is a time to remember that Christ died our death for us. Instead of ashes of death on our head, we have received the water of baptism. God has been so merciful to give us life through Jesus Christ.

O Lord, grant us grace this Lent to prepare for a right celebration of Easter by rightly remembering our Lord's death. Amen.

Paul J. Schulze/Feb. 27, 1963

THE KING OF KINGS

Tell the daughter of Zion, Behold,
your King is coming to you, humble,
and mounted on an ass, and on a colt,
the foal of an ass. Matthew 21:5 RSV

*A*mid the palms on Jerusalem Way rode the greatest King the world has ever known. It was the Savior, Christ the Lord. Ever since, we have echoed the cries of that first Palm Sunday, singing to the Lord of lords and King of kings.

The Scriptures repeatedly describe Christ as King. In Jerusalem the Wise Men asked, "Where is He that is born King of the Jews?" (Matthew 2:2 KJV). After the miraculous multiplication of food, the satiated crowd wanted to make Him their king. Pilate's interrogation during the precrucifixion hours was highlighted by a key question, "So You are a king?" Contrary to the protests of His enemies, a caption was placed on His cross reading, "Jesus of Nazareth, King of the Jews."

The Scriptures document His kingship. Yet Christ indicated clearly that His kingdom was not of this world, but is rather the kingdom of heaven. With our spiritual palms in hand, we hail Christ as our King. He rules our hearts and minds, having sacrificed Himself for our sins. In rising again he assures the world that He rules also over death. Truly, He is our Lord of lords and King of kings.

"Wondrous King, all-glorious, Sov'reign Lord victorious, Oh, receive our praise with favor." Amen.

Ihno A. Janssen/April 4, 1982

375

A New Meal

He said to them, "I have eagerly desired
to eat this Passover with you before I suffer."
Luke 22:15

*B*efore our Lord went to the cross, He paused to celebrate the Passover meal with His disciples. He took time to recall God's great deliverance of His people from Egypt.

As God used Moses to lead His people to the Promised Land, so He called on Jesus to lead all His people to the promised home of heaven. The next day Jesus would accomplish that deliverance and open the door to salvation.

But there was more than the Passover meal. Jesus gave His disciples the meal of His precious body and blood. As the Passover meal recalled the deliverance from Egypt, so Holy Communion recalls God's love for humanity that Christ fulfilled on the cross. But it does more than recall.

In His meal of Holy Communion our Savior gives us what He used to purchase our forgiveness and salvation: His precious body and blood. Not only do we recall His suffering and death each time we partake of this meal, but we also receive the forgiveness of sins, salvation, and the power of Christ for our faith and life. What spiritual nourishment this is!

Lord Jesus, we do thank You for Your body and blood in this holy meal and for the blessings of our salvation. Amen.

Victor A. Constien/March 31, 1988

THE CRUCIFIED CHRIST

And they crucified Him. Mark 15:24 RSV

When you visit Jerusalem, no one can point out with absolute certainty the spot where Jesus was crucified. Yet there is no doubt in the mind of reasonable people anywhere that He was crucified.

This means much to you and me. It means that our Christian faith rests not merely on some pious and beautiful wish or abstract thought, but on a real historical person who performed for us a very real historical act to save us. This fact stands. No matter how the devil may rage, our salvation is an historic fact, achieved by the historic person Jesus, the God-man. No person, no event, no power can undo this fact.

To understand the meaning of this fact is most important for us. Many who grant that Jesus was crucified fail to understand *why* He was crucified.

The truth is, you and I could not in a thousand years ever guess why Jesus let Himself be crucified. Did not the Spirit of God Himself make this clear to us? Fortunately for us, the Spirit of God does this. He tells us: Jesus bore our sins in His own body on the tree. He was wounded for our transgressions. He is the Lamb of God that took away the sins of the world. This is the message of this day, which is why we call it *Good* Friday.

Blessed Spirit of God, enable each of us poor sinners to look up with faith and say, "This is my Lord, who has redeemed me." Amen.

Otto A. Geiseman/March 31, 1961

THE CLOSED DOOR

[Joseph] laid Him in a sepulchre.
Mark 15:46 KJV

On Good Friday afternoon the body of Jesus was taken from the cross and placed into the tomb. A stone was placed in front of the opening with the seal of the governor affixed.

The door to Jesus was closed. What a contrast to His active ministry! The door to Jesus was always open for young and old, sick and well, rich and poor to come into His presence.

It seems like a permanent closing with the heavy stone and governor's seal. Many must have wondered that Saturday whether that door would ever be opened again. Some may have said, "Why want it open? There is nothing but the dead body of Jesus." But already today we peek toward the grave and see the door open and the dead Jesus alive. This door will not remain closed.

We have closed the door to the grave of a loved one. For the moment it seems like a permanent closing. As little as the door to Christ's grave could remain closed, so we know the door to the graves of loved ones will not remain closed. Someday our own grave will be closed. Just as the closed grave of our Savior was opened, so we believe our grave will open at the resurrection.

Lord Jesus, we praise You because You rested in the tomb. We know our stay in the grave will be only temporary. Amen.

Walter C. Loeber/April 5, 1980

EASTER LIFE—NOW AND FOREVER

*I came that they may have life,
and have it abundantly. John 10:10 RSV*

*I*n all of life nothing so defeats us, nothing so causes our world, plans, hopes, and dreams to come crashing down to earth in hopeless and irrevocable chaos as death. Death is the great destroyer, the great curse.

But the first Easter Sunday changed all this for all who accept the gift of Easter. That gift is life in exchange for death—life now and forever.

We live in a world of death. We cannot escape the persistent reminders of death that we meet almost daily in life. And we build our lives and make our plans with the knowledge that all earthly life has its terminal point.

But Christ Jesus, our Lord, entered our world of death and did battle with death itself, and the result was a glorious one. He came to give us life—abundant life. From the moment this Easter victory of our Lord becomes ours through faith in Him, our life, here and now, is new—dramatically and completely new. The awful defeat of death no longer awaits us like a grinning skull. We are living a life that will never end.

Jesus is our bridge between time and eternity. We have so much to look forward to as we wait to enter the glory of our Lord.

O deathless Savior, grant us the glorious vision of the life You have won for us, now and forever. Amen.

Arnim H. Polster/April 19, 1961

379

THE KING OF GLORY

*When He had spoken these things, while they
beheld, He was taken up; and a cloud received
Him out of their sight. Acts 1:9 KJV*

On the 40th day after His resurrection Jesus led His disciples to Bethany, where He blessed them for the last time. Before their eyes He was taken up into glory. Paul writes, "[He] ascended up far above all heavens, that He might fill all things" (Ephesians 4:10 KJV).

In His ascension Christ was crowned with glory and honor. He was greeted with the triumphal shouts of angels and archangels and of all the company of heaven. Cherubim and seraphim acclaimed Him the King who had triumphed over sin, death, and hell for all humanity. So He received the crown of glory, because on earth He was willing to wear the crown of thorns and bear the shame of death on the cross. Having done all this for us, He ascended victoriously into heaven.

His victory is our victory. In Christ we have conquered sin and death. On this Ascension Day we, too, earthbound but heaven destined, shout to acclaim Him our victorious Savior. It is the shout of faith. One day we shall follow Him to heaven, then be with Him forever and ever. By His blood and death He has become the King of glory, the Lord strong and mighty, the King of kings, and the Lord of lords.

Risen, ascended Lord, glory and honor be to You now and forever because You have overcome our enemies by Your death. Amen.

Paul G. Barth/May 7, 1970

380

THE PENTECOST FAITH

The just shall live by faith. Romans 1:17 KJV

*T*he Christian church was born on Pentecost Day by the pouring out of the Holy Spirit and His creative power. On this day the apostle Peter stood before thousands and preached a sermon. Its theme would become the fundamental message of the Christian church through the ages.

The church proclaims to the world that Jesus Christ is the Lord and Savior of all. By dying on the cross for our sins and being raised from the dead, He has reconciled us to His Father. All those who believe in this Jesus and have received Him into their hearts are called the children of God. This faith is created in us by the Holy Spirit.

All believers in the true God compose the Christian church. The church is more than a human organization. The church is here because of the creative act of the Holy Spirit. We were called to faith into the church by God's saving grace, not because we are nicer and better people. We are new creatures in Christ and His atoning cross, and we bear witness in our fast-changing world with the fears and powers of hell all around us, that God's unchanging Word still is true: "The just shall live by faith"!

"We now implore God the Holy Ghost For the true faith, which we need the most, That in our last moments He may befriend us And, as homeward we journey, attend us. Lord, have mercy." Amen.

Richard Z. Meyer/June 10, 1962

381

A Question of Reading God's Mind

Who has known the mind of the Lord,
or who has been His counselor? Or who has
given a gift to Him that he might be repaid?
Romans 11:34–35 RSV

*T*he Bible tells us much about the triune God, but there is so much more we would like to know about Him. How is He one God in three persons? How can He be all-powerful, all knowing, and present everywhere? How could He become one of us in the person of Jesus Christ?

Oh, if only we could read God's mind! If only we knew His reasons for the unexplainable times in our life when we cry out in bewilderment, anger, pain, or tears: "Why, Lord?" But then, if we fully understood His mysterious ways and dealings, we would have mastered Him—and He would no longer be our God and Master.

Thank God that His thoughts and His ways are not our thoughts and ways! He sees us from His eternal perspective, and His will for us is always for our everlasting good. We praise Him especially today, Trinity Sunday, for coming into our heart through His Word and sacraments and clearly revealing Himself as the personal God of our salvation. That's what He really wants us to know about Him!

Father, Son, and Holy Spirit, when we vainly try to fathom Your mysteries and read Your mind, turn our attention to Your Word of truth and reveal Your heart of love in our Savior. Amen.

Martin J. Schmidt/June 10, 1979

THE GOOD SHEPHERD

I am the Good Shepherd: the Good Shepherd
giveth His life for the sheep. John 10:11 KJV

Of all the pictures our Lord gives of Himself, surely
none is more precious and meaningful than that of
the Good Shepherd. It's so personal. "All we like sheep
have gone astray," writes Isaiah (53:6 KJV). Left to ourselves, we remain scattered and lost. But the Good
Shepherd sacrifices Himself for the safety and salvation of
the sheep. He goes out to seek everyone who is lost; He
gathers us into His own precious flock to nourish us and
keep us safe forever.

Today is Mother's Day. We remember God's gifts to us
through loving and sacrificing mothers and the blessings
that are ours in the "little flock" we call our family.

What better example for the way we live together in
our families than that of the Good Shepherd! "Love one
another even as I have loved you," Jesus says (John 13:34
RSV). Day after day we have opportunity to practice that
love toward parents, spouses, children. We cannot do for
one another what Jesus did for us, but we can reflect His
love. We can be patient, quick to forgive, anxious to
serve rather than to be served. As He has laid down His
life for us, so let us use our redeemed lives to serve one
another.

*Lord Jesus, our Good Shepherd, fill our hearts, our
homes, our families with Your abiding love. Amen.*

August T. Mennicke/May 13, 1984

383

The Joy of Humility

Humble yourselves before the Lord, and He
will lift you up. James 4:10

*A*s a young graduate, in cap and gown with diploma in hand, walked down the street, he met "the world." On being asked by the world, "Whom have we here?" the young man replied, "Why, evidently you don't know me. I am John Jay Richards, A.B." To which "the world" responded, "Young man, come with me, and I will teach you the rest of the alphabet."

Humility is not easy to achieve. In our success-oriented world, it seems to be hard for us not to "blow our own horn." After all, if we do not blow it, who will?

Our Lord would have us think differently, though. In Matthew 23 He tells us that whoever exalts himself will be humbled, and whoever humbles himself will be exalted. St. James echoes the same thought, making us realize that without the humbling experience of repentance, the exaltation of forgiveness through Jesus' merits is not possible, nor do we deem it necessary.

Perhaps we can "boast a little" from time to time about our achievements, but in the presence of the Lord Jesus, the humility of a heart that is truly sorry for its sin can accomplish vastly more: It will lift us up.

O Lord, be merciful to me, a sinner. Amen.

Carlos H. Puig/Jan. 18, 1988

A Lasting Memorial

*Wherever this Gospel is preached in the whole
world, what she has done will be told in
memory of her. Matthew 26:13 RSV*

On Memorial Day people go to cemeteries to remember the dead. They place flowers or other decorations on the graves of loved ones. We do not know where the above-mentioned Mary is buried, but we can honor her even if we cannot put flowers on her grave. As we read this text, we remember again the loving act she performed for Jesus when she anointed Him with a precious ointment. Jesus praised her for serving Him, calling her act a memorable one.

We too can give lasting memorials. True, we cannot anoint Jesus for His burial; that has already been accomplished. But we can honor Jesus by attending Holy Communion in remembrance of Him. We can honor Him by carrying out His command to be witnesses to the fact that He died and rose again for the salvation of all. We can honor Him by feeding the hungry and by helping others in their needs. In doing this, we give lasting and living memorials, as our Lord has said. "As you did it to one of the least of these My brethren, you did it to Me" (Matthew 25:40 RSV). What we do for Jesus is a lasting act.

*Lord, You have done a very memorable thing for us.
Lead us to give living memorials for You. Amen.*

Clarence H. Born/May 27, 1985

385

A Question about Fatherly Love

What father among you, if his son asks for a
fish, will instead of a fish give him a serpent; or
if he asks for an egg, will give him a scorpion?
Luke 11:11–12 RSV

Would a father give his son a snake instead of the requested fish, a scorpion instead of the requested egg? Of course not! A real father wants only the best for his sons and daughters.

On this Father's Day, how good it is to know that Jesus uses these questions to bring out the truth that God is our loving Father who wants only our spiritual good. Our Savior adds: "If you then, who are evil, know how to give good gifts to your children, how much more will the heavenly Father give the Holy Spirit to those who ask Him!" (Luke 11:13 RSV).

Fathers, are you asking your heavenly Father, for Jesus' sake, to strengthen you with the Holy Spirit so you set a fine example and serve your Savior as the Christian head of the family? Children, are you asking God to make you strong to live in loving appreciation of your father as God's gift to you? Wives and mothers, are you asking the Lord for power to live as God-pleasing helpmates with your husbands, together praising Him for your children?

God, we thank You that in Jesus You are our Father. Thank You for the gift of fatherhood and for our earthly father. Amen.

Martin J. Schmidt/June 17, 1979

Keep Busy!

Do not labor for the food which perishes.
John 6:27 RSV

*L*abor Day is not a church holiday, yet its observance is certainly a concern of God's people. Labor is part of the economy of God. Going back to the creation account, we read that after God created man, He put him in a garden, not to spend a vacation but to tend it. God's will, by precept and example, is that people do something.

Labor should be directed by God. When it is, it will be honest and God-pleasing. Just look at the lives of great men and women of the Bible. They worked hard to earn their daily bread. Abraham, Moses, David, Amos—just to mention a few—were herdsmen. Rebecca and Rachel tended gardens and raised their families. Elisha put his hands to the plow. Paul was a tentmaker and Peter a fisherman. Lydia was a businesswoman.

However, they did not merely labor for the food that perishes. They had given their hearts to God and were moved by His love to extend helping hands to others. They were concerned with food for the soul, which is the Gospel of Christ. It assures us of God's love, which forgives our sins. Living and laboring with this objective, we are laying up treasures in heaven that will pay dividends throughout eternity.

Lord Jesus, grant us Your Spirit that we labor not merely for food that perishes but for the bread of life. Amen.

Lewis E. Eickhoff/Sept. 3, 1979

387

THE THANKFUL LIFE

And be thankful. Colossians 3:15 RSV

*T*o say "Thank you!" is a necessary part of accepted social manners. We impress it on our children. We resent its neglect in our life together. We have made it a national institution by setting aside each year a special Thanksgiving Day.

All of the new life in Christ is a thankful life, and so also this day is rich in meaning for us. When we thank God, we acknowledge our complete dependence on Him for all we need in body and soul. We confess that by ourselves we have not deserved the least of all His mercies. We declare ourselves in His debt, obligated to express our gratitude, not with our lips alone but with our life of service to Him as well. And we put forth the prayer that, as His mercy has been with us in the past, so His blessings may be ours in abundant measure also in the days to come.

This is the thanks He would have us bring to Him today. For the sake of Jesus, He accepts it. In His eternal love He will continue to bless us that we may bring Him our thanks all the days of our life. "Bless the Lord, O my soul: and all that is within me, bless His holy name. Bless the Lord, O my soul, and forget not all His benefits" (Psalm 103:1–2 KJV).

"Praise God, from whom all blessings flow! Praise Him, all creatures here below! Praise Him above, ye heavenly host! Praise Father, Son, and Holy Ghost!" Amen.

Daniel E. Poellot/Nov. 26, 1970

The Keepers of Christmas

Let us now go even unto Bethlehem, and see this
thing which is come to pass, which the Lord hath
made known unto us. Luke 2:15 KJV

Millions of people today are strangely uniting in
keeping Christmas. The shepherds hasten to
Bethlehem. They are the common folk on life's road
working hard to have food, clothing, shelter. In
Bethlehem they find a Savior who makes every burden
lighter and brings peace and the hope of heaven to their
hearts.

The Wise Men journey to Bethlehem. They are privileged people, whose wealth has given them the best things
of life. They come because they have discovered that the
riches of this world do not satisfy the hunger of the soul.
They need the greater treasures of forgiveness and peace
and the certainty of salvation. These they find only in Jesus.

Sinners hasten to Bethlehem today, realizing their sins
have closed the door on salvation. We come to be made
over and to start life anew by the grace of God in this babe
in the manger.

The saints come in joyous expectation, recognizing
that they are what they are by the grace of God. They
marvel at the greatness of God's love as they behold their
own worthlessness.

All Christians this morning are on the way to
Bethlehem to adore the Christ Child. Let us join them.

*Thanks to You, Lord God, for this greatest of gifts.
Amen.*

George J. Beto/Dec. 25, 1961

389

THE CHRISTMAS AFTERGLOW

The shepherds returned, glorifying
and praising God for all they had heard and
seen, as it had been told them. Luke 2:20 RSV

*A*s you and I bask in the afterglow of Christmas, we are reminded of a line from a favorite Christmas carol: "How silently, how silently, the wondrous gift is given!"

In the stillness of the first Christmas night, God did indeed give us the gift of salvation in Jesus. It didn't seem so earthshaking at the time. But the baby Jesus certainly proved to be God's most wondrous gift to our world. Isn't that typical of the way God deals with us?

Although the rush and the turmoil of our Christmas celebration is over, God is still with us. In the quiet, day-to-day flow of events, He will be there.

Our challenge today is to rise above the sounds of our usual routine and to hear the voice of our Savior inviting us to fellowship with Him and to enjoy His gift of sins forgiven. Jesus Christ is waiting to lead us gently in God's way. If we are willing to listen to His tender and loving voice, all His wondrous gifts will be ours throughout the coming year. Then we will have His wonderful truths to sustain us when temptations and trials come on us.

Heavenly Father, fill us with Your Spirit that we may follow our Savior as He leads us into Your way. Amen.

Elmer J. Knoernschild/Dec. 26, 1980

HAVE A GOOD DAY!

This is the day which the LORD has made; let
us rejoice and be glad in it. Psalm 118:24 RSV

*T*his just isn't my day!" We've all had days when nothing seems to go right, when we perhaps wonder why
we ever got out of bed in the morning. Perhaps we feel
that way even on birthdays.

But wait a minute! Any day, even my birthday, is not my
own. It's God's day! It's just like every other day the Lord
gives us. The sun shines. The flowers bloom. Fruit and
vegetables ripen. It's a beautiful day, full of God's care and
love in Jesus Christ.

If the day is ruined, it's because of what I've done to it—
or what someone else has done to spoil God's beautiful
handiwork. That old specter of sin injects itself into God's
perfect day. It happens all the time in our imperfect world.

Every day Christ offers me forgiveness of my sins, a
new beginning. Every day He gives me a new life—24
hours more to serve Him. I can rejoice and be glad
because of His presence in this day. Thank God for His
mercy and forgiveness, new every morning!

Thank God for another birthday! The day is good
because it is God's day. Your birthday brings God's goodness into sharper focus. Have a good day! Have a God
day!

*I will make a joyful noise to You, O Lord, for Your
steadfast love endures forever. Help me to serve You
with gladness. Amen.*

Louise Mueller/June 1985

391

I Come to the Lord's Supper Remembering

This do in remembrance of Me.
1 Corinthians 11:24 KJV

We come to the Lord's Supper remembering that table in the Upper Room at which were gathered 12 men and their Master, who was God and man. They were all dusty and weary from travel along the crowded roads of Palestine. I close my eyes—and I seem to see the Lord, girded with a towel, washing the feet of the disciples. By this humble service, He rebuked and silenced their complaining and vainglorious wrangling. Then my own false pride and morbid concern for glory and recognition fade away into nothingness. I confess quietly, "Just as I am, without one plea, but that Thy blood was shed for me."

We remember how He prayed in the garden; how He gave Himself up to the lynch mob; how He gave His cheek to the smiters and His back to the scourge; how He gave His life to the death of crucifixion, till His blood ran down to the ground and His spirit cried out in utter loneliness to His Father; how He sacrificed Himself for us.

Then I remember that table in the Upper Room again—and I am amazed at how it has stretched out around the world and across 20 centuries. On that dark night it served 12 men; now it serves millions who trust in that broken body and that shed blood for the remission of their sins.

"Lord, may Thy body and Thy blood Be for my soul the highest good." Amen.

David A. Preisinger/Aug. 21, 1961

THY WILL BE DONE

"Not My will, but Thine, be done."
Luke 22:42 KJV

*T*hese words of Jesus have set the pattern for thousands upon thousands of prayers spoken by Christ's followers. Sometimes what we say doesn't accurately portray what we are thinking. We easily fall into the habit, even when we pray that God's will be done, of thinking that by prayer we bend God's will to conform to our own. Nothing could be more opposite the truth. It is our will that needs bending to conform to the ruling will of God.

A major cause of the restless, unsatisfied feeling and the frictions that spoil the soul's peace is that God wants one thing and we desperately want another. God says, "Do this." Our will says no to that. This spells civil war within. Then, like Jesus, we need to come to our Gethsemane and touch our knees to the gravel there and say no to self and yes to God. No matter how hard or difficult the process may be, we shall find God's peace, a wonderful sense of liberation and serenity, just as Jesus found. This peace the rigors of life cannot destroy. So much of our fretting and pouting is done because we do not get our way. But we can have our way if it is the way of God. The quickest and surest and only way to peace and contentment is to ask God to bring our will into line with His.

Savior, Master of our lives, help us to bring our wills into line with Yours and grant us Your peace. Amen.

Arnold G. Kuntz/Jan. 13, 1967

393

SCRIPTURE INDEX

Jeremiah

17:7–8	Aug. 14
18:4	Jan. 14

Daniel

12:1	Oct. 29

Jonah

2:2	Feb. 4
4:6	Aug. 10

Micah

5:2	Dec. 15, Dec. 19

Malachi

3:1	Dec. 7
3:6	April 7

Matthew

2:1–2	Jan. 6
2:11	Jan. 7
3:3	Dec. 4
5:8	Jan. 11
5:44	Jan. 15
5:48	Sept. 24
6:10	Feb. 1, Dec. 5
6:33	Feb. 15
8:3	Jan. 10, June 29
9:2	May 20
9:2, 6	Sept. 18
9:12	Sept. 10
9:20–21	March 3
11:28	Oct. 11
11:29–30	Aug. 17
14:20	Aug. 16
14:27	July 12
14:30	Sept. 9
16:17	June 14
16:21	March 4
17:8	Transfiguration
17:8–9	Feb. 7
18:14	Sept. 6
18:19–20	Jan. 18
18:21	Oct. 3
19:14	Aug. 4
21:5	Palm Sunday
21:22	Feb. 22
22:4	June 4
23:13	Aug. 5
24:36	Nov. 25
26:10	Feb. 13
26:13	Memorial Day
26:29	April 9
26:52	April 11
27:19	March 31
27:45	April 15
27:46	Aug. 29
28:10	July 28
28:20	May 23

Mark

4:20	Feb. 6
5:36	Feb. 26
6:31	Sept. 11
6:50	Feb. 16
8:34	May 24
10:14	Nov. 15
10:47	March 7
14:33	March 2
14:69	April 12
15:24	Good Friday
15:46	Holy Saturday
16:3	April 20

Luke

1:28	Dec. 8
1:38	Dec. 13
1:68	Dec. 10
1:76	Dec. 2
2:4	Dec. 20
2:7	Dec. 23
2:8	Dec. 22
2:15	Christmas Day 1
2:20	Dec. 27, Christmas Day 2
2:21	Jan. 1
2:22	Feb. 2
2:29	Dec. 31
2:30–32	Dec. 29
2:42	Aug. 19
2:46	May 7
2:48	April 3
2:49	June 22
4:16	May 11
5:5	Oct. 13
5:19	Oct. 22
5:20	Feb. 17
7:11	July 29
7:16	April 25
8:11	March 21
8:12	Nov. 19
8:49	Jan. 20
9:35	Feb. 9
9:60	Feb. 20

13:5	Jan. 4
13:8	April 7

James
1:22	Sept. 13
4:8	Nov. 13
4:10	Oct. 30,
	Graduation
4:11	Sept. 17

1 Peter
1:12	Sept. 26
1:13	March 11
1:15	Sept. 20
4:1	Oct. 16
5:12	Aug. 3

1 John
2:25	Jan. 26, Oct. 1
3:15	July 22
3:20	June 30
4:10	March 25
4:16	Dec. 28
5:4	July 18

Revelation
3:20	July 31
5:14	Oct. 28
16:15	Nov. 16